Rembrandt *by himself*

Sponsored by Thames & Hudson

Rembrandt *by himself*

EDITED BY
Christopher White and Quentin Buvelot

ESSAYS
Ernst van de Wetering, Volker Manuth and Marieke de Winkel

CATALOGUE
Edwin Buijsen, Peter Schatborn, Ben Broos and Ariane van Suchtelen

NATIONAL GALLERY PUBLICATIONS LIMITED, LONDON
and
ROYAL CABINET OF PAINTINGS MAURITSHUIS, THE HAGUE

Distributed by Yale University Press

Sponsor's Preface

Fifty years ago Thames & Hudson was founded by Walter Neurath, an art historian who also strongly felt himself to be a man of his own times. Art, for him, was not to be regarded as an 'elite' subject; the opportunity to enjoy and understand it should be offered to everyone. He acted on his dream to bring art closer to the general public and to this day it is his conviction and passion that remain the guiding principles of our publishing house.

In those post-war years the response from the public was immediate. Artists and art galleries were enthusiastic supporters of Thames & Hudson's mission and Philip Hendy, then the director of the National Gallery, became a great friend as did Michael Levey who followed him. This link with the National Gallery happily continues in our friendship with the present director, Neil MacGregor, who for many years has given us a home for our annual Walter Neurath Memorial Lecture.

The exhibition of Rembrandt's self portraits gives us at Thames & Hudson a most welcome opportunity on our fiftieth anniversary to join the Gallery in supporting the brilliant plan of showing, for the first time, this very special aspect of the artist's work. Rembrandt's penetrating psychological curiosity about the person behind the face and its expression found liberation in self-portrayal, for that freed him from the expectations of a sitter or those who had commissioned him. Artists like Rembrandt, or for that matter Shakespeare or Beethoven, seem to break through the bondage of their particular time in history and reach out into a profoundly humane language which will remain 'modern' for generations to come.

We hope that this exhibition and the intensity of the artist's search into the essence of the human condition will inspire an appreciation of what art's function in our lives can be and we feel most privileged to be associated with it.

THOMAS NEURATH, *Publisher*

Foreword

The self portraits produced by Rembrandt — painted, etched and drawn — record for posterity the artist's appearance as it developed from his earliest days in Leiden as a young man trying to establish himself as an artist until the last year of his life in Amsterdam more than forty years later. They are not only universally accepted as playing a fundamental role in his art, but also constitute the largest group of self portraits ever produced by any great artist throughout history. As a result Rembrandt's face is immediately recognisable to most people today. These works were not just occasional exercises in self-analysis, but clearly had a meaning and purpose for Rembrandt and, we may presume, for contemporary lovers and collectors of art. What that significance was — and it was very probably not the same throughout Rembrandt's life — remains one of the puzzles of the history of art. As well as giving us an opportunity, never attempted before in an exhibition, to study the artist's appearance and, no less revealing, the changing guises in which he presented himself, this show attempts to provide a solution to this question. It is our hope that the visitor will leave the exhibition with a new understanding of Rembrandt and how he and his art, as far as it was centred on himself, were viewed by his contemporaries. To round out our picture of the artist and his circle, a number of self portraits by Rembrandt's pupils have been included.

In an ideal world we would have liked to have exhibited every self portrait produced by Rembrandt, but, owing to questions of conservation and individual restrictions on loans, this was clearly never going to be possible. But we are pleased to have been able to borrow such a substantial and representative group of paintings, etchings and drawings, and we are deeply grateful to those collections, both public and private, who have generously agreed to our requests. We are especially grateful to Her Majesty Queen Elizabeth II, His Grace The Duke of Sutherland, Robert Anderson, Mària van Berge-Gerbaud, Jetteke Bolten-Rempt, Rolf Bothe, Julius Bryant, Gilles Chazal, Denis Coutagne, Chris Dercon, Alexander Dückers, Erik Ebbinge, Jan Piet Filedt Kok, Olle Granath, Jacob M. de Groot, Ulrich Großmann,

Anne Hawley, Ed de Heer, Christian von Holst, Ronald de Leeuw, Tomás Llorens, Christopher Lloyd, Ekkehard Mai, John Murdoch, Konrad Oberhuber, Earl A. Powell III, Malcolm Rogers, Peter Schatborn, Bernhard Schnackenburg, Peter-Klaus Schuster, Wilfried Seipel, George T.M. Shackelford, Alan Shestack, Julian Spalding, Baron H.H. Thyssen-Bornemisza, Annamaria Petrioli Tofani, Julian Treuherz, Bret Waller and two private owners who wish to remain anonymous. Their generosity will be warmly appreciated by tens of thousands of visitors.

From the very beginning *Rembrandt by Himself* has been a joint project of the National Gallery in London and the Mauritshuis in The Hague. Many dedicated people have combined to make the undertaking a success. We must express our gratitude to our colleagues for supporting our requests for loans of valuable and fragile works of art: Holm Bevers, Marian Bisanz-Prakken, Marjolein de Boer, Helen Braham, Görel Cavalli-Björkman, Michael Clarke, Ian Dejardin, Jeroen Giltaij, Hilliard Goldfarb, Antony Griffiths, Wouter Kloek, Friso Lammertse, Sylvie Menant, Herman Mildenberger, Mark O'Neill, Konrad Renger, Martin Royalton-Kisch, Karl Schütz, Manfred Sellink, Christiaan Vogelaar and Arthur Wheelock. We also wish to thank Christopher Brown, formerly Chief Curator at the National Gallery, and now Director of the Ashmolean Museum, Oxford. For acting as intermediaries, we would like to acknowledge the invaluable help given by His Excellency A. Christiani, the Austrian Ambassador to the Netherlands, His Excellency J.T.H.C. van Ebbenhorst Tengbergen, the Dutch Ambassador to Austria, His Excellency B. de Faubournet De Montferrand, the French Ambassador to the Netherlands, His Excellency F.P.R. van Nouhuys, the Dutch Ambassador to Japan, and Egbert Haverkamp Begemann, Roman Herzig, Simon Levie and Robert Noortman.

We are indebted to the various people who took part in the technical research on the two panels in Nuremberg and The Hague (cat. nos. 14a-b): Ulrich Großmann, Martina Homolka, Daniel Hess, Frank Matthias Kammel, Jørgen Wadum, Caroline van der Elst, Christopher White, Edwin Buijsen and Adri Verburg. On 7 and 8 October 1998 both paintings were examined side by side in the conservation studio of the Germanisches

Nationalmuseum in Nuremberg by the staff of the museum and a delegation from the Mauritshuis.

We would like to thank all those members of staff at the National Gallery in London for their tireless work on this exhibition and its catalogue. Rik van Koetsveld, Deputy Director of the Mauritshuis, was responsible for the organisation of the exhibition in The Hague; he was assisted by Peter van der Ploeg, Senior Curator, and Quentin Buvelot, Curator. Lieke Vervoorn, Head of Communications, with Carola Visser and their staff, carried out the marketing and publicity campaign for the Dutch venue, while Ariane van Suchtelen, Curator, was responsible for the presentation. Henk Douna, Facility Manager, and his staff realised the installation of the exhibition as well as overseeing the general logistics as well as the building of the Rembrandt pavilion. Albert Verhaar, Finance Manager, controlled the ticket sales and the financial arrangements connected with the project. We would particularly like to thank the exhibition's sponsors: in London, Thames & Hudson; in the Hague, ING Group. The publication of the catalogue has also received generous support from the Basil Samuel Charitable Trust.

The scholarly editing of the catalogue was carried out by Christopher White and Quentin Buvelot, who skilfully unified the essays and entries written by the various authors, several of whom are leading Rembrandt scholars. To give the catalogue a more universal appeal, every work attributed to Rembrandt, which may have some reasonable claim to be considered as a self portrait, whether it is in the exhibition or not, has been illustrated and discussed. We would especially like to thank the authors, who have ensured the success of the publication: Ernst van de Wetering, Volker Manuth, Marieke de Winkel, Edwin Buijsen, Peter Schatborn, Ben Broos and Ariane van Suchtelen. They have produced a stimulating and highly informative enquiry into the art of self-portraiture as practised by Rembrandt. Rudi Ekkart, Director of the Netherlands Institute for Art History in The Hague, has given advice on the entries on the painted self portraits.

We are enormously grateful to the members of the Rembrandt Research Project, and in particular to Ernst van de Wetering, for their contribution to the scholarly preparation of the exhibition and accompanying publication by agreeing to our consultation of the manuscript of the forthcoming fourth volume of the *Corpus*, which at the time was only partly completed. When the exhibition catalogue went to press, a number of entries for the *Corpus* were still being written and edited, so that discrepancies between the two publications may well occur.

Many have worked tirelessly on the editing, picture research, translation and production of the catalogue and we are indebted to the publishing team at National Gallery Publications Limited. Quentin Buvelot skilfully edited the English and Dutch editions, as well as coordinating the English, French and German translations. The English translation of the essays and the biography was in the capable hands of Michael Hoyle, while the entries and Volker Manuth's essay were fluently translated by Beverley Jackson and Rachel Esner respectively. Jean Raoul Mengarduque was responsible for the French translation, while Axel Rüger carried out the German translation of the entries and biography, and Susanne Karau and Volker Manuth the introductory essays. Manuth's essay, written in German, was translated into Dutch by Marieke de Winkel.

The elegant design of the catalogue is the work of Isambard Thomas. Finally we wish to thank Wim Waanders, of Waanders Publishers and Printers, and his staff, particularly Henk Diele, Henk van de Wal, Hans van de Willige and Marjoleine van Nielen. It was their achievement that this book was published in time.

We thank all those who have contributed to this unique project, and hope that the show will live up to the expectations of Jakob Rosenberg, in the impassioned fantasy of his famous monograph on Rembrandt of 1948: 'If it were ever possible to assemble all the painted self-portraits of the master in one exhibition, we should be surprised to find so little repetition in arrangement and expression, and so consistent and intense an interest in the psychological content. The scope of Rembrandt's emotional life and the diversity of his moods would be strikingly brought out by such an exhibition and the visitor could not fail to be impressed by the ceaseless and unsparing observation which the paintings reflect.'

NEIL MACGREGOR
Director
The National Gallery,
London

FREDERIK J. DUPARC
Director
Royal Cabinet of Paintings
Mauritshuis, The Hague

The Multiple Functions
of Rembrandt's Self Portraits

Ernst van de Wetering

MANY MORE FACES have been erased by death and cast to the shadows than artists could ever have recorded for posterity. This was true of Rembrandt's time, although proportionately more faces were captured in a variety of ways in the Netherlands than in any other country in the seventeenth century. Dr Ekkart has estimated that 50,000 (approximately 1.5 per cent) of the 3 million people who populated the northern Netherlands over three generations probably had their portraits painted.[1] Occasionally there is more than one portrait of an individual – the Prince of Orange or his wife, a naval hero, a scholar or a famous clergyman (figs. 1–3). These, though, are exceptions.

It seems fairly self-evident that the seventeenth-century artists who painted the famous, the mighty or the rich, would also have recorded their own likenesses, and a relatively large number of self portraits were indeed made.[2] The features of many artists, though, are simply unknown to us.

Some artists made more than one self portrait, but rarely produced more than a handful. It is understandable, then, that the fact that Rembrandt's features appear in such a remarkably large number of paintings came as a surprise to scholars in the nineteenth and early twentieth century, when they began surveying his oeuvre as a whole. They discovered that he had painted himself before the mirror on at least forty occasions, had etched himself thirty-one times, and had made a handful of drawn self portraits.[3] This segment of his oeuvre is unique in art history, not only in its scale and the length of time it spans, but also in its regularity. New self portraits appeared almost annually, and sometimes several times a year. In addition, it is a category that encompasses some of his most impressive paintings and etchings.

Rembrandt's uncommonly large output of self portraits does not seem to have been considered exceptional at the time. None of his contemporaries who spoke about him, no author in the decades after this death, not even an eighteenth-century writer, seems to have been so struck by this fact that he thought it worth mentioning, let alone explaining. That Rembrandt's contemporaries never realised that he was producing so many self portraits will not surprise those who believe that these were intimate documents. Why, indeed, should they have been aware of a phenomenon about which the author of a survey of the history of the self portrait wrote: 'Over the years, Rembrandt's self portraits increasingly became a means for gaining self-knowledge, and in the end took the form of an interior dialogue: a lonely old man communicating with himself while he painted.'[4] These words express a view still held by many people. However, as the present catalogue will show, it is extremely unlikely that Rembrandt made his self portraits as a personal form of self-analysis. How, then, is the phenomenon to be explained? Different aspects of this intriguing question will be dealt with in the essays and entries in this catalogue. First, though, we must reconnoitre the terrain. How did Rembrandt's self portraits originate? Are they faithful likenesses? Can one distinguish different types? It is only when this has been done that one can enquire into Rembrandt's motives.

Previous page
Self Portrait with Two Circles (cat. no. 83, detail).

Rembrandt in the Mirror

When the Dutch cineast Bert Haanstra (1916–97) was commissioned to make a short film about Rembrandt in the commemorative year 1956, 350 years after the artist's birth, he had the brilliant idea of filming the self portraits painted over a period of forty years in chronological order, one merging into the next.[5] The eyes were always in the same position on the screen, and it was around their gaze that the viewer saw Rembrandt's face gradually age. The head became broader, the double chin grew, the distinctive pouches flanking the chin became more pronounced, the tufts of brown hair on either side of the skull turned grey, and the wrinkles multiplied. It almost seemed, too, that one saw Rembrandt's personality mature before one's eyes. The very consistency of this process, which one can also see when leafing through this catalogue, is evidence that Rembrandt must have examined his face very closely in the mirror.

The painter and writer on art Cornelis de Bie (1627–after 1711) wrote in his *Gulden Cabinet* of 1661 that 'anyone depicting himself needs a mirror, in which he can only perceive himself from the front' (figs. 4 and 5).[6] There were mirrors in Rembrandt's house, as there were in many seventeenth-century homes. Two are mentioned in the inventory made at the time of his financial difficulties in 1656 and in the one drawn up after his death in 1669. The 1656 inventory actually specifies 'een groote spiegel (a large mirror)'.[7] Since Rembrandt made several monumental self portraits from 1652 on, this is not without significance, as will become clear below. In addition, a document of 1658, the year in which Rembrandt painted his largest self

fig. 1 *opposite left*
Michiel van Mierevelt, *Portrait of Johannes Wtenbogaert*, 1632. Panel, 70 × 59 cm.
Amsterdam, Rijksmuseum.

fig. 2 *opposite centre*
Rembrandt, *Portrait of Johannes Wtenbogaert*, 1633.
Canvas, 130 × 103 cm. Amsterdam, Rijksmuseum.

fig. 3 *opposite right*
Jacob Backer, *Portrait of Johannes Wtenbogaert*, 1638.
Canvas, 122.5 × 98 cm.
Amsterdam, Rijksmuseum.

fig. 4 *above right*
Johannes Gumpp, *Self Portrait before the Mirror*, 1646.
Canvas, 88.5 × 89 cm. Florence,
Galleria degli Uffizi.

fig. 5 *right*
Antonie van Steenwinkel, *Self Portrait with His Wife*, (n.d.). Canvas, 85 × 64 cm.
Antwerp, Koninklijk Museum voor Schone Kunsten.

portrait (cat. no. 71), records that his 16-year-old son Titus had given orders for the transport to Rembrandt's home of 'a large mirror in a black frame'. The mirror broke *en route*, which is why this remarkable document came to be written.[8]

The *Self Portrait with Two Circles* in Kenwood House (fig. 6, cat. no. 83) contains an interesting clue indicating that the mirror Rembrandt used must have been quite large. The genesis of this painting also sheds light on the faithfulness with which he set to work, and offers a glimpse of the complications involved in painting one's own mirror image. An X-radiograph of this impressive picture (fig. 7) shows that Rembrandt must initially have depicted himself in the act of painting, exactly as he saw himself in the mirror, with palette, brushes and maulstick in his right hand, and his left hand holding a brush, which is raised in such a way as to suggest that he was working on the canvas. One could deduce from this that his reflection in the mirror extended down to the hips. However, he evidently rejected the mirror image in this particular case, for he made major changes to the initial design. With hastily applied strokes and dabs he moved the palette, brushes and maulstick to his left hand and reduced the right hand to an indistinct blur. His decision to do so was undoubtedly prompted by the problem facing anyone painting a self portrait, and one that confronted Rembrandt time and again throughout his career: the fact that the right hand becomes a left hand in the mirror.

It should be said straight away that Rembrandt was right-handed; the hatchings in his many drawings provide incontrovertible evidence of this (cat. nos. 63 and 77). Because the painting hand of a right-handed artist becomes a left hand if the mirror image is followed faithfully (compare fig. 20), the hands in self portraits are usually omitted or just cursorily described. The right hand is unable to 'pose', because as a mirror-image left hand it is moving as the artist paints. The same is also true for the left hand, because it is holding the palette, brushes and maulstick in the 'wrong' hand. In the initial conception of the Madrid self portrait (cat. no. 59) a 'right hand' was again painted out (only to be brought to light later by a curious conservator). The 'painting hand' in the self portrait in Windsor Castle is stuffed into the clothing (cat. no. 57), while the initial designs for hands were painted out in several late works (cat. nos. 82 and 84–5). In an etched self portrait this reversal is compensated for by the fact that the impression taken from the etching plate is the mirror image of a mirror image.

One of the few paintings in which both of Rembrandt's hands are depicted in detail is the lost *Self Portrait with Pen, Inkpot and Sketchbook* of *c.*1655, which survives only in a reproduction print and a few copies (cat. nos. 70a–c). Here, and this also applies to the large self portrait in the Frick Collection (cat. no. 71) and the *Self Portrait at the Easel* in Paris (cat. no. 79), it is conceivable that another person posed for the hands. It is known that in the seventeenth century someone other than the subject, a studio assistant for example, sat to the painter for the hands,[9] since the artist could not expect his august clientele to pose for long. This may also have been the way to attain the well-nigh impossible in a self portrait: depicting the hands properly.

In the drawn self portrait in Rotterdam (cat. no. 77), Rembrandt included the drawing hand in mirror image but then

partly covered it up by hatching. This sequence of events comes closest to what must have happened when Rembrandt made the Kenwood picture: he followed the reality in the mirror faithfully and then swiftly reversed the hands. If this reconstruction is correct, it sheds light on Rembrandt's fidelity when working in front of a mirror. It would also mean that the mirror used for the Kenwood portrait showed him down to the hips, which the larger seventeenth-century mirrors were perfectly capable of doing.

In genre pieces one sometimes finds mirrors approximately eighty centimetres high.[10] Those in a palace were no larger, as demonstrated by the much-debated mirror in the background of Velázquez's *Las Meninas* (fig. 8). This is an indication that it was technically impossible to make larger mirrors from a single sheet of glass in Rembrandt's day. It was not until 1688 that Bernard Perrot discovered a way of casting glass for larger mirrors. Until then mirror glass was blown just like ordinary glass. The hot, flexible bubble of molten glass was cut down the middle and spread out flat. A text of 1674, written shortly before Perrot's invention, records that a certain Lady Clayton bought 'a very large mirror', but it was not big enough to show her entire mirror image, merely 'her ugly face and body to the middle'.[11] Since a mirror image is smaller than the reality (because one sees someone apparently standing as far behind the mirror as one is in front of it), Rembrandt could well have seen himself to the hips in a mirror that was large by contemporary standards. However, he often must have stepped up to it in order to study his face more closely. Is that, however, a guarantee that his self portraits are faithful likenesses?

fig. 6 *opposite left*
Self Portrait with Two Circles (cat. no. 83).

fig. 7 *opposite right*
X-radiograph of *Self Portrait with Two Circles*
(cat. no. 83; London, Courtauld Institute).

fig. 8 *above*
DIEGO VELÁZQUEZ, *Las Meninas*, 1656.
Canvas, 323 × 276 cm. Madrid, Museo del Prado.

Rembrandt's Face

Anyone seeing photographs of Vincent van Gogh (1853–90) or of a meticulous realist like Dick Ket (1902–40) gets the odd sensation of looking at someone other than the person so familiar from his self portraits (figs. 9–12). Even if we are convinced that we know Rembrandt's face well, we would still like a portrait of him viewed through a second artist's eyes. That desire is undoubtedly the reason for the attempts that have been made to discover portraits of Rembrandt by other artists (see p. 117, fig. 14f).[12]

Jan Lievens (1607–74), his friend from his Leiden period, made a history painting in which he included Rembrandt's face distorted by fear (fig. 13), but what a find it would be to uncover a true portrait of Rembrandt by someone like Frans Hals (c.1580–1666). In 1956, Dirk Vis tried to persuade the world that he had done just that. He was convinced that Hals's *Portrait of a Painter* of the early 1650s depicted Rembrandt as seen by Holland's most brilliant portrait painter of the day (figs. 14–15).[13] Vis attributed the differences between the head in Hals's painting and those in Rembrandt's self portraits to the effect just noted in connection with Van Gogh and Ket. He wrote: 'Suddenly I saw the hitherto familiar lineaments of Rembrandt's face amplified with what had always been hidden: the utterly relaxed look of the eyes that the self portrait can never capture. It was a meeting with this man as . . . his contemporaries met him.'[14] Vis's hypothesis never found any real support, and I too am convinced that he was wrong. Nevertheless, I will compare the head of Hals's painter (fig. 15) with Rembrandt's head as depicted in his self portraits

fig. 9 *top left*
Vincent van Gogh at the Age of 18, c.1871.
Photograph (Amsterdam, Van Gogh Museum archives).

fig. 10 *top right*
VINCENT VAN GOGH, *Self Portrait at Approximately 34 Years Old*, 1887. Canvas, 42 × 34 cm. Amsterdam, Van Gogh Museum (Vincent van Gogh Foundation).

fig. 11 *above left*
JOHAN MEKKINK, *Dick Ket in his Studio at Approximately 36 Years Old*, c.1937–8. Photograph (The Hague, Netherlands Institute for Art History [RKD]).

fig. 12 *above right*
DICK KET, *Self Portrait at the Age of 29*, 1931.
Canvas, 72 × 51 cm. Amsterdam, Stedelijk Museum.

fig. 13 *right*
JAN LIEVENS, *Samson and Delilah*, c.1627–8.
Panel, 27.5 × 23.7 cm. Amsterdam, Rijksmuseum.

fig. 14 *above*
FRANS HALS, *Portrait of a Painter*, 1650.
Canvas, 100.3 × 82.9 cm. New York,
The Frick Collection.

fig. 15 *above right*
Detail of fig. 14.

fig. 16 *right*
Self Portrait (cat. no. 65, detail).

(fig. 16) because a rebuttal of his hypothesis presents a good opportunity to get a better idea of Rembrandt's physiognomy and the structure of his head.

It is true that the painter portrayed by Hals has a rather round face with a slightly cleft chin, as Rembrandt does in his self portraits. He also has Rembrandt's double chin and the familiar little moustache and the tuft of hair immediately below the bottom lip. There are, however, fundamental differences in the anatomy of the eyes. The man in Hals's painting has heavy eyelids, while those in Rembrandt's self portraits are narrow and hooded by a fold of skin above each eye. In most of the self portraits, this fold hangs further over the right eye (to the beholder) than the left. There are also essential differences in the forehead and nose. Rembrandt's nose in the paintings looks much squatter than that of the man in Hals's portrait, and ends in a bulbous tip. The three-quarter-length self portraits (fig. 17; see also cat. no. 84) show that the tip of Rembrandt's nose must have been quite protuberant. His nose ran in an undeviating line to the tip (fig. 18), and the nasal bone must have looked almost straight when seen from the side. Viewed from the front, however, the thickening of the nose is very apparent. Rembrandt clearly indicated this in his three-quarter-length self portraits. The nose of the man in Hals's painting, on the other hand, is narrow, the tip appears to be more pointed and the wings less flaring. It looks more as if the unknown man had a beaky nose, for Hals painted an undulating line between light and shadow as if the side profile was not straight, as it was in Rembrandt's case.

Finally, there is the furrow between the eyebrows in almost all of Rembrandt's self portraits from 1630 on. It was undoubtedly the lack of this crease in Hals's painting that gave Vis the idea that this was Rembrandt painted in a relaxed mood, for a furrow like the one Rembrandt depicts appears when one is staring (or thinking) intently and can disappear when one relaxes.

Raupp has pointed out that furrows of this kind can be found in the portraits and self portraits of other painters, and believed that they could be read as an 'attribute' of the emancipated artist.[15] That emancipation was associated with the growing awareness among painters that they should be regarded more as intellectuals and practitioners of a liberal art than as craftsmen. On the forehead, which was a 'prominent feature that determined one's appearance' and 'the reflection of the thoughts, aye the book of the heart', as was said in the seventeenth century,[16] the frown could symbolise the artist as thinker.

However attractive the latter hypothesis may be, Rembrandt's frown cannot be viewed solely as a 'pasted-on' attribute of the emancipated artist. He really must have had one, whether or not it was caused by peering into the mirror. The furrows in the various self portraits resemble each other so closely that he must have studied them in the mirror time and again, and the same applies to the asymmetrical folds above the eyes. The furrow, too, is asymmetrical. It is not in the centre of the forehead but a little to the left, from our viewpoint, and extends down into the eye-socket. Occasionally Rembrandt depicted a short, far less pronounced indentation to the right of the nose (compare cat. no. 73).

It is difficult to imagine that Rembrandt's face did not have a trace of the furrows when the muscles were relaxed. As with so many people, they appear to be a permanent part of his facial 'landscape'. If the faint cluster of short brushstrokes above the nose of the man in Hals's portrait is meant to indicate a furrow, it is at any rate too far from the centre of the forehead relative to Rembrandt's. Moreover, the position of this furrow, if that is what it is, contributes to the impression that the nose of Hals's sitter sprang more or less directly from the forehead, whereas the deep-set root of the nose is one of the key features of Rembrandt's physiognomy.

Will we ever find an answer to the question of whether Rembrandt's self portraits are accurate likenesses? Each of his self portraits shows a slightly different individual, just as our own successive passport photographs do. That being said, no one can shake off the feeling that Rembrandt's personality and even his physiognomic peculiarities crystallise, as it were, when one surveys his self portraits as a group. You feel that you recognise him. It looks like him. The truth, however, will never be known. Anyone who has drawn or painted a portrait will have learned from the reactions of members of the sitter's family that likeness is something that is difficult to pin down and is, ultimately, subjective.

The Changing Experience of Self

The term 'self portrait' did not exist in Rembrandt's day, and that is not without significance. If, in the seventeenth and even eighteenth centuries, one wished to speak of a Rembrandt self portrait one described it as the 'contrefeitsel van Rembrandt door hem sellfs gedaen (Rembrandt's likeness done by himself)',[17] or 'het portrait van Rembrandt door hem zelf geschildert (the portrait of Rembrandt painted by himself)'. In the 1639 inventory of the paintings belonging to King Charles I of England (1600–49), Rembrandt's self portrait of c.1630–1 (cat. no. 26) is listed as 'his owne picture & done by himself'.[18] This may appear to mean the same as the term 'self portrait', but there is a subtle difference. It is demonstrated by an incident involving a French contemporary of Rembrandt's, the painter Nicolas Poussin (1594–1665). When the French art-lover Paul Fréart de Chantelou (1609–94) decided that he wanted a portrait of this much-admired artist, Poussin cast around for a painter to do the job, since he did not consider himself to be a portraitist. He failed to find a suitable candidate and also felt that the prices he had been quoted were excessive. He eventually resolved the impasse by painting the picture himself (fig. 19).[19] For the patron, De Chantelou, and for Poussin, there was evidently no fundamental difference between a portrait of Poussin painted by another artist and one by Poussin himself.

'Self portrait' only came into use in the nineteenth century,[20] and this was no coincidence. Inherent in the concept of 'self portrait' in the nineteenth and twentieth centuries was a form of self-awareness that had a specific existential connotation, because from the end of the eighteenth century the experience of one's own individuality was very different to that current in Rembrandt's century. It was in the 1970s, not all that long ago, that people began speaking of a new 'me generation'. Such

fig. 17 *opposite left*
Self Portrait with Beret and Turned-Up Collar,
(cat. no. 74, detail).

fig. 18 *opposite right*
Self Portrait (cat. no. 60, detail).

fig. 19 *right*
NICOLAS POUSSIN, *Self Portrait*, 1650.
Canvas, 98 × 74 cm. Paris, Musée du Louvre.

Under the influence of literature in particular, and later of psychology, the highly personal form of self-reflection associated with this has become such an integral part of our image of mankind in general that we can barely imagine that man's self-experience was different in the pre-Romantic period. It is this unconsciously held 'Romantic' view of mankind that has set a heavy stamp on the interpretation of the phenomenon of Rembrandt's self portraits. Rosenberg, in his influential monograph on the artist of 1948, spoke of the 'ceaseless and unsparing observation which [Rembrandt's self portraits] reflect, showing a gradual change from outward description and characterisation to the most penetrating self-analysis and self-contemplation ... Rembrandt seems to have felt that he had to know himself if he wished to penetrate the problem of man's inner life.'[23]

fig. 20
ATTRIBUTED TO GIOVANNI BATTISTA PAGGI,
Self Portrait with an Architect Friend, c.1580–90.
Canvas, 81 × 62 cm. Würzburg, Martin von
Wagner Museum.

Such a passage demonstrates that we can barely, if at all, avoid reading into Rembrandt's face latent emotions and forms of self-awareness that were only possible in and after the Romantic era. The most recent monograph on Rembrandt's self portraits, by Chapman in 1990, demonstrates just how tenacious (and evidently attractive to the public) this anachronistic view of Rembrandt's self portraits is. On the cover, Chapman's study is presented as 'fascinating evidence that they [Rembrandt's self portraits] were the result of a necessary process of identity formation: they represent a conscious and progressive quest for individual identity in a truly modern sense'.[24] In the book itself, Chapman states in her discussion of Rembrandt's last self portrait (cat. no. 86) that 'a drive to self-exploration continued to motivate Rembrandt until the very end of his life'.[25]

Raupp, in a 1980 publication on self portraits, endeavoured to shake off the influence of the Romantic view of human nature in his attempt to fathom the standpoint from which the self portrait must have been regarded in pre-Romantic times. He, too, is convinced that the prevailing view of the self portrait as a means for 'self-examination' is an anachronism when applied to the period before 1800.

He argues cogently that the experience of the individual in the pre-Romantic era was governed first and foremost by categories of Christian and humanistic ethics, and by the doctrine of the temperaments and dispositions, topped off with a liberal dose of astrology.[26] In the literature of Rembrandt's day, the image of personality and character was so shaped by the model proposed by classical authors like Plutarch (c.46–120) and

Cornelius Nepos (first century BC) that personality was seen primarily as being bound to certain immutable types. The introspection of an exceptional man like Michel de Montaigne (1533–92), who opened his *Essais* of 1580–8 with the words 'It is myself that I paint. . . . I myself am the subject of my book', should likewise not be confused with a Romantic, individualistic desire for self-knowledge. Montaigne's search for his 'I', nourished by countless references to classical writers, is directed more towards what unites him with the rest of mankind than what sets him apart. His attempt to 'paint himself' leads him to a personal system of ethics (and morals) in which the doctrines of the Stoics, Epicureanism, a sceptical attitude to life and a moderate Catholicism all have a place. Montaigne's self-aware reflection has little to do with Romantic self-expression.

Raupp concluded that when an artist of Rembrandt's day painted a self portrait, he 'did not step to the mirror with questions and doubts, but with a carefully planned programme'.[27] Does this apply to Rembrandt? What might his programme have been? Could he have had more than one?

The Various Types of Self Portrait

As already indicated, the most obvious 'programme' is that Rembrandt's self portraits were intended as portraits of Rembrandt by Rembrandt (along the lines of the portrait of Poussin by Poussin mentioned above). As I hope to show below, that was merely one part of their function. The often unusually informal character of these works makes it hard to interpret them solely as portraits like the formal self portraits by Poussin, say,

fig. 21
HANS VON MARÉES, *Self Portrait with Franz Lenbach*, 1863. Canvas, 53 × 61 cm. Munich, Bayerische Staatsgemäldesammlungen, Neue Pinakothek.

or those (p. 47, fig. 11) by Peter Paul Rubens (1577–1640). We must start by noting that not every work by Rembrandt that we label a 'self portrait' can be comprehended as a 'portrait of Rembrandt'. This applies especially to several of the early ones.

In the first place, there is the group of early etchings in which Rembrandt depicted himself with different facial expressions (figs. 22–5). These are generally regarded as studies of emotions, of moods that figures in history paintings could display. It is known that Rembrandt's pupil Samuel van Hoogstraten (cat. no. 96) advised his own pupils to empathise as closely as possible with the emotions of the figures in history pieces while looking into a mirror: 'thus must one reshape oneself entirely into an actor … in front of a mirror, being both exhibitor and beholder.'[28]

It is very likely that Van Hoogstraten based this advice on his own experiences in Rembrandt's studio. The latter's early, etched 'self portraits' displaying a variety of grimaces appear to be the best illustrations of this studio practice. In other words, it was not a question of an artist's personal physiognomy but of the possibility of studying a specific distortion of the features under the influence of an emotion, albeit one faked in the studio. It is known from the autobiography of Constantijn Huygens (1596–1687) that Rembrandt was seen as, and probably saw himself as, an artist with an uncommon ability to portray the emotions of the figures in his history paintings,[29] or as Rembrandt himself put it, 'meeste ende die naetueertelste beweechgelickheijt (the greatest and most natural emotion)'.[30]

Likewise, a specific physiognomy was not the most important point about these self portraits, which should really be seen as

tronies, or heads. They were usually busts of imaginary figures decked out in a variety of costumes which must have had specific connotations for the seventeenth-century viewer: piety, bellicosity, the strange and exotic, youth, old age, transience and so on. Although the sitter's identity was not a priority, models were used when painting *tronies* (fig. 26).[31] However, the artist could also portray himself, which had the advantage of being both inexpensive and practical. Some of Rembrandt's early self portraits can be regarded as *tronies*. As Marieke de Winkel demonstrates in her essay, the Nuremberg self portrait (cat. no. 14a) belongs in this category, and the same is true of several etchings (cat. nos. 41–2 and 49). As it happens, the 'lovers of art' discussed below would certainly have recognised Rembrandt's face, which means that a painted or etched *tronie* could also have functioned as a portrait of Rembrandt. The *tronie* self portrait, however, probably served principally as the vehicle for a specific connotation.

De Vries suggested that the bulk of Rembrandt's self portraits should be interpreted as *tronies*.[32] He based this on his belief that Rembrandt's face would not have been recognised as such by the buyers of these works. One could counter this by pointing to documents from which it can be deduced that Rembrandt's likeness was recognised from early on in his career.[33] This also has an important bearing on another category of self portraits – the figures with his own features that Rembrandt included in a few history paintings. We can take it that he knew that his face would be recognised in the history pieces in which he appeared as a 'bit player', or in the handful of self *portraits historiés*.

fig. 22 *opposite above left*
'Self Portrait', Wide-Eyed (cat. no. 20).

fig. 23 *opposite above right*
'Self Portrait' with Angry Expression (cat. no. 21).

fig. 24 *opposite left*
'Self Portrait', Smiling (cat. no. 22).

fig. 25 *opposite right*
'Self Portrait', Open-Mouthed (cat. no. 23).

fig. 26 *right*
Rembrandt pupil, *An Artist painting an Old Man*.
Pen in brown ink and brush, 91 × 139 mm.
Paris, Institut Néerlandais, Frits Lugt Collection.

That was undoubtedly the case with *The Raising of the Cross* commissioned by the stadholder Frederick Henry (1584–1647; fig 27), in which Rembrandt depicted himself as one of the men helping to raise the Cross. If he was not recognised, the opportunity for the owner or someone from his immediate circle to point out Rembrandt's 'hidden' self portrait must have been one of the attractions of the work. That would also have been true of *The Stoning of Saint Stephen* from his first Leiden period (fig. 28) and the Leiden *History Piece* (cat. no. 1). People in the circle from which the commissions for these pictures came would no doubt have recognised Rembrandt's features instantly.[34]

Inserting one's own likeness in a history painting was a long-established practice (see p. 41), and Rembrandt's public would have been aware of it. A contemporary of Rembrandt's, the painter Joachim von Sandrart (1606–88), saw it as a way of 'including his own portrait for the sake of remembrance', with an eye to his mortality.[35] That may have been Rembrandt's underlying thought when he painted his own features into a history piece. It is known that many self portraits by other artists must have been intended as *memoriae*, for as Sluijter has demonstrated, they often contain unambiguous allusions to life's transience (see fig. 5).[36] In most cases, though, these artists rarely left more than one likeness of themselves. None of Rembrandt's many self portraits makes an explicit reference to transience. The hypothesis put forward later in this essay in connection with the function of these works will make it clear why this is so.

There are two obvious examples of the self *portrait historié* in Rembrandt's oeuvre. In one of them he cast himself as the apostle Paul (cat. no. 81), and in the other as Zeuxis, the painter from classical antiquity (cat. no. 82). Such paintings, too, were part of a tradition.[37] An owner of the *Self Portrait as the Apostle Paul* knew in 1695 that the person depicted was Rembrandt (see p. 51). That information must have accompanied the picture from the time it was made, in so far as Rembrandt's physiognomy was not known from his etched self portraits, which, like his other etchings, were avidly collected in all their states in order to make up a complete 'set'.[38]

Therefore it is clear that Rembrandt's self portraits can be divided into several categories; Marieke de Winkel will demonstrate that this division can be broken down even further. The main purpose of the discussion so far has been to show that some of the works that we call 'self portraits', particularly several of the early etchings and *tronies*, were not made with the idea that the artist would be recognised. However, this was the case with the other categories, such as the self *portrait historié* and the multi-figured scenes in which he incorporated his self portrait. Does this mean then that contemporaries saw these works purely as portraits of Rembrandt 'done by himself'? In order to answer this question it is necessary to form an idea of Rembrandt's public.

'Lovers of the Art of Painting'

The fear of elitism is so pervasive in these democratic days that we hesitate to divide the seventeenth-century art public into separate, clearly defined categories. With the present norm of cultural dissemination and education, we automatically tend to assume that even back then there was a homogeneous public for

art. That was definitely not so. Our present-day, ideal public, queuing to get into museums and keeping informed about record auction prices and major exhibitions through the press, is in fact a colossal enlargement of just one segment of the sixteenth- and seventeenth-century population, namely the art-lover.

In Rembrandt's day there was a fast-growing but clearly distinguishable public that was interested in art and artists, a public that was designated as 'Liefhebbers van de Schilderkonst' (Lovers of the Art of Painting).[39] Not every purchaser of a painting was necessarily an art-lover, for seventeenth-century pictures also served decorative and other purposes. Anyone who studies the interiors in seventeenth-century genre works will soon discover that paintings then, as indeed today, were used to adorn walls, generally in a symmetrical hang. This, of course, does not rule out the possibility that members of a family and their guests could be pleasantly intrigued by the depiction and the illusionism, as well as being edified or amused by the subject of the paintings.[40] An art-lover, on the other hand, did not need to be a purchaser or collector of paintings, although as a rule he would have been. His main purpose was to understand paintings so as to be able to discuss them with other devotees, and preferably with painters as well (fig. 29; see also p. 65, fig. 10).

When the surviving writings from classical times were studied during the Renaissance, scholars discovered numerous, often brief passages about artists, mainly painters, from Greek and Roman antiquity.[41] The exegesis of those passages, many of which are anecdotes, supplied the building blocks for a theory of art which further refined the potential for an exchange of ideas

about painting. One outcome, the importance of which for art history can barely be overstated, was the elevation of the discourse about painting and its creators to a laudable way of passing the time by the sixteenth-century diplomat and writer Baldassare Castiglione (1478–1529; p. 170, fig. 53b) in *Il Cortegiano*, his extremely influential manual for courtiers published in 1528.[42] The growing status of painting led to the phenomenon of the princely collection; rulers were *ex officio* lovers of painting.[43]

The rise of the lover of art, and of painting in particular, has not halted since and, incidentally, also resulted in a growing army of amateur draughtsmen and painters. In addition, many an art-lover joined the artists' Guild of St Luke or one of the later artists' confraternities.[44] As their knowledge of painting, whether or not inspired by classical authors, gradually became more refined and familiarity with artists and their works grew, books were published.[45] In the Netherlands, Karel van Mander (1548–1606) was the first to synthesise the historical, theoretical and practical information about painting in his *Schilder-Boeck* of 1604. That knowledge had been the preserve of the leisured class in Castiglione's day, but a century later the Hague schoolmaster David Beck (1594–1634) wrote in his diary for 29 February 1624: 'I read for no less than an hour in Van Mander's *Schilder-Boeck*.' On 25 April he relates how he made the acquaintance of a cabinetmaker called Master Anthony on the horse-drawn ferry to Delft, 'with whom I conversed endlessly about art'.[46] Beck, incidentally, was another art-lover who took up the brush himself.

As noted above, the art-lover's knowledge of art included a form of art history involving legendary artists and legendary art-

fig. 27 *opposite left*
REMBRANDT, *The Raising of the Cross*, 1633.
Canvas, 95.7 × 72.2 cm.
Munich, Bayerische Staatsgemäldesammlungen,
Alte Pinakothek.
(for detail of self portrait see p. 88, fig. 1f)

fig. 28 *opposite right*
REMBRANDT, *The Stoning of Saint Stephen*, 1625.
Panel, 89.5 × 123.6 cm.
Lyon, Musée des Beaux-Arts.
(for detail of self portrait see p. 88, fig. 1b)

fig. 29 *right*
FLEMISH SCHOOL, *Cognoscenti in a Room hung with Pictures* (detail), *c.*1620. Panel, 95.9 × 123.5 cm.
London, National Gallery.

lovers. Anecdotes recorded by classical writers about the special relationship between Alexander the Great (356–23 BC) and his court painter Apelles (fig. 30), and the almost equal footing that Titian (active by 1510; died 1576) enjoyed with Emperor Charles V (1500–58), gave both the painter and the art-lover of Rembrandt's day the possibility of identifying with great role models of the past in their mutual relationship and the importance of their pursuit.

Much of the communication between the art-lover and painter took place during studio visits (figs. 31 and 32; see also p. 65, fig. 10). In a French manual for art-lovers of 1635 known as the *Brussels Manuscript*, the author concludes his introduction as follows: 'Therefore, to know how to discourse on this noble profession ["painting on a flat surface, one of the most noble arts of the world", as he had described it earlier], you must have visited the studio and disputed with the masters, have seen the magic effects of the pencil, and the unerring judgement with which the details are worked out.'[47] It is known that Constantijn Huygens, the secretary to three successive stadholders and a great devotee of art, visited painters in their studios. His account of his visit to Rembrandt in *c.*1629 is one of the most oft-quoted and detailed sources on the young artist.[48]

When reading the works written by artists for art-lovers, and some by the latter themselves, one gets the idea that the knowledge gained from studio visits mainly concerned the miracle of the illusion of reality on a flat surface (fig. 33), and the painterly and technical means that went into the creation of that illusion. Part of the miracle, for example, was the ability of some

fig. 30
WILLEM VAN HAECHT, *Apelles painting Campaspe* (detail), *c.*1630. Panel, 104.9 × 148.7 cm. The Hague, Mauritshuis.

fig. 31 *below left*
FRANS VAN MIERIS THE ELDER, *A Visitor in the Painter's Studio*, *c.*1655–7. Panel, 63.5 × 47 cm. Dresden, Staatliche Kunstsammlungen, Gemäldegalerie Alte Meister.

fig. 32 *below*
JOB BERCKHEYDE, *Visitors in the Painter's Studio*, 1659. Panel, 49 × 36.5 cm. St Petersburg, Hermitage.

painters to convey a figure's emotions convincingly. One passage
that is often quoted is Huygens's analysis of the penitent Judas
in Rembrandt's ambitious picture of 1628–9, in which Christ's
betrayer returns the thirty pieces of silver (fig. 34).[49] Art-lovers
appear to have regarded the subject of the painting as a whole as
the occasion for this magic rather than its real *raison d'être*. They
seem to have been most interested in the 'unerring judgement
with which the details are worked out' (fig. 35), to quote the
Brussels Manuscript. That explains why so little attention was paid
to iconography in painters' treatises, whose extensive title pages
show that they were intended as much for artists as for 'lovers
of art'.[50] The fact that the former did not consider the subject
as being of primary importance, but admired paintings
as demonstrations of a painter's mastery will prove to be one
of the keys to understanding Rembrandt's self portraits.

Form and Content

Needless to say, many paintings were made to serve a specific
function, and there the iconography was crucial. The subject
justified the picture for groups other than art-lovers. That
applied to ecclesiastical art, of course, but also to portraits,
and topographical and moralistic scenes. However, in the
case of a painting in which the subject was paramount, its
importance for the art-lover could shift to the extent that it
became above all the vehicle for the specifically artistic qualities
of a particular painter.

This form of interest was particularly important for artists.
It even justifies the question of whether the enormous upsurge

and variation that took place in painting from the Renaissance onwards was not caused in part by the fact that there was so much expert interest, leading to growing rivalry between artists. Rembrandt's contemporary, the painter Joachim von Sandrart, relates how apprentices and art-lovers went to look at the paintings he had made for churches and monasteries. They did so not for religious reasons. As he recalls, they travelled in droves to see seven works he had made for an isolated monastery because they believed that those pictures constituted 'a perfect school of painting'.[51] Earlier, in 1584, Raffaello Borghini had described how sixteenth-century art-lovers toured Florentine churches, holding critical discussions about the quality of the drapery or the anatomy, the poses of the figures, or the rendering of the human skin in the painted altarpieces and frescoes.[52]

Such an image of the way the seventeenth-century amateur experienced art contains echoes of *l'art pour l'art* – a concept which we think only arose in the nineteenth century. One outcome of a situation in which a painting has priority as an end in itself rather than as a means of communicating content is that the viewer's interest shifts from the scene to the maker. The economist Montias carried out a statistical survey using data from seventeenth-century probate inventories in the city archives of Delft, and this led him to observe that a gradual change took place in the designation of paintings in the course of the seventeenth century. In the framework of his quantitative analysis of the many Delft inventories he had examined, he wrote: 'If my surmise is correct, notaries and their clerks became distinctly

more conscious of the importance of appending an artist's name to a painting in the 1640s and 1650s. This represents a significant change in the attitude towards the painted objects described in inventories. There is no greater step in the metamorphosis of craft into art than the recognition that an object is the unique creation of an individual and that its worth to potential amateurs [art-lovers] will depend, at least in part, on the information they have about its maker.'[53]

Montias noted that this trend applied mainly to paintings, but was also noticeable in the case of drawings and prints, works of art that were akin to paintings and were executed chiefly by painters. This confirms the special position that painting occupied among the other arts in the seventeenth century. Montias's observation of the growing emphasis on the names of the makers of paintings ties in perfectly with the fact that Rembrandt's pupil, Samuel van Hoogstraten, writing about contemporary collectors of paintings in his *Inleyding tot de hooge schoole der schilderkonst* (Introduction to the Art of Painting) of 1678 (fig. 36), spoke of 'name buyers', adding, 'of whom there are so many these days'.[54]

'Name Buyers'

A phenomenon like the 'name buyer' can only arise when a substantial number of painters enjoy a certain measure of fame. This applies not only to legendary artists of the past but to contemporary ones as well. It emerges from the fact that drawing up lists of the names of historical and contemporary painters was one of the activities pursued by art-lovers.[55] Rembrandt's name

appeared on such a list very early on in his career. In 1628, the lawyer and 'Lover of the Art of Painting' Arnold van Buchel (1565–1641) mentioned Rembrandt in his notes as 'a miller's son from Leiden' who was 'highly regarded, albeit prematurely'.[56] Rembrandt was 22 at the time. The growing fame of both Rembrandt and his Leiden colleague Jan Lievens, with whom he may have shared a studio, undoubtedly played a role in Huygens's decision to call on them in *c*.1629. Huygens (fig. 37) wrote in his autobiographical fragment the following year, at the beginning of his lengthy discourse on the painters he knew (or wished to know): 'I am always eager to be on friendly terms with famous men.'[57]

It is against the background of this remarkably modern-sounding symbiosis between seventeenth-century artists and art-lovers, in which fame was the catalyst, that we must conceive of Rembrandt's activity as a maker of self portraits.

Fame as a Spur to producing Self Portraits

The wide dissemination of Rembrandt's etched self portraits undoubtedly contributed to his burgeoning reputation. Prints were one of the most effective ways of garnering fame, as seventeenth-century artists were well aware.[58] It can now be taken as read that Rembrandt was famous far beyond the borders of the Dutch Republic, and remained so until his death. The myth that he was a 'neglected artist' is admittedly tenacious, but it has been overtaken by the facts.[59]

As Manuth explains in his essay, one of the consequences of the public's interest in famous people was a growing demand for

fig. 36 *opposite*
Title page of Samuel van Hoogstraten's
Inleyding tot de hooge schoole der schilderkonst,
Rotterdam 1678.

fig. 37 *above*
THOMAS DE KEYSER, *Portrait of Constantijn Huygens
and his Clerk*, 1627. Panel, 92.4 × 69.3 cm.
London, National Gallery.

images of celebrities. The faces of *uomini famosi* (famous men) were gathered together in portrait galleries, in print series or as prints in biographies, such as the portraits of painters and other artists in the books of Vasari (p. 42, fig. 2), Von Sandrart (fig. 38) and Houbraken (fig. 39). That there is a direct connection between someone's fame and the number of images of him or her in circulation is self-evident today, but it applied equally in the seventeenth century. It was Rembrandt's fame, even during his lifetime, that must have been an important motive for his large output of self portraits. Raupp and Naumann have already come to this conclusion. But is it confirmed by seventeenth-century sources? They are extremely meagre on this point, but telling nonetheless.

The locations of only three Rembrandts during the artist's lifetime are known: two were in royal collections (cat. nos. 26 and 85) and one was with a famous art dealer (see p. 67).[60] However, that does not mean that he kept the rest himself. On the contrary, not a single self portrait is mentioned in the remarkably detailed inventory of Rembrandt's possessions and stocks drawn up in 1656.[61] Self portraits appear in documents in the decades after his death, mainly in the inventories of amateurs and royalty. It is not possible to prove that they were all there during Rembrandt's lifetime, although they probably were.

If we accept that the correlation between fame and the demand for portraits and self portraits is the main explanation for the exceptional scale of Rembrandt's production of paintings and etchings bearing his likeness, how are we to account for the fact that there are only four painted self portraits by Rubens

(leaving aside the three in which he included other members of his family),[62] who was unquestionably more famous than Rembrandt? People wanting his portrait had to make do with an engraving after a painted self portrait (see p. 144, fig. 32d). There must have been another factor that would explain why Rembrandt made so many painted and etched self portraits. As discussed above, it could not have been the 'search for self', but what was it?

The Multiple Functions of the Self Portrait

When Cosimo de' Medici (1642–1723), later Grand Duke of Tuscany, made his Grand Tour in 1667 at the age of 25 and passed through the northern Netherlands with his entourage, he met numerous artists and visited fifteen in their studios.[63] Of the painters mentioned in his travel journal, three received the predicate 'famoso': Gerrit Dou (cat. no. 89), Frans van Mieris the Elder (1635–81) and Rembrandt.[64] The fact that it was these three who produced such an unusually large number of self portraits is no doubt directly associated with their fame. Naumann came to this same conclusion in his exemplary oeuvre catalogue of Van Mieris when he observed that the artist had included his likeness no fewer than thirty-one times in his paintings.[65] That this was frequently done in genre works will prove to be significant, as will Van Mieris's habit of making portraits of himself and *tronies* with his features in which he wears rich, often gleaming fabrics (figs. 40 and 41). The dozen self portraits by Dou (see cat. no. 89) are as a rule included in similar elaborate settings (figs. 42 and 43).[66]

It is understandable that Dou and Van Mieris, who were both

fig. 38 *left*
Portrait of Rembrandt. From Joachim von Sandrart's *Teutsche Academie*, Nuremberg 1675, facing p. 356.

fig. 39 *right*
Portrait of Rembrandt. From Arnold Houbraken's *De Groote Schouburgh*, vol. I, The Hague 1718, fig. M, facing p. 272. This engraving also contains the portraits of Anna Maria van Schurman (1607–78) and Jacob Backer (1608–51).

fig. 40 *right*
FRANS VAN MIERIS THE ELDER, *Self Portrait of the Artist, with a Cittern*, 1674. Canvas, 17.5 × 14 cm. London, National Gallery.

fig. 41 *far right*
FRANS VAN MIERIS THE ELDER, '*Teasing the Dog*', 1660. Panel, 27.5 × 20 cm. The Hague, Mauritshuis.

fig. 42 *below*
GERRIT DOU, *Self Portrait*, 1647. Panel, 43 × 34.5 cm. Dresden, Staatliche Kunstsammlungen, Gemäldegalerie Alte Meister.

fig. 43 *below right*
GERRIT DOU, *The Quack* (self portrait at extreme right), 1652. Panel, 112.4 × 83.4 cm. Rotterdam, Museum Boijmans Van Beuningen.

fijnschilders ('fine painters', who specialised in a glossy, enamel-like finish), made fewer self portraits than Rembrandt, given the time it took them to produce a painting. However, Van Mieris's output of depictions of his countenance in genre scenes or otherwise, was proportionately greater than Rembrandt's, his likeness appearing in no less than a quarter of his paintings.[67]

But, was the phenomenon simply a case of collectable portraits of and by these three famous men, which were sometimes inserted into genre-like settings? In my view, the route that has taken us past the art-lover offers the prospect of a second explanation. I believe that the reason Dou and Van Mieris generally incorporated their likenesses in settings that are to some extent genre-like is associated with the fact that both men owed their fame to their exceptional ability to give a convincing imitation of a multiplicity of materials. Hecht has argued persuasively that the demonstration of this skill was probably the main *raison d'être* for their paintings.[68] My central hypothesis for the argument presented in this essay is that the inclusion of their portraits in such a setting provided the purchaser with both the portrait of a celebrated artist and a display of the mastery that had made him famous in the first place.

Several documents in the archives of the Galleria degli Uffizi relating to the collection of self portraits assembled by the Medici (see p. 49, fig. 12) can be regarded as buttressing this hypothesis. The dual function of the self portrait is most explicitly summed up in an eighteenth-century document. The Jesuit and art-lover Luigi Lanzi (1732–1810) wrote the following in 1782 in connection with the Medici gallery of self portraits:

every portrait in the two rooms is a self portrait of the painter, so in each painting one has a depiction of the artist and at the same time a particular example of his style.[69]

One finds a striking parallel with this view as early as the sixteenth century. It is noteworthy that the few women painters active in that century, such as Catherina van Hemessen (1528– after 1587) and Sofonisba Anguissola (*c*.1532–1625), produced a relatively large number of self portraits, generally showing them before their easels (figs. 44 and 45). Woods-Marsden has cogently demonstrated the dual function of Sofonisba's self portraits:

As it was, Anguissola's several self-images in the act of painting were understood by contemporaries as embodying *two* 'marvels', as the humanist Annibale Caro put it: the rarity of a work created *by* a female, and a simulacrum *of* its prodigious creator.[70]

The dual function of the self portrait that I am proposing could of course be achieved in another, far more explicit way if the maker included a sample of his work in the picture. A well-known instance of this is the request that Van Mieris hold a small painting 'of the kind he usually paints' in a self portrait that had been commissioned from him. Other painters (and an engraver) depicted themselves thus in their self portraits.[71] Van Mieris, however, did so just once. Whereas a landscapist like Pieter Jansz van Asch (1603–78) must have felt obliged to include a miniature landscape in order to identify his specialism (fig. 46), the settings into which Van Mieris and Dou usually inserted their likenesses were themselves characteristic of their art as *fijnschilders*.

This concept of the multiple function of the self portrait, on the one hand as a portrait of an *uomo famoso* and on the other hand as an autograph specimen of the reason for that fame – an exceptional painting technique – can likewise be applied to Rembrandt's painted and etched self portraits. However, the contemporary admiration for Rembrandt involved aspects of his art other than the imitation of textures that gave rise to the fame of Dou and Van Mieris.

The Self Portrait as a Specimen of Rembrandt's Exceptional Technique

'The miracle of our age' was how the South German art-lover Bucelinus (1599–1681) commented on the 58-year-old Rembrandt in his list of 1664 of 'The Names of the Most Distinguished European Painters'. Rembrandt's was the only one of the 166 names in the list to attract such a tribute.[72] In attempting to discover why he was such a wonder one discovers that Bucelinus must have been alluding to his technique.[73] His main informants were two painters, one of whom, Samuel van Hoogstraten, was a pupil of Rembrandt's, while the other, Joachim von Sandrart, must have known Rembrandt and his work at very close quarters.

A third painter who had been acquainted with Rembrandt, Gerard de Lairesse (1640–1711), was full of praise for him in his book of 1707: 'Everything that art and the brush can achieve was possible for him [Rembrandt], and he was the greatest painter of the time and is still unsurpassed.'[74] De Lairesse especially praises Rembrandt's use of colour and handling of light.

fig. 44 *opposite left*
Catherina van Hemessen, *Self Portrait*, 1548.
Panel, 31 × 25 cm. Basel, Kunstmuseum.

fig. 45 *opposite right*
Sofonisba Anguissola, *Self Portrait*.
Canvas, 66 × 57 cm. Lancut, Muzeum Zamek.

fig. 46 *above*
Pieter Jansz van Asch, *Self Portrait*.
Panel, 51.5 × 43.5 cm. Amsterdam, Rijksmuseum.

Similar admiration is found in the writings of Bucelinus's informants, Van Hoogstraten and Von Sandrart. They too commended Rembrandt's exceptional painterly qualities, notwithstanding their criticism of his transgressions of the 'rules of art' by the lights of nascent Classicism.[75] The feature that they mostly singled out was Rembrandt's ability to break colours up, group them, and use them to suggest space and depth, which was considered innovative. It emerges from Van Hoogstraten's book that Rembrandt's skill in rendering human skin was also greatly admired. After expatiating on the need to follow 'true naturalness' in depicting the skin so that 'it appears to be flesh', he adds: 'I shall say nothing of Rembrandt and others, who hold this part of art to be of the utmost importance.'[76]

Apart from these, however, there were aspects of Rembrandt's technique that were held to be not only remarkably good but also unusual, not to say peculiar. In a play of 1648, for instance, the skill in embroidery displayed by one of the main female characters was compared to Rembrandt's art of painting. It was said of this figure, Dorothea, 'that her needle outshines the paintings of Rembrandt himself, acting as a brush with which she paints with gold'.[77]

The theatregoers were evidently expected to know who Rembrandt was and to have such an idea of his paintings that the association with Dorothea's gold embroidery spoke for itself. Many had probably visited the Doelen (Civic Guard Hall) to goggle at 'The Night Watch' completed in 1642 (fig. 47), six years previously, in which the gold embroidery painted in heavy impasto on the clothes of Lieutenant Ruytenburch must have

fig. 47 *left*
REMBRANDT, *The Company of Captain Frans Banning Cocq and Lieutenant Willem van Ruytenburch, known as 'The Night Watch'*, 1642. Canvas, 363 × 437 cm. Amsterdam, Rijksmuseum.

fig. 48 *above*
Detail of fig. 47.

fig. 49 *opposite*
Self Portrait as the Apostle Paul (cat. no. 81, detail).

caused great amazement. We know from the testimony of one of Rembrandt's pupils, Bernhard Keil (1624–87), that the Amsterdam public (and it would have included more than art-lovers alone) were astounded by the extreme illusionism of the figure of Ruytenburch (fig. 48).[78]

Rembrandt's colleagues and the 'Lovers of the Art of Painting' would have had a deeper understanding of this unusual aspect of his technique. It is perfectly possible that Rembrandt's own remark in a letter of 1639 that his paintings should be hung in a strong light so that they could 'voncken (sparkle)' relates to an aspect that appealed to the art-lover's imagination.[79] I have argued elsewhere that this 'sparkle' might be associated with the fact that he, more than any of his contemporaries, used impasto, locally thick paint, particularly in the lighter passages.[80] The light reflecting off the irregularities of its surface structure could have been described by Rembrandt as sparkle. It comes out best in the gold embroidery and the depiction of golden and other gleaming fabrics. When imitating other surface structures, such as human skin, the sparkle contributes to the extraordinary force of the light that is such a characteristic of Rembrandt's paintings, including his self portraits (fig. 49).

That Rembrandt's impasto must have been a subject of discussion in his own day is evident from what Keil told the Italian art-lover Baldinucci. Among other things, he speculated on the origins of Rembrandt's impasto.[81] In his life of the master, Arnold Houbraken (1660–1719) he tells of a portrait 'in which the paint had been applied so thickly that one could lift the painting from the ground by the nose'. He added that works painted 'with impasto have a powerful effect, even from a great distance'.[82]

The unusual, wilful nature of Rembrandt's technique, for which he attracted the highest praise for his achievements, must be regarded as the key to why he was so admired in his own day. But he was renowned not only for his painting technique. Baldinucci had included Keil's remark about Rembrandt's impasto in a book that was actually about printmaking. Rembrandt is the only Dutch graphic artist of his generation discussed in the book, which was aimed at art-lovers and collectors. What he wrote about Rembrandt as an etcher throws, in a different way, a sharp light on the unusual image that his contemporaries had of him. Baldinucci called Rembrandt's etching technique 'una bizzarissima maniera (a most bizarre manner)'. He was particularly struck by Rembrandt's unusually free hand, the traces of which he described as 'tratti irregolari (irregular lines)'.[83] One should bear in mind that, at a time when the highly disciplined practice of engraving shaped the face of graphic art, such freedom must have caused great astonishment (figs. 50 and 51). The liberties that Rembrandt permitted himself in the finish of his etchings would also have been considered bizarre (see for the sketchiness of Rembrandt's etchings cat. nos. 2, 6 and 11).[84]

This idiosyncratic attitude towards the 'unfinished' is also a feature of many of Rembrandt's paintings. The great variation in the finish of the details in his paintings and etchings, which also strikes one in his self portraits, was regarded as one of the most remarkable properties of his art (fig. 52). This is known from the biography of Rembrandt that Houbraken wrote on the basis of information he had received from a number of the master's pupils. Houbraken spoke of paintings he had seen 'in which some things were worked up in great detail, while the remainder was smeared as if by a coarse tar-brush, without consideration for the drawing. He was not to be dissuaded from this practice, saying in justification that a work is finished when the master has achieved his intention in it.'[85]

A self portrait like the one in Karlsruhe (cat. no. 60) can almost be interpreted as a statement of principle on this point. The extremely delicate handling of details like the lips and the modelling of the forehead is in stark contrast to the sketchy strokes indicating the body. Yet this kind of painting, which Rembrandt signed and evidently considered complete, was highly desirable to the amateur. The unknown person who bought it from Rembrandt – one of the later owners was the French court painter Hyacinthe Rigaud (1659–1743) – may have been identifying with the Greek and Roman art-lovers of whom Pliny wrote in AD 77:

It is a very unusual and memorable fact that the last works of artists and their unfinished paintings … are more admired than those which they finished, because in them are seen the preliminary drawings left visible and the artists' actual thoughts.[86]

The Karlsruhe self portrait is by no means the only one that must have appeared only partly finished to Rembrandt's contemporaries.

Rembrandt's pictorial innovations with colour, light and

space (which connoisseurs and initiates appreciated along with the sparkle of gold brocade and other impasto passages), his freedom of handling (regarded as bizarre) and his idiosyncratic ideas about finish must have been qualities that made his works the unusual products of a wayward but extremely gifted painter, not so much in their conception as in their execution.

On top of this there was the convincing illusion of reality, even when Rembrandt worked with a visible brushstroke, and this illusionism was the most important criterion for the appreciation of his art. It also applied to his self portraits, as demonstrated by a passage in Houbraken's biography of Rembrandt:

> Among a multitude of his portraits that were worthy of fame there was one … that he had painted after his own likeness which was so artfully and powerfully elaborated that even the most vigorous brushwork of Van Dyck and Rubens could not match it, aye the head appeared to protrude from it and address the beholders.[87]

We do not know which picture Houbraken was talking about (see pp. 53–4), but when he wrote this, before 1718, it belonged to the wealthy art-lover Jan van Beuningen (1667–1720).[88]

Conclusion

In the section devoted to 'Lovers of the Art of Painting' I argued that this specific group, which was of key importance for the artist, considered the subject of a picture far less interesting than its execution and the fame of its creator. It was not the scene that counted, but the fact that it displayed certain features of the creator's art. Every Rembrandt, every self portrait by Rembrandt,

fig. 50 *opposite left*
Self Portrait with Beret (cat. no. 58, detail).

fig. 51 *opposite centre*
Reinier van Persijn after Joachim von
Sandrart after Raphael (p. 170, fig. 53b),
Portrait of Baldassare Castiglione (detail), c.1641.
Engraving, 262 × 193 mm. Amsterdam,
Rijksmuseum, Rijksprentenkabinet.

fig. 52 *right*
Self Portrait (cat. no. 65, detail).

was no more and no less than a specimen of his art in the eyes of the art-loving collector. The added advantage of the self portrait, however, was that it also portrayed its creator.

That leaves us with the question of why there were not as many self portraits by equally famous, if not more famous artists like Rubens and Poussin. The answer must be that their self portraits were probably not regarded as typical specimens of their art. Both artists were history painters *pur sang* who, the sources suggest, had no desire to fritter away their time painting self portraits for art-lovers, royal or otherwise. Anyone who wanted their portraits could buy a print. Rembrandt's fame, by contrast, was based to a large extent on his *tronies*. The single figures and half-lengths make up the majority of his painted and etched oeuvre. Contemporaries must therefore have seen them as representative of his art. A self portrait by Rembrandt also fell into this category, making it a typical Rembrandt. I have rejected De Vries's hypothesis that the master's self portraits can be regarded as *tronies* on the grounds that he assumed that contemporaries would not have recognised that the figure was Rembrandt. However, De Vries is probably correct in saying that contemporaries must have counted the self portraits as belonging to the *tronies* genus, which was felt to be typical of Rembrandt.

They were not seen solely as anonymous heads, though, but simultaneously as portraits of the *uomo famoso* Rembrandt.

The magnificent variety of both the painted and etched self portraits demonstrates that Rembrandt saw them as experimental forcing-grounds for his painterly and graphic adventures, as he did most of his other works. The purchasers of these portraits must have regarded them as typical works by Rembrandt which had an added attraction in that they also showed the face of the creator. That, however, does not exhaustively explain their meaning. Raupp has pointed out that self portraits, not just those by Rembrandt, could contain messages about art and the status of the artist,[89] and Marieke de Winkel will further substantiate this theory in her essay with the aid of her analysis of the costumes in which Rembrandt portrayed himself. The costumes were part of a complex 'visual language' that must have been comprehensible to initiates, the 'Lovers of the Art of Painting'. The statements made in that visual language, however, were not the *raison d'être* for Rembrandt's self portraits. Rather, they added an extra layer of meaning to the paintings that were collected as portraits of Rembrandt 'done by himself', and perhaps above all, as exemplars of his manner, which was experienced as both wondrous and bizarre.

Translated from the Dutch by Michael Hoyle.

This essay is based on research conducted within the framework of the Rembrandt Research Project, which has been subsidised by the Netherlands Organisation for Scientific Research in The Hague from 1968 to 1999, and was sponsored by DSM from 1990 to 1998. I am grateful to Volker Manuth, Marieke de Winkel and Wardy Poelstra for their helpful comments.

1   Oral communication from Dr R.E.O. Ekkart, Netherlands Institute for Art History (RKD) in The Hague.

2   Van Hall 1963.

3   The following monographic studies have been published on Rembrandt's self portraits: Von Bode 1876; Pinder 1950; Erpel 1967; Wright 1982 and Chapman 1990.

4   Gasser 1961, p. 88.

5   *Rembrandt: Schilder van de mens*, premiered in 1957 (duration: 20 minutes).

6   De Bie 1661, p. 398.

7   Strauss/Van der Meulen 1979, no. 1656/16, no. 72: 'Een Spiegel in een ebben lijst (A mirror in an ebony frame)'; no. 126: 'Een groote spiegel (A large mirror)', and no. 1669/5, no. 7: 'Een spiegel (A mirror)'; no. 50: 'Een oude spiegel met een capstok (An old mirror with a hat-stand)'.

8   Strauss/Van der Meulen 1979, no. 1658/13.

9   Weyerman 1726, p. 733. According to Weyerman in 'De achtste 't Zamenspraak tusschen Pieter Paulus Rubens, Anthony van Dyk en Godefroi Kneller, drie beruchte Schilders', this was the standard practice in Godfried Schalcken's studio. His female English customers complained that he made a habit of painting, in the rather podgy hands of his studio assistant.

10   Philadelphia/Berlin/London 1984, nos. 59, 72, 109–10.

11   Child 1990, p. 19.

12   Leiden 1968, no. 25; Wright 1982, p. 25.

13   Vis 1965, pp. 15–47.

14   Vis 1965, p. 18.

15   Raupp 1984, pp. 115–23, especially p. 122.

16   Goeree 1682, p. 108; Van Mander 1604a, Chapter VI.

17   Amsterdam, Gemeentearchief, PA 234, inv. no. 309, dated 6 September 1685.

18   Bredius 1915–22, vol. I, p. 221, vol. III, p. 957, vol. IV, p. 1240; Strauss/Van der Meulen 1979, no. 1639/11.

19   Blunt 1964, pp. 119, 126, 132, 139, 143, 145, 147.

20   *Woordenboek der Nederlandsche Taal*, s.v. 'Zelfportret'.

21   *Grote Winkler Prins* (8th edn), 25 vols., Amsterdam/Antwerp 1979–84, vol. XIX, s.v. 'Renaissance'.

22   Glaser/Lehmann/Lubos 1973, p. 142.

23   Rosenberg 1964, p. 37.

24   Chapman 1990, cover.

25   Chapman 1990, p. 131.

26   H.-J. Raupp in Brunswick 1980, p. 7.

27   H.-J. Raupp in Brunswick 1980, p. 8.

28   Van Hoogstraten 1678, pp. 109–10.

29   Heesakkers 1987, p. 86.

30   Strauss/Van der Meulen 1979, no. 1639/2.

31   J. van der Veen in Melbourne/Canberra 1997–8, p. 71.

32   De Vries 1989, pp. 185–202, especially pp. 194 and 197.

33   Strauss/Van der Meulen 1979, no. 1639/11.

34   Schwartz 1984, pp. 24–7.

35   Von Sandrart 1675, p. 41.

36   Sluijter 1998.

37   See *Corpus*, vol. IV, nos. 21 and 22.

38   On the desire to collect all of Rembrandt's etchings see, for example, Houbraken 1718–21, vol. I, p. 271.

39   Van Hoogstraten 1678, unpaginated. On this subject see Van de Wetering 1995, pp. 264–70.

40   E. de Jongh et al. in Amsterdam 1976. See also the numerous publications that flowed from this project.

41   Franciscus Junius was the first to make an inventory of these classical writings and fragments that aimed at completeness (see Junius 1638/1694).

42   Castiglione 1528, pp. 81–6.

43   Von Schlosser 1978, pp. 28–127; Brown 1995.

44   Van Keulen 1996.

45   Many of the printed sources relating to art (compare Von Schlosser 1924), even when they appear to be intended solely for artists, state that they are actually directed at 'all who love this noble, free and exalted art in any way whatsoever'.

46   Beck 1624, pp. 54 (29 February) and 82 (25 April).

47   *Brussels Manuscript* 1635, vol. II, pp. 766–9.

48   Heesakkers 1987, pp. 84–90.

49   Heesakkers 1987, p. 86.

50   The various title pages in *Het Schilder-Boeck* mention not only artists but art-lovers as the public Van Mander was addressing (see also note 45).

51   Von Sandrart 1675, p. 40.

52   Stumpel 1988, p. 148; Borghini 1584.

53   Montias 1982, p. 227.

54   Van Hoogstraten 1678, unpaginated, 'aen den Lezer' (note to the Reader).

55   E. van de Wetering in Melbourne/Canberra 1997–8, pp. 58–68, especially pp. 58–60.

56   Strauss/Van der Meulen 1979, no. 1628/1.

57   Heesakkers 1987, p. 74.

58   Van Hoogstraten 1678, p. 195.

59   Slive 1953; Emmens 1968; E. van de Wetering, 'The miracle of our age: Rembrandt through the eyes of his contemporaries', in Melbourne/Canberra 1997–8, pp. 58–68.

60   Strauss/Van der Meulen 1979, nos. 1639/1 and 1657/2; Langedijk 1992, p. 151.

61   Strauss/Van der Meulen 1979, no. 1656/12.

62   Rubens's four painted self portraits are in Florence (Galleria degli Uffizi, *c*.1615), London (The Royal Collection, 1623; see p. 47, fig. 11), Antwerp (Rubenshuis, *c*.1630) and Vienna (Kunsthistorisches Museum, *c*.1635–40). On Rubens's self portraits and the prints associated with them see Vlieghe 1987, nos. 133–7.

63   Hoogewerff 1919.

64   Hoogewerff 1919.

65   Naumann 1981, vol. I, p. 126 (see note 67).

66   Baer 1990, nos. 20, 30, 46, 56, 75, 79, 88 and 112. Four self portraits are not accepted by Baer: formerly Henle Collection (Martin 1913, p. 13, ill.); formerly Frankfurt am Main, De Rothschild Collection (Martin 1913, p. 19, ill.); formerly Paris, Warneck Collection (Martin 1913, p. 21, ill.) and Salzburg, Residenzgalerie (p. 238, fig. 89b). If her rejection is correct, these portraits may well be copies after lost originals.

67   Naumann 1981, vol. I, p. 126. Five of these paintings can be regarded as true self portraits, although it is difficult to draw the line demarcating the *tronie*-like self portrait. There are twelve known works that fall into one of these two categories. The remaining nineteen pictures in which Naumann detects the face of Frans van Mieris are genre pieces.

68   P. Hecht in Amsterdam 1989–90, passim.

69   Prinz 1971, pp. 230 and 182.

70   Woods-Marsden 1998, p. 192.

71   Naumann 1981, vol. I, p. 125.

72   Schillemans 1987, pp. 25–37.

73   E. van de Wetering in Melbourne/Canberra 1997–8, pp. 64–8.

74   De Lairesse 1707, vol. I, book V, p.325.

75   E. van de Wetering in Melbourne/Canberra 1997–8, pp. 63–8; Van de Wetering 1997, pp. 269–72.

76   Van Hoogstraten 1678, pp. 226–8, especially p. 228. On the painting of flesh colours see also Angel 1642, pp. 54–5 (Hoyle/Miedema 1996, p. 248).

77   Zoet 1648; see Slive 1953, p. 45.

78   Baldinucci 1686, p. 78.

79   Strauss/Van der Meulen 1979, no. 1639/4.

80   Van de Wetering 1997, pp. 251–2.

81   Baldinucci 1686, p. 80.

82   Houbraken 1718–21, vol. I, p. 269.

83   Baldinucci 1686, p. 80, quoted from Slive 1953, p. 106, note 1.

84   *Corpus*, vol. IV, Chapter II.

85   Houbraken 1718–21, vol. I, p. 259.

86   *Naturalis Historia*, XXXV, xl, lines 143–6 (see Pliny 1968).

87   Houbraken 1718–21, vol. I, p. 269.

88   Houbraken 1718–21, vol. I, p. 269; On Van Beuningen see Broos 1995, pp. 20–6.

89   Raupp 1984, passim.

Rembrandt and the Artist's Self Portrait: Tradition and Reception

Volker Manuth

'And so it is certain that the faces of the dead live on in painting' (Leon Battista Alberti, *Della pittura*, Florence 1436).

In Oscar Wilde's *Picture of Dorian Gray* (1891), the painter Basil Hallward gives a surprising answer to Lord Henry Wotton's query about his refusal to exhibit the portrait of Dorian Gray:

every portrait that is painted with feeling is a portrait of the artist, not of the sitter. The sitter is merely the accident, the occasion. It is not he who is revealed by the painter, it is rather the painter who, on the coloured canvas, reveals himself.[1]

Here, Hallward is making an indirect reference to the Renaissance concept of the artist who, no matter what his subject, unconsciously puts something of his own personality and soul into all his creations. Stemming from the rhetorical practices of antiquity, this conviction had already found its classic formulation by the end of the fifteenth century in the Italian adage 'Ogni pittore dipinge sé (every painter paints himself)'.[2] Although figuratively applicable to all genres of painting, the phrase's literal meaning takes on an entirely new dimension in Rembrandt's numerous self portraits, in which he repeatedly – and consciously – made himself the focus and theme. No other artist before him (and hardly any after) has left behind such an extensive group of works, ranging from small-scale drawn or etched studies in expression to independent paintings of considerable size. Despite the many problems of attribution, it is now generally accepted that there are more than seventy surviving self portraits, executed in various techniques over a period of some forty years.

This group of pictures has often been interpreted as a kind of painted autobiography, an extraordinarily personal document of the vicissitudes of Rembrandt's life.[3] It has also been seen as the manifestation of a complex artistic psyche, and as the visual incarnation of his search for the self.[4] Increasingly, analyses of the self portraits have concentrated on Rembrandt as a member of society, whose practice reflected varying aspects of contemporary public and artistic life, as well as ideas expressed in art theory.[5] These have made it clear that it is necessary to revise the traditional and widely accepted notion that the self portrait results from purely internal needs.

In conceiving his self portraits, Rembrandt had a long tradition at his disposal, with roots stretching back to antiquity. His engagement with the genre is therefore less surprising than the extraordinary number of pictures he produced, and the dogged persistence with which he explored all means of self-representation throughout his career. In his self portraits he relied partially on conventions that had emerged since the Renaissance, which he both modified and further elaborated upon. At the same time, he apparently sought to satisfy the growing demands of art-lovers and collectors, who exhibited a great interest in his self portraits. Rembrandt's place within the established practice of the artist's self portrait, the significance of this form for the contemporary public, and aspects of the history of collecting such works are the main focus of this essay.

Previous page
History Piece (cat. no. 1, detail).

Rembrandt and the Self Portrait Tradition

The history and evolution of the independent self portrait is inexorably linked to the changing status of the artist, and in particular to his desire for improved professional standing, which had begun to develop in the early Renaissance.[6] Although numerous medieval painters and sculptors incorporated their likenesses into their figural compositions, this practice appears to have been religiously motivated (the desire for salvation) and not an expression of the creative individual's pride in either themselves or their works of art. It was only with the gradual emergence of the artist from the collective strictures of the guilds, and his greater artistic freedom resulting from the revival of the notion of *artes liberales* (liberal arts), that the foundation was laid for a new self-understanding and social advancement. The Renaissance admiration of antiquity also led to the revival of the notion of individual glory and was equally attributed to artists. The artists of ancient Greece served as models: Apelles, Zeuxis and Parrhasios, whose names had been handed down by Pliny (61/2–114) and others. This enhancement of the artist's standing was paralleled by a growing interest in his personal history. The increasing admiration of the public for artistic personalities was given a visible form in *c*.1490, when Lorenzo de' Medici (1449–92) erected a monument – with a portrait – to the painter Fra Filippo Lippi (*c*.1406–69) in the cathedral at Spoleto.[7]

By the fifteenth century it was no longer unusual to find artists' self portraits incorporated into compositions.[8] This remained a popular form of self-representation in the centuries that followed. Interestingly, the young Rembrandt also began his long series with self portraits incorporated into history paintings: for example, in his earliest known work, *The Stoning of Saint Stephen* (1625; p. 22, fig. 28), and the still unravelled composition in Leiden, painted in 1626 (cat. no. 1).[9] Partly hidden by the commander's sceptre, the painter – easily recognisable by his curly head of hair – stares out at the viewer (fig. p. 39). Here, he is merely a participant in a larger event; it was not until the end of the 1620s that he completed the move into the realm of the independent self portrait, with which he drew attention to his personality and art as commensurate elements in the creative process.

The independent self portrait began to develop in the fifteenth century, but its evolution was slow. This explains why examples from this period are relatively rare.[10] Where exactly this pictorial form originated is unclear, as there are striking analogies between Southern and Northern Europe. One possible candidate for the earliest, independent self portrait of the modern era is Jan van Eyck's *Man in a Turban* in London (fig. 1). The painting has retained its original frame, which, in addition to the name of the artist and the date (21 October 1433), also bears the painter's personal device – 'Als ich can (As I can)' – partially written in pseudo-Greek capitals.[11] Around the same time, the Italian architect and theoretician Leon Battista Alberti (1404–72) painted his own self portrait. In the sixteenth century, it still hung in the Palazzo Rucellai in Florence, which he had designed. Today we know it only from the copy by Christofano dell'Altissimo (died 1605) in the Uffizi.[12] The artist depicts himself in near-profile, a reference to the portrait conventions

fig. 1
JAN VAN EYCK, *A Man in a Turban*, 1433.
Panel, 33.3 × 25.8 cm. London, National Gallery.

of coins and medals. Alberti also made two self-portrait plaquettes based on antique numismatic representations of rulers, an indication of the growing self-confidence among the artists of his time.[13]

Outstanding personalities from political and intellectual life – known during the Italian Renaissance as *uomini illustri* or *famosi* (famous men) – were often celebrated in series of portraits.[14] From the sixteenth century, artists were included among their ranks. Paolo Giovio (1483–1552), Bishop of Nocera, for example, commissioned a group of likenesses of poets, philosophers, artists, popes and kings – both living and dead – for his villa on Lake Como. On his death, the collection encompassed approximately 400 pictures.[15]

It was, however, the various artists' biographies illustrated with their portraits that helped generate and sustain the public's growing interest in the life and work of famous painters, sculptors and architects. Most important among these was the second edition of *Le Vite de più eccellenti Pittori, Scultori e Architettori* (The Lives of the most excellent Painters, Sculptors and Architects), by the Italian painter and art historiographer Giorgio Vasari (1511–74), published in 1568.[16] Here, the unillustrated first edition of 1550 was embellished with 144 woodcuts after artists' self portraits. The bust-length, oval likenesses are set within an architectonic framework, with attributes and personifications referring to each artist's *métier* (fig. 2). Vasari, whose *Lives* forms the first comprehensive self-portrait anthology, also encouraged art academies to establish their own collections of such works. The statutes of the Accademia del Disegno in Florence, for example,

which he helped formulate in 1562–3, already recommended that Tuscany's most famous artists be depicted on the walls of the assembly hall.[17] Although this project was never carried out, the first president of the Accademia di San Luca in Rome, Federico Zuccari (1540/1–1609), soon took up the idea. He donated his own self portrait to the academy and copies were made of those by other famous painters; from then on, portraits and self portraits of all academy members were added continually.[18]

The collection of the Académie Royale de Peinture et Sculpture in Paris, founded in 1648, was formed more systematically. On the day of their admission to the academy, candidates for full membership were required to deliver trial pieces on assigned subjects in their area of specialisation, so-called *morceaux de réception* (literally 'reception pieces'). Among these were self portraits or portraits of other members, executed according to specific rules and conventions.[19] The most important type was the *portrait d'apparat* (fig. 3), an elaborately staged, imposing image, with various props and details serving to underline the sitter's distinguished status. Even art had to satisfy the purposes of the 'Sun King' Louis XIV (1638–1715) and his absolutist state. Academic painters adapted this form, originally reserved for the nobility, by including the tools of their profession. Hence, their portraits became an expression of their own 'noble' status and the importance of art: the artist as aristocrat.

In formulating his own self portraits, Rembrandt was particularly influenced by a series of Dutch artists' portraits of the sixteenth century: the twenty-three engravings published by the humanist Domenicus Lampsonius (1532–99) in Antwerp in

1572, entitled *Pictorum aliquot celebrium Germaniae inferioris effigies*.[20] The engravings were executed by Jan (1549–*c*.1618) and Hieronymus Wierix (1553–1619), Cornelis Cort (1533–78) and Hieronymus Cock (*c*.1510–70), some of them after self portraits by artists already deceased. This extraordinarily popular compilation was re-issued a total of four times in the years before 1600. In 1610, the Hague engraver and publisher Hendrick Hondius (1573–1649) increased the number of portrait prints to sixty-eight.[21] Hondius's richly detailed backgrounds enlivened the relatively uniform Lampsonius series, in which the bust-length figures are set against a neutral background and the artists are rarely shown with their professional attributes or at work. The painters' elegant contemporary clothing draws attention to their elevated social status. In addition to preserving the memory of those already dead, the series was also intended to champion a specifically Northern artistic tradition. By reproducing the presumed likenesses of the brothers Jan (active 1422; died 1441) and Hubert van Eyck (*c*.1385/90–1426) at the very beginning of the Lampsonius series, and by integrating important painters from outside the Netherlands into the Hondius group – for example, Hans Holbein the Younger (1497/8–1543), Albrecht Dürer (1471–1528) and Isaac Oliver (*c*.1560–1617) – the compilers fostered the notion of an enduring and important Northern European school of painting, that was both different and independent from that of Italy.

Rembrandt repeatedly turned to the prints of Lampsonius and Hondius for inspiration, particularly in the late 1630s. His etched self portrait with a feathered beret of 1638 (fig. 4), for example, seems to have been modelled on the Lampsonius likeness of Jan Gossaert (active 1503; died 1532) (fig. 5).[22] In addition to the formal similarities, it is interesting to note how closely Rembrandt has imitated the sitter's clothing. As in a number of other works (for example, cat. no. 54), he is dressed according to sixteenth-century fashion in a conscious effort to place himself among his older colleagues, who had played a decisive role in the development of the Northern European painting tradition. Another important artist in this regard was Lucas van Leyden (active 1508; died 1533), a native of Rembrandt's home town (p. 69, fig. 13). In the seventeenth century he was considered a venerable figure in Northern painting, an honour he shared with Dürer, with whom he had been personally acquainted. In his *Schilder-Boeck*, published in 1604, the art historiographer Karel van Mander (1548–1606) noted that they had had a special affinity, and that both had found fame outside their own countries.[23]

Van Mander never tired of praising Dürer's dual talent for engraving and painting, which even the Italians had been forced to recognise. In his biography of Dürer he also mentions the artist's predilection for self portraits. Van Mander describes both those incorporated into history paintings and those created independently – all works he himself had seen.[24] Rembrandt, who purchased a large number of Dürer's engravings and woodcuts at an auction in 1638, must have read these passages with great interest.[25] Here, after all, was a famous artist of the North whose numerous self portraits were widely admired and, consequently, eminently collectable.

fig. 2 *opposite left*
Unknown artist, *Portrait of Michelangelo*. Woodcut. From the second edition of Giorgio Vasari's *Lives*, Florence 1568, vol. III, p. 717.

fig. 3 *opposite right*
GÉRARD EDELINCK after Rigaud, *Portrait of Hyacinthe Rigaud* (after the painted self portrait), 1698. Engraving, 478 × 364 mm. Amsterdam, Rijksmuseum, Rijksprentenkabinet.

fig. 4 *right*
Self Portrait in Sixteenth-Century Apparel (cat. no. 49).

fig. 5 *far right*
Unknown engraver, *Portrait of Jan Gossaert* (detail), 1572. Engraving, 209 × 124 mm. From Lampsonius/Cock 1572, no. 7. Amsterdam, Rijksmuseum, Rijksprentenkabinet.

As already mentioned, Rembrandt's earliest self portraits – like Dürer's – are found in his history paintings. But, in his independent self portraits there are traces of his deep involvement with his renowned predecessor. In a picture completed in 1640, Rembrandt once again posed in a costume dating from the period 1520–30 (fig. 6). Two major sixteenth-century Italian works are generally thought to have served as his exclusive models: Raphael's *Portrait of Baldassare Castiglione* (p. 170, fig. 53b) and Titian's *Portrait of a Man* (p. 170, fig. 53a). Both works were in Amsterdam when Rembrandt painted his self portrait, and he even made a drawing after the Raphael (p. 172, fig. 53c), which was auctioned in April 1639.[26] Nonetheless, there are equally obvious connections with Dürer's self portrait of 1498 (fig. 7), particularly in the treatment of the arm resting on the balustrade. In contrast to Titian's sitter, who seems to be leaning only on his elbow – difficult though this is to discern due to the fullness of his sleeve – Rembrandt, like Dürer, rests his entire forearm on the ledge. Furthermore, an X-radiograph of Rembrandt's self portrait reveals that it achieved its final form only after a revision of the original composition (p. 173, fig. 54a).[27] Initially, the painter had also planned to show the fingers of his left hand, which would have related the two works still more closely.

Dürer's self portrait had been in the collection of King Charles I of England (1600–49) since 1636, a gift from the city of Nuremberg. It had been brought to him by Thomas Howard (1585–1646), Earl of Arundel, whose journey back to London had taken him through the Netherlands (Arnhem and The Hague),

where Rembrandt could conceivably have seen it.[28] It is also possible that he modelled his work on a drawing, or even a pre-1640 copy. The portrait was of a particularly popular type in Northern Europe in the first half of the sixteenth century, as indicated, for example, by the *Portrait of a Young Man of the Van Steynoert Family* (fig. 8) painted by an anonymous Dutch artist around 1520. Rembrandt's 1640 self portrait appears to mark the climax of a phase in the late 1630s in which Dürer's work, including his various forms of self-representation, played an influential role in his art. In this way, Rembrandt consciously made himself part of the great Northern European tradition to which he owed so much, and he did so in such a way that his contemporaries could not fail to notice.

Judging from the depiction of a fictitious collection of paintings (fig. 9) attributed to Jan Brueghel II (1601–78), the promotion of an independent painterly tradition stretching back to the fifteenth century was a topical subject in the Netherlands. To the left and right of the archway in the room with the personification of Painting executing a flower still life, hang numerous portraits. With three exceptions, these are all likenesses of famous Dutch artists of the fifteenth and sixteenth centuries: Hubert van Eyck, Lucas van Leyden, Quinten Metsys (c.1465–1530), Gossaert and Pieter Coecke van Aelst (1502–50). The only non-Dutch painter included, besides the Italians Michelangelo (1475–1564) and Raphael (1483–1520), is Dürer. In Brueghel's allegory of the art of painting, these portraits suggest which famous figures of the past should provide inspiration for the artists of the present. The fact that portraits of Northern

European artists are in the majority indicates a certain amount of pride in their accomplishments and a growing interest in the origins of the Dutch school.[29]

The most influential series of artists' portraits – also in terms of the development of Baroque portraiture in general – can be traced back to Anthony van Dyck (1599–1641). His so-called *Iconography*, a group of eighty engraved portraits of famous contemporaries, was first published in Antwerp by Maerten van den Enden (active *c*.1630–54) between 1632 and 1641.[30] The bulk of prints depict southern Netherlandish artists and connoisseurs. The series also includes princes, officers, scholars and diplomats, but these are in the minority. The concept governing Van Dyck's *Iconography*, and the element binding all the figures depicted, is the aristocratic notion of *virtù*: the belief in a fundamental link between a virtuous way of life and intellectual or artistic activity. In these portraits, Van Dyck captures the sitter's character through a lively depiction of his external appearance (fig. 10). Both physique and pose are made to express his moral standing. Elegance and noblesse have now become attributes of the artist as well; he has reached the status of an aristocrat.

Rembrandt certainly knew this series, which appeared in an expanded second edition of one hundred prints in 1645 (see p. 70, fig. 15). There is, however, little evidence that he used them as models for his self portraits.[31] Van Dyck's *virtuosi* exhibit a rich variety of gesture. The sitter's arms and hands – shown shoved into their clothing, raised as if in speaking, or pointing towards themselves or at something beyond the frame – their poses and the dynamic handling of drapery, are meant to emphasise mental

fig. 6 *opposite left*
Self Portrait (cat. no. 54), detail.

fig. 7 *opposite right*
ALBRECHT DÜRER, *Self Portrait*, 1498.
Panel, 52 × 41 cm. Madrid, Museo del Prado.

fig. 8 *above*
ANONYMOUS DUTCH PAINTER, *Portrait of a Young Man of the Van Steynoert Family, c.1520.*
Panel, 41 × 32.4 cm. New York, The Metropolitan Museum of Art, The Friedsam Collection.

fig. 9 *right*
JAN BRUEGHEL II, *Lady Pictura painting Flowers.*
Copper, 48 × 75 cm. The Netherlands, Private Collection.

agility. Even in those rare instances when Rembrandt abandoned the half-length format, his hands play only a subordinate role, doing nothing more than holding his painter's tools – pencil, palette, brush or maulstick. Arnold Houbraken (1669–1719) remarked in 1718: 'One rarely sees a well-painted hand by him [Rembrandt], as he usually hides them in shadow – particularly in portraits. Unless of course it is the hand of a wrinkled old woman.'[32] In any case, unlike Van Dyck, in most of his self portraits, Rembrandt remained rooted in a formal tradition originating long before the appearance of his Antwerp colleague's series.

Rembrandt's Self Portraits in Princely Collections of the Seventeenth and Eighteenth Centuries

King Charles I's large collection included numerous artists' self portraits.[33] Although the English monarch had a preference for Italian – particularly Venetian – painting of the sixteenth century, he did own several works by Dutch and Flemish artists. During the first years of his reign, his favoured portrait painter was Daniel Mytens (c.1590–1647) from Delft, who was appointed court painter by James I in 1618. Even before he ascended the throne in 1625, however, Charles had established contact with Peter Paul Rubens (1577–1640) – although he ultimately failed to keep the artist at court. He requested Rubens's self portrait in 1623; it was hung, together with one by Mytens (London, The Royal Collection), in St James's Palace, and then in Whitehall (fig. 11).[34] These works were later joined by a self portrait by Van Dyck, who became the most celebrated

portraitist of the royal family and the English aristocracy from 1632.

In 1625, Charles I granted the Dutch artist Abraham van der Doort (1575/80–1640) the post of keeper of 'all our pictures of Us, Our Heires and Successors'. His task was 'to prevent and keepe them from being spoiled or defaced, to order marke and number them, and to keepe a Register of them'.[35] According to Van der Doort's catalogue of 1639, the self portraits by Rubens, Mytens and Van Dyck hung in the king's breakfast chamber.[36] This seems to have been a sign of his admiration for these three contemporary court painters, each of whom had been in his service, if only temporarily. The fact that Rubens and Van Dyck were widely recognised as important members of their profession, and as remarkable personalities who could carry themselves with confidence and sophistication at court, certainly also influenced his choice.

These pictures were not, however, the only artists' self portraits in Charles I's collection. In addition to the likenesses of the three Netherlandish painters, he owned a number of sixteenth-century Italian self portraits. Most of these were hung in the so-called Long Gallery at Whitehall. They reflect his preference for Italian painting, which had developed over the course of time into a particular veneration for the Venetian and Florentine schools of the sixteenth century. Abraham van der Doort's catalogue mentions self portraits by Titian (active by 1510; died 1576), Giovanni Antonio da Pordenone (active 1504; died 1539), Agnolo Bronzino (1503–72) and Giulio Romano (1499?–1546).[37]

fig. 10 *left*
AFTER ANTHONY VAN DYCK, *Portrait of Theodoor van Loon, Painter*. Engraving from Van Dyck's *Iconography*, 281 × 174 mm. Amsterdam, Rijksmuseum, Rijksprentenkabinet.

fig. 11 *opposite*
PETER PAUL RUBENS, *Self Portrait*, 1623. Panel, 85.9 × 62.3 cm. London, The Royal Collection.

Nonetheless, Charles did not set out to create a collection of artists' self portraits systematically, as was later the case with Leopoldo de' Medici (1617–75) and his nephew Cosimo III (1642–1723). This is borne out by the two self portraits of Northern European painters – Dürer and Rembrandt – in his possession. Both these works were presents, and thus came into his ownership purely by accident. As we have seen, Dürer's self portrait of 1498 was given to Charles in 1636 as a gift from the city council of Nuremberg (fig. 7).[38] The Rembrandt self portrait, along with two other works attributed to him, entered the collection in 1633, a gift from Robert Kerr (1578–1654), the first Earl of Ancrum. On the basis of the description in Van der Doort's catalogue, it is likely that this was the self portrait now in Liverpool (cat. no. 26) of c.1630–1:

the picture done by Rembrant, being his owne picture & done by himself in a Black capp and furrd habbitt with a lit[t]le goulden chaine uppon both his Should[rs] In an Ovall and a square black frame.[39]

The measurements recorded in the inventory are also nearly identical to those of the work in Liverpool.

As Charles I's faithful ally, Kerr was asked to undertake a diplomatic mission to Holland in 1629. Here he met the stadholder's secretary, Constantijn Huygens (1596–1687), who probably drew his attention to the promising young painters Rembrandt and Jan Lievens (1607–74). In his (fragmentary) memoirs, begun the same year, Huygens (p. 27, fig. 37) praised the two artists, whom he had visited in their shared studio in Leiden.[40] It is likely that it was he who established the contact that eventually led to the commission for the self portrait, which Rembrandt completed around 1630–1. Lievens, too, profited from this connection to the English aristocrat: Kerr purchased both his portrait of an old woman (p. 134, fig. 26a) – mistakenly listed in Van der Doort's catalogue as a work by Rembrandt – and a signed and dated study of the head of a Capuchin monk, which has remained in the family's possession.[41] In addition, shortly before his death in exile in Amsterdam, he commissioned his own portrait from Lievens (Edinburgh, Scottish National Portrait Gallery).[42]

Kerr was Charles I's confidant. He cannot, however, be counted among the greatest collectors of his day. It therefore seems safe to assume that the Rembrandt was intended from the outset as a gift to his sovereign and personal friend. However, it is remarkable, although not altogether incomprehensible, that he chose a self portrait by a young artist little known outside his native land. The years between Kerr's sojourn in The Hague and the completion of Rembrandt's picture were marked by the artists' close relations with the Orange court. Following Huygens's visit to their studio – if not before – both Rembrandt and Lievens could rely on his support and assistance in obtaining commissions. It was thanks to Huygens, for example, that Stadholder Frederick Henry (1584–1647) bought Rembrandt's *Capture of Samson*, painted in 1629/30 (p. 156, fig. 41a), and, in all likelihood, his *Simeon praising Christ* of 1631 (The Hague, Mauritshuis) before 1632.

At this time, Rembrandt also enjoyed the court's patronage as a portraitist, as his likeness of the stadholder's wife, Amalia of Solms (1602–75), dated 1632, demonstrates.[43] At the time of

Kerr's visit, then, everything indicated that Rembrandt was destined for a successful career and an enduring relationship with the House of Orange. The same was true of Lievens, whose *Gypsy Fortune-Teller* (Berlin, Gemäldegalerie) was also in Frederick Henry's collection by 1632.[44] Encouraged by Huygens's favourable judgement, the English diplomat must have felt assured that in purchasing works by the two young men he was acquiring pictures by artists with a great future. This must have led Kerr to consider Rembrandt's self portrait an appropriate gift for the English monarch.

The early appreciation of Rembrandt's work, even outside the northern Netherlands, stimulated interest in the painter as a person. Van der Doort's correct identification of the sitter in the self portrait of 1630–1 indicates that by 1639 Rembrandt's features were already widely known. Almost from the beginning, then, Rembrandt could count on being recognised in his painted self portraits. The dissemination of his etched likenesses certainly played a decisive role. The fact that one of his self portraits had found its way into the possession of the king of England at the very start of his career was both an acknowledgement of his talent and an incentive. In London, his likeness became part of a small but discerning group of artists' self portraits, which already included works by his more famous Flemish colleagues, Rubens and Van Dyck. This collection in many ways anticipated a statement made by Johan van Gool (1685–1763) more than one hundred years later. According to Van Gool, portraits, once removed from the family context, tend to be neglected, since they are difficult to sell on the open market. He continued: 'Even in

famous collections they have no place, unless of course we are talking about portraits of such figures as Rubens, Van Dyck, Rembrandt and, occasionally, Frans Hals.'[45] Charles I's collection is a striking example of this phenomenon.

As I have discussed, the choice of self portraits in Charles I's possession reflected his personal taste and preferences. In addition, the social standing of the artist portrayed also seems to have been an important factor. In contrast, these criteria played no role in the formation of the largest and most significant group of artists' self portraits: the Galleria degli autoritratti (self portrait collection) in the Uffizi in Florence, which was famous in Italy and far beyond.[46] The origins and history of this unique collection are inseparable from Medici patronage and the family's passion for owning works of art. It was begun by Cardinal Leopoldo de' Medici. As a non-governing member of the family, with many and sundry ties to scholars and intellectuals throughout Europe, he devoted himself from an early age to the acquisition of drawings, coins, books and specimens of natural history. On his death, he left behind some 700 paintings, about 80 of which were artists' self portraits.

A number of works by famous painters of the Renaissance – already hanging in the Palazzo Vecchio as part of a series of *uomini illustri* brought together by Cosimo I (1519–74) – formed the basis of the collection. Among them were likenesses of Brunelleschi (1377–1446), Alberti, Leonardo (1452–1519), Michelangelo, Titian and Dürer. This array was augmented by purchases, inheritance, gifts and, from 1664 on, commissions.[47] After Leopoldo's death, his nephew, Cosimo III, Grand Duke

fig. 12
Self portrait gallery in the Uffizi, Florence; entrance to the corridor with portraits of painters from the Northern European schools. Pen drawing, 386 × 560 mm. Vienna, Österreichische Nationalbibliothek, Cod. min. 51, fol. 6.

of Tuscany since 1670, continued his work. In 1681, the pictures were transferred from the Palazzo Pitti to a special gallery in the Uffizi; by 1714, the collection comprised a total of 186 paintings (fig. 12).[48]

It was during his extended travels as heir to the duchy that Cosimo III began purchasing artists' self portraits for Cardinal Leopoldo. His two trips to the Netherlands, in 1667–8 and 1669, were particularly important in the collection's development.[49] Dynastic ties to the court of Elector Johann Wilhelm von der Pfalz (1658–1717) in Düsseldorf also proved useful for acquiring further self portraits by Netherlandish artists. This art-loving prince and enthusiastic collector married Cosimo's daughter, Anna Maria Luisa, in 1691, and brought a number of his favourite Dutch and Flemish painters to Düsseldorf. He not only used his position to broker commissions from his father-in-law, but also made him gifts. The earliest catalogue of the Düsseldorf collection, compiled by the court painter and 'curator' Gerhard Joseph Karsch in 1719, reveals that Johann Wilhelm owned several artists' self portraits,[50] among them works by Luca Giordano (1634–1705), Rubens, Van Dyck and Anton Schoonjans (1656–1726/7).

The collection also included a self portrait – or a copy after one – by Rembrandt. This painting was hung in the same room in the Düsseldorf gallery as the artist's seven-part so-called *Passion Series*, commissioned by Frederick Henry (p. 22, fig. 27).[51] The portrait was exactly the same size as the pictures in the series. The fact that it was placed together with these history paintings testifies to a growing interest in the artist as a person, whose self portrait gives visual expression to an individuality inseparable from his artistic creations. Cosimo III was also interested in this connection between the artist's personality and his oeuvre. In order to create a certain unity among the self portraits he commissioned, he prescribed both the size and portrait-type the artists were to follow. The painters were required to show themselves at work and to depict a 'painting within a painting' that would reveal their area of specialisation.[52]

At the time of the earliest inventory, compiled between 1663 and the end of 1671, Leopoldo de' Medici's collection contained only a few self portraits by Netherlandish painters: Justus Sustermans (1597–1681), Jan Fyt (1611–61), Van Dyck and Rembrandt.[53] Since two of the three (so-called) Rembrandt self portraits entered the Galleria degli autoritratti after the cardinal's demise, the work listed in the inventory can only be the late self portrait apparently painted shortly before Rembrandt's death (cat. no. 85).[54] We know from the journal of Cosimo III's stay in Holland, kept by his travelling companion Filippo Corsini, that the *Gran Principe* visited a number of artists' studios in Amsterdam on 29 December 1667, apparently with the intention of acquiring some paintings. The entourage also called on Rembrandt:

His Excellency went to Mass, and then with Blaeu and Ferroni to see pictures by several masters – the draughtsman Van der Velde, the famous painter Rembrandt … and others. Since none of these had any finished works, they continued their search elsewhere.[55]

No mention is made of Cosimo having purchased a Rembrandt self portrait. He may have acquired it only on his second visit to

Amsterdam, in June 1669.[56] However, since there is no allusion to a renewed visit to Rembrandt's studio in the travel records, this remains purely speculative. If we assume Cosimo bought the work directly from the artist, then the late self portrait in the Uffizi must have been executed between December 1667 and Rembrandt's death in October 1669. It is thus, with the self portraits in London (cat. no. 84) and The Hague (cat. no. 86) – both dated 1669 – one of Rembrandt's last works. The visit by the Italian group to his studio, and the epithet 'pittore famoso (famous painter)' applied to him, indicate how prominent and admired the elderly Dutch artist was, even outside the Netherlands. This is also confirmed by the handwritten list of 163 artists compiled by the German clergyman Gabriel Bucelinus (1599–1681) at Kloster Weingarten in 1664: among them, only Rembrandt's name is annotated 'nostrae aetatis miraculum (the miracle of our age)'.[57]

Rembrandt's self portraits – or portraits believed to be such – were clearly desirable collectors' items. The likeness of a young man with a beret and iron gorget, executed around 1639–40, only entered the Galleria degli autoritratti in 1818 (fig. 13). Elector Johann Wilhelm had given the painting to the Gerini family in Florence, and in 1724 it was exhibited at the Accademia del Disegno as a self portrait;[58] it was also described as such in the illustrated catalogue of the Gerini collection in 1759. Though we now doubt both the identity of the sitter and the attribution, this does nothing to change the enormous value placed on it by the owners themselves, who clearly treasured their presumed Rembrandt. Their admiration was even expressed in the

decoration of the Palazzo Gerini: in a fresco by Giuseppe Zocchi (1711–67) – an allegory of the arts – a personification of Painting is shown gazing at a large book being held up to her by two little boys. The book – the aforementioned collection catalogue – is open at the page with the engraving after the Rembrandt self portrait (fig. 14).[59]

The most extensive collection of artists' portraits north of the Alps originated in the late seventeenth century and, in the eighteenth century, was housed at Schloss Leopoldskron, near Salzburg. Here, Laktanz, Count Firmian (1712–86), nephew and heir to the Prince-bishop of Salzburg, Leopold Anton, Count Firmian (died 1744), amassed a large number of painters' self portraits following the death of his uncle.[60] In 1783 he owned 248 examples by 240 different artists, and at his death he left behind a 'painters' gallery with 304 portraits of the most famous artists of the past and present, from various schools and nations'.

An Italian source of 1767 indicates that as early as 1690 Leopold Anton had asked Cosimo III for permission to make copies of the portraits in the Medici collection. The request was denied and so a group of painters was sent to Florence to make the replicas in secret. Before being discovered, they managed to duplicate ninety works and send them back to Salzburg.[61] Over the course of time, Laktanz supplemented this group – which was more or less of the same size and painted on brass – with copies after engravings and new self portraits by contemporary artists. The collection began to be broken up and sold in 1822; we know its composition today only from a surviving list of artists' names.[62] Among the numerous other Netherlandish painters –

fig. 13
Tronie of a Young Man with Gorget and Beret
(cat. no. 52).

fig. 14 *opposite*
GIUSEPPE ZOCCHI, *Allegory of the Arts*. Fresco.
Florence, Palazzo Gerini.

such as Pieter Bruegel the Elder (active 1550/1; died 1569), Hendrick Goltzius (1558–1616), Adriaen Brouwer (1606?–38) and Gerard van Honthorst (1592–1656) – is Rembrandt. We do not know whether this portrait was an illegal replica made in Florence, or a copy after an etched self portrait. But, in any case, the Leopoldskron collection, formed under the influence of the Galleria degli autoritratti in Florence, documents the continuing interest in such series as an essential part of any princely collection.

Rembrandt's Self Portraits in Non-Aristocratic Collections of the Seventeenth and Eighteenth Centuries

Even during his lifetime, several of Rembrandt's self portraits appear to have been in the hands of his non-aristocratic contemporaries. Given the large number of these images, it is no surprise to discover that most of them were, in fact, made for sale. Thanks to the few surviving references in inventories and notaries' records of the seventeenth century something is known of their fate. However, most of the descriptions in these documents are rather vague and they contain no information on the exact circumstances of the acquisitions. Whether the owner commissioned the self portrait directly from the artist, inherited it, or bought it on the free market cannot be known for sure.

Just how well Rembrandt and his family were known can be gauged from a barter agreement drawn up in 1647. In exchange for ships' fittings, Marten van den Broeck of Amsterdam offered his business partner five Rembrandt paintings. Among them were three portraits, described as 'a portrait of Rembrandt's wife', 'a portrait of Rembrandt' and 'Rembrandt's nurse'.[63] What is remarkable is that Van den Broeck apparently not only owned a likeness of the painter himself – probably a self portrait – but also one of Saskia and one of Geertje Dircx, Titus's nurse. Though it is not clear how or when he acquired these paintings, this incident indicates that Rembrandt sought to satisfy the demand for his work not only with self portraits, but also with portraits of members of his household. Originally all such paintings were intended for sale, but a number of them did remain in the family after the artist's death. In 1677, Adriana van Gheyn, the widow of Titus's guardian, owned 'a portrait of Rembrandt van Rijn and his wife'; and Magdalena van Loo (1642–69), Titus's own wife, bequeathed a 'portrait of [her] father-in-law'.[64] This, too, was most likely a self portrait.

Rembrandt's likeness could also be found in collections of seventeenth-century art-lovers outside the Netherlands, among them that of Everhard Jabach (1607/12–95), a native of Cologne. The 1695 inventory of his Paris collection lists around 650 paintings, some of them of extraordinary quality. Under number 123 we find a 'portrait of Rembrandt, with a white cloth wrapped around his head, in half-length, life-sized, by himself'.[65] This is probably his *Self Portrait as the Apostle Paul* (cat. no. 81).

In most cases, the reasons for acquiring a single artist's self portrait remain mysterious. Various motivations for the creation of portrait collections among burghers, however, can be ascertained from the following examples. 'Every century produces great men, but not always in such great numbers', wrote Charles Perrault (1628–1703) in the introduction to his edition of

Les hommes illustres qui ont paru en France pendant ce Siècle (Paris 1696–1700). Here, biographies of outstanding French politicians, theologians, officers and scholars are illustrated with their portraits. A number of painters were also included: Poussin (1594–1665), Le Brun (1619–90), Callot (1592–1635), Mignard (1612–95) and Vouet (1590–1649). Perrault's book is just one example of how the tradition of amassing engraved portraits of important personalities – with its roots in the *uomini illustri* series of the Renaissance – continued to live on throughout the seventeenth and eighteenth centuries. Likenesses of artists were an essential part of these often large collections, which were intended to give history a palpable form by documenting its major figures. The engraver's medium gave the less wealthy a chance to assemble their own collections of artists' portraits.

One unique example is the print collection of Samuel Pepys (1633–1703), which has survived virtually intact.[66] His library naturally included a copy of Perrault's book. Pepys, largely known for the diary he kept between 1660 and 1669, was Secretary to the English Admiralty, and was responsible for overseeing the building and supply of the fleet until 1689. He also engaged in various scientific pursuits, becoming a member of the Royal Society in 1665 and its president in 1684. He owned a large library, today held by Magdalene College, Cambridge, part of which was a systematically assembled collection of prints and drawings, purchased from dealers in Rome, London and Amsterdam. One of the hallmarks of Pepys's collection is its breadth.[67] There are approximately 1800 portraits, which, like all the other engravings, were kept in albums. They were arranged according to hierarchic, historical, and topographical criteria. The collection's universal character is revealed in Pepys's own categories:

royal family / sovereign princes foreign / noblemen, great ministers / ambassadors / gentlemen, virtuosi, men of letters, merchants / ladys & virtuosae / seamen / soldiers, churchmen / lawyers / physicians, chirurgeons, chymists / poets, comedians, musicians / paynters, [en]gravers, statuarys, architects / trades arts, mechanics, exempts as not comprehended in any of the praeceding classes.[68]

The group of painters, engravers, sculptors and architects comprises a total 118 portraits of English, German, Flemish, Dutch, Italian and French artists of various centuries. There seems to be no strict criteria for the choice of portraits. Oddly enough, the collection does not include a Rembrandt self portrait, although Pepys owned several of his etchings of biblical themes. Amsterdam artists of Rembrandt's period are represented by Govert Flinck (cat. nos. 93 and 94) and Jacob Backer (1608–51), whose portraits are placed side by side with that of the Fleming Frans van den Wijngaerde (1614–69) (fig. 15).

Samuel Pepys collected artists' self portraits not because he was particularly interested in the fine arts, but because he sought to thoroughly document the world and its most important protagonists. The relative cheapness of the print medium allowed him to achieve his aim. Forming a collection of painted artists' portraits, on the other hand, was much more difficult and expensive, which explains why it remained mostly the prerogative of the nobility. One of the very rare exceptions was to be found in Rembrandt's native city in the eighteenth century. Here, over the course of a lifetime, the former burgomaster Johan van der

Marck (1694–1770) succeeded in assembling an enormous collection of painted, drawn and engraved portraits of Dutch painters and draughtsmen of the seventeenth and eighteenth centuries. He also owned numerous genre and history paintings by artists of his favoured Leiden school: works by Gerrit Dou (cat. no. 89), Frans van Mieris the Elder (1635–81), Pieter van Slingelandt (1640–91), Arie de Vois (c.1632–80) and Carel de Moor (1656–1738), as well as by other, lesser known *fijnschilders* (fine-painters).[69] The auction catalogue of the collection, which was sold in Amsterdam on 25 August 1773, lists 97 painted, around 120 drawn and several hundred engraved portraits of mostly Dutch painters.[70] A large number of the paintings are self portraits, others are executed by colleagues, and some were copies after prints. Number 446 was a self portrait by Rembrandt, described as follows: 'In this work, this hero of the art world has depicted himself, dressed in a cloak, with a velvet cap on his head. Painted on copper in a very powerful manner.'[71] The notation of both the support and the measurements allow us to identify this picture as a self portrait now in Stockholm (cat. no. 18).

Although there are numerous other references to Rembrandt self portraits in documents and auction catalogues of the late seventeenth and early eighteenth centuries, these can rarely be identified with surviving works.[72] The artists' biographer Arnold Houbraken, for example, mentions a self portrait by Rembrandt in the collection of Jan van Beuningen (1667–1720) in Amsterdam. He describes it as so 'artful' and 'powerfully executed' that it surpasses even the works of Van Dyck and Rubens.[73] If, as recently suggested, the painting meant is the

fig. 15 *opposite*
Page from an album with engraved portraits of Frans van den Wijngaerde, Govert Flinck and Jacob Backer. From Album no. 2980 (p. 254a-c) of Samuel Pepys's collection of prints. Cambridge, Magdalene College, Pepys Library.

fig. 16 *above*
REMBRANDT, *Head of a Man with a Feathered Beret*. Panel, 62.5 × 47 cm. The Hague, Mauritshuis.

famous *Head of a Man with a Feathered Beret* (fig. 16), then it is not a self portrait.[74]

The two other documented Dutch collections of artists' portraits – one formed around 1700, the other around the middle of the eighteenth century – are completely different from Van der Marck's. The first is the famous *Pan Poeticon Batavum*, a group of portraits of Dutch poets attributed to the Amsterdam painter and engraver Arnoud van Halen (1673–1732) (fig. 17).[75] Van Halen depicted his figures *en grisaille*, on small ovals of tin, using engravings and drawings as his models. The title of the group is misleading: in addition to poets, painter-writers such as Van Mander, Otto van Veen (1556–1629), Samuel van Hoogstraten (cat. no. 96) and Houbraken are also included. Even Cornelis Ketel (1548–1616), Rubens and his Flemish colleague Bonaventura Peters (1614–52) are represented.

In 1719, Van Halen commissioned a special walnut cabinet with eighty-two drawers to hold the framed and captioned portraits. A year later, the poet Lambert Bidloo (1633–1724) composed a descriptive ode on his collection.[76] At that time, it already encompassed some 200 portraits. In 1773, when the Leiden poetical society *Kunst wordt door arbeid verkregen* (Art is attained by effort), then owner of the collection, decided to publish it – along with various laudatory poems and the captions – it had grown to 324 portraits.[77] Of these, seventy-seven are now housed in the Rijksmuseum in Amsterdam.[78]

A comparable collection, although limited to painters, was formed by the Rotterdam artist Jan Stolker (1724–85) in the course of the eighteenth century. On his death, he left behind 155 oval copperplates bearing the portraits of Dutch and German painters of the fifteenth, sixteenth and seventeenth centuries, contained, like Van Halen's, in a specially-made cabinet. An unsuccessful attempt was made to auction the collection in 1786, and so it remained in the artist's family for some time before it was finally dispersed.[79] In recent years, small groups and individual portraits have repeatedly surfaced on the art market (fig. 18).[80]

Stolker based his images on several of the well-known portrait series of the sixteenth and seventeenth centuries. Among models were the engravings of the Wierix brothers, Cornelis Cort and Hieronymus Cock for the 1572 Antwerp Lampsonius edition, discussed above. There is also evidence that he relied on the portraits in Hondius's expanded edition of 1610, and Van Dyck's *Iconography*. Finally, Stolker also drew on the illustrated biographies of Cornelis de Bie (*Het Gulden Cabinet*, 1661), Arnold Houbraken (*De Groote Schouburgh*, 1718–21) and Joachim von Sandrart (*Teutsche Academie*, 1768 edition). Some of the miniatures indicate the names of their original creators in the form of signatures or monograms on the front. Stolker noted the sitters' names on the back.

Judging by the works which have survived, the series stretched from Hugo van der Goes (active 1467; died 1482) and Dürer to Bruegel the Elder and Goltzius, to Emanuel de Witte (1615/17–91/2) and Rembrandt. In several instances, Stolker took self portraits as his models. This was the case with Rembrandt (fig. 19). He copied the likeness from an etching of 1636 depicting the painter and Saskia (cat. no. 46), closely cropping it to

fig. 17 *left*
ARNOUD VAN HALEN, *Self Portrait*.
Copper, 14.5 × 12.5 cm (oval).
Amsterdam, Rijksmuseum.

fig. 18 *opposite*
JAN STOLKER, *Series of 20 painted Artists' Portraits*.
Copper, *c*.10.2 × 8.2 cm (oval).
Present whereabouts unknown.

fig. 19 *right*
JAN STOLKER, *Portrait of Rembrandt*.
Copper, 10.2 × 8.3 cm (oval).
Present whereabouts unknown.

eliminate Rembrandt's wife. In composing the series, one of Stolker's aims was undoubtedly to underline the grandeur of the Dutch and German schools that had grown up since the late Middle Ages. In terms of form, his oval portrait busts are reminiscent of the woodcuts in the second edition of Vasari's *Lives* (fig. 2), although Stolker eliminated the elaborate framing devices. Although of a far lesser quality than the models copied, Stolker's miniatures are nonetheless painted on copper, and they were kept in a special cabinet, giving them an even more ambitious character than contemporary collections of drawn and painted artists' portraits.

In summary, we may conclude that Rembrandt's self portraits were created at least partially as a response to the ever-increasing interest in eminent artistic personalities. Since the Renaissance, painters, sculptors and architects had found a permanent place among the *uomini illustri*. With the second, illustrated edition of the *Lives*, Vasari had made the artists' external appearance as important as information about his work. In the course of the seventeenth century, the painter's self portrait became an independent category for collectors. Already during his lifetime, some of Rembrandt's self portraits found their way into royal and princely collections outside the Netherlands, and some were even to be discovered in non-aristocratic collections of the seventeenth and eighteenth centuries. Although a number of his contemporaries owned his self portraits from early on, in most cases the reasons for these acquisitions cannot yet be satisfactorily determined.

Rembrandt's numerous self portraits document not only the final emancipation of his profession, but also the growing interest in artistic personalities. Remarkable here is that he so often took up elements found in sixteenth-century Northern European artists' portraits. Contemporary formulations played only a subordinate role. In terms of both composition and costume there are obvious parallels with Dutch and German portraits of the early sixteenth century, particularly those of Albrecht Dürer and Lucas van Leyden. In this way, Rembrandt consciously placed himself within the tradition of his famous precursors, who had contributed significantly to the development of an independent Northern European school. His inspiration was drawn, among others, from the well-known portrait series of Lampsonius and Cock. That artists' portraits continued to be used to advocate Dutch and German painting well into the eighteenth century is demonstrated by the work of Jan Stolker. His 155 miniature portraits of artists of the fifteenth, sixteenth and seventeenth centuries are a kind of painted history of Northern European art since the late Middle Ages. Many of Rembrandt's self portraits clearly express his awareness that he, too, was part of this great tradition.

Translated from the German by Rachel Esner.

1 Wilde 1988, p. 10.

2 See Kemp 1976 and Zöllner 1989.

3 For example by Pinder 1943 and Rosenberg 1964, pp. 36–55.

4 See Waetzoldt 1908, pp. 313, 320–1, 342–4, 361; Chapman 1990, pp. 10–34.

5 On Rembrandt's self portraits as an expression of his social standing and ambitions see De Jongh 1969 and Sullivan 1980. On the art-theoretical implications see, most recently, Raupp 1984, pp. 166–81.

6 On the origins and history of the independent self portrait in the fifteenth century see, most recently, Schweikhart 1993, pp. 18–22.

7 Prinz 1971, p. 20.

8 For the development of the various categories of portraits incorporated into compositions see Boehm 1985, pp. 231–50 and Schweikhart 1993, pp. 11–18.

9 An analysis of Rembrandt's self portraits in his history paintings is given in Raupp 1984, pp. 250–5, and Chapman 1990, pp. 105–20.

10 Schweikhart 1993, pp. 18–22.

11 Davies 1968, pp. 53–4; Campbell 1990, p. 12, plate 21 and fig. 22. The usual designation of the headgear as a 'turban' is misleading. It is not an oriental but rather a contemporary form of headdress known as a *chaperon*.

12 Prinz 1966, pp. 24–5 and fig. 10.

13 For Alberti's medallion self portraits see Badt 1957–8.

14 On the *uomini illustri* series of the Renaissance see Prinz 1971, pp. 17–20, Liebenwein 1977, pp. 91–3, Joost-Gaugier 1982 and, most recently, Donato 1987.

15 Prinz 1971, p. 20, and, more recently, De Vecchi 1977 and Klinger 1991.

16 The following comments on the woodcuts in Vasari's *Lives* are based on the work of Prinz (1966) and Ragghianti-Collobi (1971 and 1972). See also Hope 1985, and the discussion of Vasari's book illustrations in Gregory 1998, pp. 94–122.

17 Prinz 1971, p. 25.

18 The history of the Accademia di San Luca's collection is examined in Susino 1974, pp. 201–70.

19 On the art collection of the Académie Royale de Peinture et de Sculpture, and the conditions regarding the *morceaux de réception* see Klingsöhr 1986. The transformation of the painted portraits into prints is discussed in Kingston 1982.

20 The most thorough analysis of the Lampsonius/Cock engravings – in the context of a study of artists' portraits – can be found in Raupp 1984, pp. 18–23.

21 On the Hondius series see Raupp 1984, pp. 23–31 and Orenstein 1996, pp. 132–3, 175, nos. 37–42, 136–59, 267–71.

22 See T. Döring in Brunswick 1997, p. 12, figs. 3 and 4.

23 Miedema 1994-, vol. I, fol. 209 verso, lines 18–20.

24 Miedema 1994-, vol. I, fol. 209 recto–209 verso.

25 Rembrandt made his acquisitions at the Gommer Spranger auction, which took place in Amsterdam from 9–13 February 1638 (Strauss/Van der Meulen 1979, p. 150, no. 1638/2). The author is currently preparing an article examining the role of this auction in the reception of Rembrandt and his circle.

26 On Titian's and Raphael's portraits as models see Raupp 1984, pp. 168–71 and P. van Thiel in Berlin/Amsterdam/London 1991–2, no. 32, as well as, most recently, A. Blankert and M. Blokhuis in Melbourne/Canberra 1997–8, no. 13. S. de Bussière (Paris 1986, p. 100, figs. 72–3) has also associated Dürer's 1498 self portrait with the London Rembrandt. However, she emphasised the painting's close relationship to Italian art, failing to acknowledge properly the Northern European elements in both works.

27 For an analysis of the X-radiographs see *Corpus*, vol. III, no. A 139, as well as London 1988–9, no. 8 and fig. 68.

28 Hervey 1921, p. 366. For Thomas Howard's diplomatic mission of 1636 see Springell 1963.

29 See Schwartz 1993 and Phoenix/Kansas City/The Hague 1998–9, no. 9. The portraits were identified by Buijsen (1993).

30 On Van Dyck's *Iconography* see Mauquoy-Hendrickx's *catalogue raisonné* (1956). Raupp (1984, pp. 45–160) gives an in-depth analysis of the art-theoretical suppositions and implications of this series.

31 See Marieke de Winkel's contribution to the present catalogue.

32 Houbraken 1718–21, vol. I, p. 261.

33 On Charles I's collection see Millar 1958–60 and Haskell 1989.

34 Müller Hofstede 1989, pp. 369–92 and Müller Hofstede 1992–3, pp. 108–9. On the works by Rubens and Mytens in the collection see also Haskell 1989, p. 152, plate 22, and p. 192, plate 62.

35 Millar 1958–60, p. xiv.

36 Millar 1958–60, p. 37, no. 2 (Rubens); p. 38, no. 4 (Van Dyck); and p. 38, no. 5 (Mytens).

37 Millar 1958–60, p. 16, no. 11 (Titian); p. 44, no. 16 (Bronzino); p. 45, no. 19 (Pordenone); and p. 45, no. 21 (Romano).

38 Haskell 1989, p. 217. On Thomas Howard's diplomatic mission of 1636 see Springell 1963.

39 Quoted after Millar 1958–60, p. 57, no. 84.

40 See Heesakkers 1987, pp. 84–90.

41 On the so-called *Portrait of Rembrandt's Mother*, formerly attributed to Rembrandt and now to Lievens, see White 1982, pp. 101–3, no. 158, and *Corpus*, vol. I, no. A 32, as well as vol. II, Corrigenda and Addenda, pp. 839–40, no. A 32. On Lievens's study of a monk's head, now in Newbattle Abbey, Collection of the Marquess of Lothian, see Schneider/Ekkart 1973, p. 107, no. 64, and Brunswick 1979, p. 15, fig. 1.

42 Schneider/Ekkart 1973, p. 334, no. 244, and Brunswick 1979, pp. 113–15, no. 38, ill.

43 On Rembrandt's connection with the court at The Hague and his commissions from Stadholder Frederick Henry and his wife, Amalia of Solms, see, most recently, The Hague 1997–8, nos. 9 and 21–3.

44 The Hague 1997–8, no. 17, ill.

45 Van Gool 1750–1, vol. I, p. 35.

46 For the history of the gallery see Prinz 1971. On the Dutch self portraits see Langedijk 1992.

47 Prinz 1971, pp. 232–6.

48 Prinz 1971, pp. 213–14.

49 See Hoogewerff 1919.

50 This catalogue was reprinted in Van Gool 1750–1, vol. II, pp. 531–67.

51 See Van Gool 1750–1, vol. II, pp. 538–9.

52 See Langedijk 1992, p. xviii.

53 See Langedijk 1992, pp. xvii, xxiii, and nos. 8, 28 and 34.

54 Bredius/Gerson 1969, no. 60; see also Langedijk 1992, pp. 148–52, no. 28.

55 Translated from the original document as reprinted in Hoogewerff (1919, p. 67).

56 See also E. van de Wetering in Melbourne/Canberra 1997–8, p. 62.

57 Schillemans 1987 and Schillemans 1991; and, most recently, E. van de Wetering in Melbourne/Canberra 1997–8, pp. 58–60.

58 *Corpus*, vol. III, no. B 11; see also Langedijk 1992, pp. 140–3.

59 See Ewald 1976, p. 355, fig. 25.

60 See Garas 1981, pp. 134–7.

61 See Meloni Trkulja 1978, p. 81.

62 Reprinted in Buberl 1916, pp. 297–9.

63 See Strauss/Van der Meulen 1979, p. 254, no. 1647/1.

64 See Hofstede de Groot 1906, documents 130 and 336.

65 Quoted and translated from the inventory printed in De Grouchy 1894, p. 255, no. 123.

66 See Van der Waals 1984 and Chamberlain 1994.

67 Pepys himself stresses this aspect in his hand-written introduction to 'My collection of heads en taille-douce & Drawings', noting that it was 'originally designed for & principally re-strained to natives of England, but occasionally taking-in some of other nations' (Chamberlain 1994, p. 1). His aim was apparently to create an almost encyclopaedic picture of the world, its history and protagonists. This is demonstrated by the system of categories, and the various focal points according to which the collection was organised. We can discern four groups in total: portraits, topography, a systematic general group, and the frontispieces; the collection also included bound series of engravings and illustrated books.

68 Quoted after Van der Waals 1984, p. 251.

69 See E.J. Sluijter in Leiden 1988, pp. 45–6.

70 See Van der Marck 1773, pp. 139–69, nos. 394–491.

71 Quoted after Van der Marck 1773, p. 156.

72 A list of so-called Rembrandt self portraits mentioned in documents of the seventeenth, eighteenth and nineteenth centuries can be found in Wright 1982, pp. 129–33. The extraordinarily brief descriptions make critical examination and attempts at identification with known Rembrandt self portraits extremely difficult.

73 Houbraken 1718–21, vol. I, p. 269. On Van Beuningen see Broos 1995, pp. 20–6.

74 See *Corpus*, vol. III, no. C 98. On Houbraken's identification of Van Beuningen's so-called Rembrandt self portrait with the picture in The Hague, see B. Broos's not entirely convincing argument in his contribution to the Mauritshuis catalogue of portraits (in preparation).

75 See Heeren 1919.

76 See Bidloo 1720.

77 See *Genootschap* 1773, pp. x-xxii, with a list of artists represented and the portraits by other artists added after Van Halen's death.

78 See Van Thiel 1976, pp. 723–36.

79 See Stolker 1786.

80 New York (Christie's), 21 May 1992, lot no. 116 (portraits of Van Dyck, Hans Holbein the Younger, Frans Hals, Dürer and Rembrandt). A group of 20 Stolker portraits were also included in an auction in Amsterdam: (Christie's), 3 December 1997, lot no. 153, ill.

Costume in Rembrandt's Self Portraits

Marieke de Winkel

Costume is one of the key elements of Rembrandt's self portraits. Its great diversity and often emphatic treatment make a major contribution to the variety that is such a feature of this large segment of his oeuvre. What could have been his reasons for depicting himself time and again in different guises? A cartoon published in *The New Yorker Magazine* in 1987 (fig. 1), shows Rembrandt standing before his easel and asking Hendrickje to 'bring in the funny hats' because he feels another self portrait coming on. Should his varied garb be seen as a fairly random selection from a fancy-dress wardrobe, or was there more to it than that?

As demonstrated by Van de Wetering and Manuth in the two previous essays, it seems that the idea that Rembrandt 'felt a self portrait coming on' cannot be accepted without question. He seems not to have painted his self portraits out of a need for self-analysis, as is sometimes thought, but in order to appeal to the purchasing public. He was probably well aware that they were collected by art-lovers and hung in several major royal and princely collections. This must have influenced the way in which he presented himself. Dress is an important way of creating the image that a person wishes to project. This justifies analysis of costume as a bearer of meaning, and that in turn makes it a very interesting aid in the study of self portraits. What is Rembrandt saying about himself in his choice of attire? Did he wish to present himself to the world as a prosperous burgher, a learned gentleman, or was he making statements about himself as an artist? Because we have scarcely any personal statements by Rembrandt as to how he saw himself as an artist, unlike the

famous Flemish painter Peter Paul Rubens (1577–1640; p. 47, fig. 11), the self portraits are the prime source for probing behind the surface.

'A head by Rembrandt, being his likeness'
Dress in Rembrandt's earliest self portraits

Costume plays a very minor role in Rembrandt's earliest self portraits (cat. nos. 2, 5–7, 15, 21 and 23), primarily because they do not extend below the shoulders and appear mainly to be studies of facial expressions or contrasts between light and shadow. They could be used in history paintings or serve as *tronies*, the two categories in which the young painter specialised during his Leiden period. *Tronie*, derived from the old French *troigne*, was the seventeenth-century word for head or face, but it was also used to refer to paintings showing distinctive heads of different types of people (see also pp. 21-2 and 95-6), such as a wrinkled greybeard, an attractive young girl, an oriental or a soldier. Unlike portraits these heads were intended for the open market and, although most were made from live models, the identity of the sitter appears to have been of secondary importance.[1]

It is striking that in his early period Rembrandt depicted himself either as one of the figures in a history painting (cat. no. 1), or in a way closely related to the *tronie* type. An important feature of the latter was the unusual attire of the figure in exotic or historicising garb. On several occasions Rembrandt chose to wear 'picturesque' articles: caps of various kinds (cat. nos. 9 and 28) and gold chains (for instance, cat. nos. 26 and 35–6). He often combined garments that referred back to the past with

Previous page
The Painter in his Studio (cat. no. 17, detail).

60

contemporary oriental accessories, so it is difficult to say precisely whether these pictures are self portraits *à l'antique* or as an oriental. One example is the '*Self Portrait' as an Oriental Potentate* of 1634 (cat. no. 41), in which the plumed beret and draped chain echo historical costume, while the sword is of an oriental type and looks very much like a Javanese kris. In the self portrait of 1629 (fig. 2), Rembrandt is wearing a similar costume combined with a scarf that has gold stripes – an accessory that had decidedly oriental overtones in the seventeenth century.

The question that arises with these *tronie*-like self portraits is, just how much importance was attached to the identity of the sitter? What is certain is that seventeenth-century probate inventories contain entries like 'Een trony van Rembrants sijnde sijn contrefeytsel (A head by Rembrandt, being his own likeness)'.[2] Was this, though, merely a term for the size of a painting – a head – or was it an indication that some of Rembrandt's self portraits were indeed regarded as *tronies* but that people knew he had reproduced his own features in them?

Whatever the answer, from around 1629 Rembrandt painted not a faithful reflection of the face he saw in the mirror in a number of self portraits but a manipulated image. In the drawn self portraits in Amsterdam and London (cat. nos. 12 and 13), the three closely related etched self portraits (cat. nos. 6, 11 and 15) and the painting in Munich (cat. no. 7), the length of the hair is so varied that it is impossible that all five are representations of reality. In each one the artist is wearing a coat with frogging down the front – a form of decoration that was chiefly associated with military dress in the seventeenth century. Although the martial

fig. 1 *opposite*
'Hendrickje, I feel another self-portrait coming on. Bring in the funny hats', 1987. Drawing by Handelsman (© The New Yorker Magazine, Inc).

fig. 2 *above*
Self Portrait with Plumed Beret (cat. no. 10, detail).

connotations of this costume would certainly have been spotted by contemporaries, the military aspect is made explicit in the *Self Portrait with Gorget*, which was also executed around 1629 (fig. 3). As in one of the prints (cat. no. 11), the artist has a long lock of hair falling down the right side of his face. Known as *cadenettes* or lovelocks, they were fashionable chiefly in France, England and Germany at the beginning of the century. This essentially aristocratic hairstyle is extremely rare in portraits of Dutchmen, and with few exceptions is depicted in the northern Netherlands solely in portraits of aristocratic, foreign officers and members of the international court of Frederick, Elector Palatine (1596–1632). It is thus extremely doubtful that Rembrandt actually wore his hair like this. In any event, it is unlikely that this is a realistic image, painted in front of the mirror, because seventeenth-century pictorial and written sources indicate that the lovelock was always worn on the right (Rembrandt's self portrait shows him in mirror image).[3] This is illustrated, for example, in the well-known series of portraits of aristocratic army officers by Michiel van Mierevelt (1567–1641). Willem Delff (1580–1638) cut his engravings after this series in mirror image, so that the *cadenette* appears on the correct side in the impressions, namely hanging down over the right shoulder (fig. 4).[4] Rembrandt's *Self Portrait with Gorget* recalls the portraits in this series, not only in the lovelock but in the pose, with the body turned a little to the left and the head seen full face. It is possible that he modelled the self portrait on this series of aristocratic officers. The other self portraits with gorgets from this early period can also be regarded as portraits in the manner of a

soldier's *tronie*.[5] Rembrandt's large output of military heads in these years, for which he did not use himself as the model, appears to indicate that this type of painting was fairly popular.[6]

'Divine in art and mind'
Rembrandt's self portraits in fashionable dress

When surveying Rembrandt's oeuvre of self portraits one is struck by the fact that he very rarely depicted himself in a formal pose wearing fashionable dress. This is in marked contrast to his contemporaries, whose attire in their self portraits is barely distinguishable from that of their clients. Rembrandt depicted himself this way in only two paintings of 1632 (fig. 5 and cat. no. 34) and a closely related etching of 1631–3 (fig. 6). Could this manner of self-presentation have had anything to do with his move to Amsterdam at the end of 1631, and with the fact that he started out there primarily as a portrait painter?

In both the paintings and the etching he is wearing a black hat with a broad brim and an ornamented gold hatband, a black cloak with velvet facings over a plain black doublet, and a type of collar known as a falling ruff. The red cord fastening the ruff around the neck is just visible in the Glasgow self portrait (fig. 5). This type of collar consisted of numerous layers of fine linen, and was in vogue from around 1620 on. The fashion-conscious Constantijn Huygens (1596–1687; p. 27, fig. 37) wore a similar collar at this time.[7] There is a close similarity between the dress in the Glasgow picture and that in Rembrandt's *Portrait of Jacob de Gheyn III* of the same year (fig. 7), particularly the way in which the cloak is folded back at the shoulder. De Gheyn (c.1596–1641)

fig. 3 *far left*
Self Portrait with Gorget (cat. no. 14a).

fig. 4 *left*
WILLEM DELFF AFTER MICHIEL VAN MIEREVELT, *Portrait of General Christian, Duke of Brunswick*, 1623. Engraving, 420 × 296 mm. Amsterdam, Rijksmuseum, Rijksprentenkabinet.

fig. 5 *opposite top*
Self Portrait with Wide-Brimmed Hat (cat. no. 33).

fig. 6 *opposite left*
Self Portrait with Hat, Hand on Hip (cat. no. 32).

fig. 7 *opposite right*
REMBRANDT, *Portrait of Jacob de Gheyn III*, 1632. Panel, 29.9 × 24.5 cm. London, Dulwich Picture Gallery (By Permission of the Trustees of Dulwich Picture Gallery).

was also a painter, and according to Huygens he was so wealthy that he neglected painting.[8] As far as the costume in the Glasgow self portrait is concerned, Rembrandt may have been placing himself on the same social level as the sitters for his portraits. Given the large number of portrait commissions he received in this period, he must have been fairly well-off, and it is not inconceivable that he could afford to dress this way. The costly gold hatband and the velvet facings of the cloak have a certain elegance, and betray a heightened awareness of status. Even more expensive materials were introduced in the last six states of the eleven-state etching (see cat. no. 32), which probably date from 1633 (fig. 6). The lace pattern of the collar is given added emphasis, and the plain fabric of the cloak has been changed into fur-lined *caffa* (a sort of patterned velvet), so that the costume looks even more sumptuous. At first sight, the almost overstated elegance of these embellishments make it difficult to accept this attire as a reflection of reality. However, that possibility cannot be ruled out automatically, for it is striking that many of Rembrandt's fellow artists of the period portrayed themselves in fashionable and fairly opulent dress.[9] Did this correspond to reality, or did they set out to present a more flattering picture of themselves? Study of the probate inventories of seventeenth-century painters in Amsterdam reveals that there were wide differences in wealth. This had consequences for the nature and number of the artists' material possessions, of which clothing formed an important part.[10] It can be deduced from several inventories of the 1620s that a wardrobe could indeed be remarkably luxurious. Articles made of *caffa* and satin, as well as

lace collars, were no exception, so it is by no means inconceivable that a young and successful painter like Rembrandt could indulge in a fur-lined *caffa* cloak, a lace collar and a gold hatband.[11]

Although Rembrandt had the money to buy expensive clothes, it is a moot point whether, socially speaking, he could permit himself to dress like this. In the seventeenth century, an excessively sumptuous mode of attire on the part of the common burgher was considered highly undesirable, since it would break down the barriers between the various classes.[12] This view was expressed by the Reformed clergyman Willem Teellinck (1579–1629), who stated in 1620 that it was not a person's purse but his social position that determined how he should dress.[13] Criticism of sumptuous costumes also came from non-religious quarters, backed chiefly by the economic argument that many articles of clothing had to be imported from abroad.[14] Laying down rules for painters, however, proved particularly troublesome, as evidenced by a remarkable pamphlet by one J. van B., an unidentified lawyer of Amsterdam. In 1662, he argued that it was high time the authorities took steps to prohibit people wearing silk and velvet as they saw fit, since it had become almost impossible to distinguish between the various classes.[15] He proposed a regulation that would allow the nobility and members of the governing bodies of the provinces and cities to wear what they wished, for one could hardly impose laws on the lawmakers. Equally, no constraints were to be placed on merchants with capital of more than 50,000 guilders, but all other 'tradesmen, shopkeepers and craftsmen' would have to cast off their velvet and silk attire and dress in 'woollen and other stuffs that befit their

station and are more serviceable to the Fatherland'. In the author's eyes, however, painters were an exception, and he was unable to prescribe for them, 'so various are these people, and many turbulent of spirit'.[16] Some were accomplished painters, 'divine in art and mind', while others were mere 'daubers and broad-brush painters'.

It can be concluded from this that it was possible for seventeenth-century painters to break through the social stratification, with the result that established clothing conventions were less applicable to them. Thus it seems that talent and the resulting financial rewards determined a painter's prestige, with people accepting that he could dress in a way that would not be permitted under the prevailing norms.

'As he was attired in his studio'
Rembrandt's self portraits in working clothes
In a drawing that is traditionally attributed to Rembrandt (fig. 8), the artist is standing with his legs apart and his arms akimbo. He has a coat that reaches halfway down his calves and is cinched at the waist with a sash. The sleeves extend to the elbows and have a vertical split at the front. Beneath the coat is a doublet with long, close-fitting sleeves and a standing collar. He has a hat on his head and slippers on his feet. Below the drawing, which is datable to around 1650, there is an inscription in a late seventeenth-century hand: 'Getekent door Rembrant van Rhijn naer sijn selver / sooals hij in sijn schilderkamer gekleet was (Drawn by Rembrandt van Rijn after his own image / as he was attired in his studio).'

fig. 8 *far left*
Full-Length Self Portrait (cat. no. 63).

fig. 9 *left*
Self Portrait (cat. no. 65).

fig. 10 *opposite*
PIETER CODDE, *Painter's Studio*, c.1635.
Panel, 38.3 × 49.3 cm. Stuttgart, Staatsgalerie.

Rembrandt wears a similar outfit in other self portraits from this period, such as the one of 1652 in Vienna (fig. 9), and the 1660 painting in New York (cat. no. 80). It is odd that he chose to show himself in his working clothes, especially given his contemporaries' propensity for displaying themselves at their easels clad in costly silk and lace collars. In principle, an artist had no need for special studio clothes. Leonardo da Vinci (1452–1519) actually argued that since there was no heavy labour involved, painting was ideally suited to the gentleman, because he could remain clothed according to his station while he painted.[17]

The seventeenth century had no specific occupational costumes in the sense of clothing specially designed and made for various activities (like the modern-day overall). Most trades involved nothing more than protective clothing like aprons over one's everyday dress. Aprons are mentioned in the probate inventories of bakers and carpenters, alongside the 'best' and 'daily' suits.[18] It is noteworthy that neither aprons nor any other kind of working garb is mentioned in the inventories of Amsterdam painters. In a letter of 1635 by Gerard ter Borch the Elder (1582/3–1662) to his namesake son it emerges that the latter had only a 'daily' and a 'best' suit.[19] He probably wore the daily suit while he worked. It is also made clear in the letter that the suits were intended to last a long time, being turned and patched before finally being discarded.

Painters, in other words, were more likely to have worn everyday attire when they worked than special working clothes, as illustrated in a painting of c.1635 by Pieter Codde (1599–1678; fig. 10). The art-lovers visiting this painter's studio are dressed in the latest styles, while the artist wears an outmoded doublet that was in fashion a decade earlier. His garb also creates a rather informal impression, with the open doublet, slippers on his feet and a loosely tied neckcloth rather than a collar. The painter is wearing his everyday, old clothes, apart from those articles that would restrict his movements, such as a stiff collar and cuffs.

Rembrandt's own studio scene of c.1629 (p. 59) provides a clue about the clothes he might have worn at work. The young artist wears a broad-brimmed black hat and a falling ruff, as in his self portrait of 1632 (see fig. 5). He also has on a loose-fitting, grey-blue gown that reaches to his feet and is tied at the waist with a sash. Beneath it the beige sleeve of a doublet can be seen. The gown, which looks a bit unusual at first sight, is not an imaginary or historicised article of clothing, as has been suggested,[20] but a so-called *tabbaard*. Originating in the sixteenth century, it continued to be worn in the seventeenth as a house-gown, and was accordingly known sometimes as a *nachttabbaard* (nightgown).[21] The use of a long, comfortable house-gown by people, like painters, who did most of their work seated, is not surprising, especially because the fur-lined version kept them warm in winter. The *tabbaard* was also highly practical, because it could be fastened with a sash and the sleeves could be left to hang down the back, giving more freedom of movement. It is very likely, then, that the costume in this painting accorded with reality.

The theory that painters wore such gowns is buttressed by inventories. In that of 1618 listing the possessions of the Leiden painter Mattheus Jansz Hyc (1580–1650), a *tabbaard* of grey cloth is

mentioned alongside the artist's best and everyday clothes.[22] There is also frequent mention of gowns in the inventories of Amsterdam painters.[23] Occasionally they bought them second-hand. In 1621, the Amsterdam painter Adriaen Geurtsz Bogaert (b. 1587) paid 6 guilders and 10 stuivers for a 'grograin *tabbaard*' at an estate sale.[24] That these gowns were indeed worn in the studio can be deduced from the inventory drawn up for Rembrandt's *cessio bonorum* (the voluntary surrender of effects to one's creditors) in 1656. In the *schilder loos*, the attic where his pupils painted, were 'two fur gowns'.[25]

As in *The Painter in his Studio*, Rembrandt is wearing a *tabbaard* combined with a contemporary hat in the drawing discussed above (fig. 8). He also has on the same type of hat in his etched self portrait of 1648 (cat. no. 62).[26] However, it is difficult to say whether the long-sleeved garment with a standing collar, which the master wears over his doublet in this portrait, is likewise a *tabbaard*, because the etching shows only the upper half of the body. There is a closer resemblance to the drawing, as regards both attire and pose, in the Vienna self portrait of 1652 (fig. 9). The gown is brown in the painting and the doublet black. Instead of a hat, though, Rembrandt is wearing a large black beret.

In the self portrait of *c*.1655 (cat. no. 69), which is very closely related to the Vienna piece of 1652, and the one of 1660 in New York (cat. no. 80), the painter appears to be wearing a hat with a slightly curling brim rather than a beret. A hat certainly does not appear to contribute to the functionality of the working attire, and may even look odd to modern eyes. In the seventeenth century, however, men almost always wore a hat, both indoors and

out. German and English travellers were often amazed by the fact that Dutchmen kept their hats on indoors, during meals, in company and even in church.[27] In the self portrait of *c*.1655, Rembrandt also appears to be wearing a brown *tabbaard* over a doublet with a standing collar. Beneath it is a red, collarless item of apparel fastened at the front, over a white shirt. This red garment, which features in other self portraits,[28] was known as a *hemdrock* or waistcoat in the seventeenth century. It was a long-sleeved woollen undergarment, and was worn by both men and women over a shirt to provide added warmth. Probate inventories show that the waistcoat was common among all sectors of the population, and is accordingly mentioned in most of the inventories of Amsterdam painters.[29] This red undergarment was only seen in informal circumstances, which is why it never appears in portraits.

Most of the articles of clothing worn by Rembrandt in his self portraits in working garb were thus actually worn in reality in the seventeenth century. Several of them, such as the *tabbaard*, slippers, various caps and the waistcoat were considered to be extremely informal house attire, which the artist undoubtedly wore because they were both practical and comfortable. Generally speaking, artists preferred to depict themselves in formal dress. Rembrandt was an exception, repeatedly appearing in casual, everyday working clothes.

Was he making a personal statement with this type of costume? Chapman regarded Rembrandt's assumed lifelong search for individual freedom as the main reason for depicting himself in his studio clothes.[30] According to Raupp, he was presenting himself as *pictor vulgaris* (an unlearned painter), with the working clothes constituting a protest against the academic disdain for the picturesque.[31] This image of Rembrandt as a nonconformist is not new in the literature, and is based partly on the statement by the biographer Arnold Houbraken (1660–1719) that the master associated in the autumn of his days with 'common folk, and those that practised art' in order to preserve his personal freedom.[32] The remark by the artists' biographer Filippo Baldinucci (1624–96) that Rembrandt was always carelessly and shabbily dressed, and was in the habit of wiping his brushes on his clothes, can also be taken as an illustration of this assumed lack of social decorum.[33]

Although observations about occupational clothes are very few and far between in the art-historical literature, Raupp made an interesting connection between Rembrandt's self portraits in studio clothing and an anecdote related in 1590 by the author Giovanni Paolo Lomazzo (1538–1600).[34] According to him, the wearing of work clothes by a painter could be seen as a sign of his humble deference to and deep respect for the power of painting. Even famous painters who were the favourites of princes and had been knighted for their work did not succumb to pride, but retained their humility. He cited the example of Albrecht Dürer (see p. 44, fig. 7), who often went into town in his painter's clothes, as did the seventeenth-century painter Bramantino, who frequently had his brush still tucked behind his ear.

Whether Rembrandt was making a personal statement about his freedom and independence as an artist with his working dress remains hypothetical. That he was emulating Dürer is an attractive possibility (see pp. 43–4). The main point about the anecdote, though, is that if Rembrandt was indeed making a statement with his working clothes, it could perhaps equally well have been a sign of his deep respect for the art of painting as much as an expression of personal freedom or a form of protest against Classicism.

'Rembrandt's likeness à l'antique'
Rembrandt's self portraits in historicising costume

The inventory drawn up in Amsterdam in 1657 of the possessions of the merchant Johannes de Renialme, an art dealer who was also a collector, contains the entry: 'Rembrants contrefeytsel antycks (Rembrandt's likeness *à l'antique*)'.[35] Although this is generally taken to be a reference to the London self portrait of 1640 (fig. 11), it could in fact apply to any of those in historical garb executed before 1657. In the majority of his self portraits Rembrandt wears not contemporary dress but a costume that could be described as historicising. As noted above, at the beginning of his career it consisted merely of a few items, often nothing more than a beret and a cloak with a chain draped over the shoulders (fig. 2).[36] In the second half of the 1630s, however, there was a development, most notably in his etched self portraits, towards more detailed and seemingly authentic sixteenth-century dress. It can be followed from the *Self Portrait with Saskia* of 1636 (cat. no. 46), through the self portraits of 1638 (cat. no. 49) and 1639 (cat. no. 53), culminating in the London picture of 1640 (cat. no. 54). The latter displays close attention to the details of the various elements and a wide knowledge of early

fig. 11
Self Portrait (cat. no. 54).

sixteenth-century dress. Rembrandt is clad in a costume that can be dated fairly precisely as that worn in the northern Netherlands between 1520 and 1530. He is wearing a black *tabbaard* with brown, striped sleeves and a fur-trimmed collar. The edge of the characteristic horizontal neckline of the jerkin beneath the gown is trimmed with braid. Beneath the jerkin is a doublet, the high, standing collar of which can be seen at the neck. The shirt beneath is smocked at the neck and has a small ruche that is typical of the first quarter of the sixteenth century. Another element indicating that Rembrandt was dressing in the manner common a century earlier is the addition of the chain with a cross that he has over his shirt.[37] On his head is a beret with a raised brim.[38]

It is this latter item, in particular, that appears regularly and in many forms in Rembrandt's self portraits. The beret, or bonnet as it was called at the time, was typical of sixteenth-century costume.[39] Portraits and probate inventories show that it was no longer being worn by the end of the century, when it was regarded as *démodé*. This is made clear by early seventeenth-century usage throughout much of Europe, when the term bonnet was synonymous with something old-fashioned or just plain old.[40] The Amsterdamer Zacharias Heyns, who gives examples of old attire in his costume book *Dracht-Thoneel* (1601), also used the bonnet to indicate the age of certain dress.[41]

Because this article of apparel contained an inherent reference to the past, it had already been used by artists like Rembrandt's teacher, Pieter Lastman (1583–1633), in his history paintings.[42] However, by depicting himself with a bonnet, Rembrandt was employing this historic, sixteenth-century item in an entirely new context. He was the first artist to portray himself in this way. The impact of this image of the artist with a bonnet was so influential that it was immediately imitated in the self portraits of Gerrit Dou and other Rembrandt pupils (see cat. nos. 87–96), and even became the general attribute of artists in the course of the seventeenth century — an association still made today. Why did Rembrandt portray himself in such old-fashioned garb, and what sources did he have at his disposal?

Late seventeenth-century authors, like Andries Pels (1631–81) in 1681 and Baldinucci in 1686, criticised Rembrandt for his habit of collecting old-fashioned weapons and second-hand clothes and using them as studio props.[43] As Scheller rightly remarked in his important article on Rembrandt's collection, the master only used such objects incidentally and the frequency of their appearance is in no reasonable proportion to the numbers that were inventoried for the *cessio bonorum*.[44] In contrast to the large number of weapons, the inventory gives no indication of a collection of old clothes as mentioned by Pels and Baldinucci. Moreover, it is extremely unlikely that the old costumes in which Rembrandt portrayed himself would have survived intact and been available in Amsterdam a hundred years later. The only part of his collection that was clearly used in his work was the graphic art.[45] These prints and drawings were all of a very high quality and extremely varied, and in numbers alone they exceeded all the other artworks he owned.

The use of prints as sources of inspiration for a painter was recommended by seventeenth-century art theorists. In 1670,

LUCAE LEIDANO PICTORI, ET SCULPTORI.

Tu quoque Durero non par, sed proxime, Luca,
    Seu tabulas pingis, seu formas sculpis ahenas,
    Et typa reddentes tenui miranda papyro,
    Haud minimam in partem (si qua est ea gloria) nostræ
    Accede, et tecum natalis Leida, Camænæ. · D. Lampsonius.

fig. 12 *above*
Hendrick Hondius after Lucas van Leyden,
Young man With a Skull: 'Portrait of Lucas van Leyden'.
Engraving, 219 × 129 mm. From Hondius 1610.
Amsterdam, Rijksmuseum, Rijksprentenkabinet.

fig. 13 *right*
Anonymous after Albrecht Dürer, *Portrait
of Lucas van Leyden.* Engraving, 188 × 127 mm.
From Lampsonius/Cock 1572, no. 10.
Amsterdam, Rijksmuseum, Rijksprentenkabinet.

Willem Goeree (1635–1711) advised artists to make a thorough study of old morals and customs, and of 'antique' clothing and ornaments such as turbans, caps, bonnets and weapons. According to him, famous masters used to acquire that knowledge from prints by other artists.[46] Rembrandt would have studied old prints primarily with a view to his history paintings. His wide-ranging study to ensure authenticity of historical detail was singled out for special praise in 1642 by the painter Philips Angel (*c.*1618–62) and held up as an example to other painters.[47]

It turns out that Rembrandt also used graphic works by old masters for the costumes in his self portraits. What is particularly interesting is that he turned to various series of well-known artists' portraits, such as those of Hieronymus Cock (*c.*1510–70) and Hendrick Hondius (1573–1649).[48] He did not use just one model, but combined elements from different prints. For example, in the self portrait of 1640 (fig. 11) the bonnet with the notched, turned-up brim may have been taken from a print by Lucas van Leyden (active 1508; died 1533) that was included in Hondius's series as a self portrait of the famous Leiden artist (fig. 12). The square, standing collar of Rembrandt's doublet, on the other hand, is very similar to the shape of the *tabbaard* and doublet in the portrait of Lucas van Leyden in Cock's series (fig. 13). Here Lucas is wearing a fur-trimmed, black doublet, and a *tabbaard* and jerkin, which are decorated with braid. Rembrandt turned these details around in his portrait. He wears a black *tabbaard* trimmed with fur at the neck, and a doublet and jerkin, both of which have striped decoration around the edges. The two portraits of Lucas were based on an etching of *c.*1519

LVCAE LEIDANO PICTORI.

Tu quoque Durero non par, sed proxime, Luca,
    Seu tabulas pingis, seu formas sculpis ahenas,
    Et typa reddentes tenui miranda papyro,
    Haud minimam in partem (si qua est ea gloria) nostræ
    Accede, & tecum natalis Leida, Camænæ.

by Lucas himself and a drawing by Albrecht Dürer (1471–1528) of 1521. The slashings around the edges of the jerkin in Rembrandt's etched self portrait of 1638 (cat. no. 49) could have been borrowed from the supposed self portrait of Lucas van Leyden engraved by Hondius.[49]

It is tempting to associate the development in Rembrandt's self portraits, from a historicising to an authentic-looking sixteenth-century costume in the latter half of the 1630s, with his large-scale purchases of graphic art by old masters like Lucas van Leyden and Dürer.[50] Given the fame of these two as both painters and engravers, their work must have had a particular appeal for Rembrandt, who had the same ambitions (see p. 43). The London self portrait would then be not so much an emulation of Titian (active by 1510; died 1576) or Raphael (1483–1520), as has been suggested (see cat. no. 54), but a claim for inclusion in the tradition of the famous Northern portraits and self portraits. In other words, he can be seen as an artist modelling himself on his illustrious Northern predecessors rather than on an aristocratic *gentiluomo* or poet.[51]

Rembrandt also used artists' portraits in his later period. The garb in the 1658 self portrait (fig. 14) – a painting in which the abundant use of colour and the frontal, seated pose are exceptional in his oeuvre – can be characterised as an amalgam of sixteenth-century historical dress and oriental elements. Rembrandt is wearing a bonnet and a bright yellow garment with a low, horizontal neckline that has many similarities to a jerkin. Tucked into it is a brocade neckcloth of the kind found in Hieronymus Cock's portrait of Jan Gossaert (active 1503;

MARTINVS RYCHART
VNIMANVS, PICTOR RVRALIVM PROSPECTVVM ANTVERPIÆ.
Ant. van Dyck pinxit. *G. H.* *Iacobus Neeffs sculpsit.*

fig. 14 *left*
Self Portrait (cat. no. 71).

fig. 15 *above*
JACOBUS NEEFFS AFTER ANTHONY VAN DYCK, *Portrait of Maarten Ryckaert.* Engraving, 242 × 157 mm. Amsterdam, Rijksmuseum, Rijksprentenkabinet.

died 1532) (p. 43, fig. 5). The diagonal closure of this white piece of fabric under the jerkin is completely at odds with sixteenth-century practice, and was used solely for oriental attire. The sash wound twice around the waist and the cane with the silver knob which Rembrandt is holding in his left hand are accessories that also had an oriental connotation. Rembrandt seems to have borrowed some parts of this costume from a print by Anthony van Dyck (1599–1641) after the portrait of the landscape painter Maarten Ryckaert (fig. 15). Rembrandt may have known the print from Van Dyck's *Iconography*, the well-known series of portraits of artists and others that was re-published posthumously in 1645.[52] Ryckaert (1587–1631) has donned Polish dress with a kaftan (*Zupan*) tied at the middle with a sash. It looks as if Rembrandt also borrowed the frontal, seated pose from this print, along with the distinctive diagonal closure of the kaftan, the sash and the cloak.

Rembrandt was still drawing inspiration from his prints in his self portrait of 1669 (fig. 16). The fifteenth-century doublet with high fur collar and button has many affinities with the portrait of Dieric Bouts (1400?–75) by Hieronymus Cock (fig. 17).[53] The resemblance is heightened when one examines the X-radiograph of Rembrandt's painting (p. 223, fig. 84a), which reveals that he originally held a brush in his right hand, just as Bouts does.

The costume in many of the later self portraits is so cursorily indicated that it is difficult to make out whether it is historicising garb or working clothes. Only the low, square-cut neckline so typical of sixteenth-century fashion is an indication that the artist intended this to be historical dress. In addition to the

fig. 16 *right*
Self Portrait (cat. no. 84).

fig. 17 *above*
HIERONYMUS COCK, *Portrait of Dieric Bouts.*
Engraving, 194 × 118 mm. From Lampsonius/
Cock, 1572, no. 6. Amsterdam, Rijksmuseum,
Rijksprentenkabinet.

portrait in Kenwood House (cat. no. 83), this also appears to be the case in the self portrait of 1660 in Paris (cat. no. 79) and the *Self Portrait as Zeuxis* of *c*.1662 in Cologne (cat. no. 82), where the attire is so ill-defined that it is extremely difficult to see precisely what the artist is wearing.

These last paintings, in which Rembrandt portrays himself in the act of painting, show him with a white linen cap that he probably wore in real life, for his death inventory of 1669 lists ten 'men's caps' among the linen.[54] Comparison with other seventeenth-century Amsterdam inventories has shown that such 'men's caps' of white linen were very common, and were worn around the house.[55] In these three paintings, then, Rembrandt combined historical attire with contemporary working clothes. It is possible that this slight ambivalence was deliberate, in order to depict him as an 'old' master at work, in the final case as Zeuxis, the famous painter of antiquity.

The costume in Rembrandt's self portraits is anything but a random selection. It forms an essential part of the image and is one of the keys to a closer understanding of his ambitions as an artist. His likeness in the *Self Portrait with Gorget* (cat. no. 14a) has been so heavily manipulated that one must consider this to be a *tronie*-like approach to a self portrait in which no priority was attached to the sitter's identity. It did, however, play an important role in the painted and etched self portraits in which he wears formal, fashionable attire. The fact that he adopted clothes that put him on the same level as his patrons must be connected with his emergence as a portrait painter in this period. He then departs from the prevailing self portrait convention by donning the informal garb he wore at work, and in those pictures he appears to be stressing his *métier* as a painter. The bulk of his self portraits show him in historical costumes. These are particularly striking for the high degree of accuracy, which turns out to be the fruits of his study of the engraved portraits of his artistic forerunners. Here it seems that he wished to place himself within the tradition of portraits of famous masters of the past, in which public awareness of his appearance must have played a role. The reason for this strong orientation towards his celebrated predecessors and the remarkable authenticity of the costumes may be due in part to Rembrandt's work as a history painter, and possibly also to his ambition to garner fame as both painter and graphic artist, like Dürer and Lucas van Leyden before him. Finally, the wide variety of dress, from contemporary to the imagined historical, shows that Rembrandt had diverse reasons for making his self portraits. Some may have served as a form of self-promotion, while others were deliberate attempts to carve out a place for himself in a long tradition.

Translated from the Dutch by Michael Hoyle.

This article is based on my lengthier essay, 'Rembrandt's clothes: Dress and meaning in his self-portraits', Corpus, vol. IV, which was written with financial support from the Netherlands Organisation for Scientific Research in The Hague. It is cordially dedicated to all my colleagues in the Rembrandt Research Project.

1   See J. van der Veen, 'Faces from life: "Tronies" and portraits in Rembrandt's painted oeuvre', in Melbourne/Canberra 1997–8, pp. 69–73.

2   Quoted from the probate inventory of Willem Spieringh of Delft (Hofstede de Groot 1906, no. 364; Delft, Gemeentearchief, notary W. van Ruyven, Notarieel Archief 2290, deed 18, dated 31 March 1689). The inventory of Dirck van Cattenburgh of 1685 contains the entry: 'Een stuck schilderij sijnde een tronye door Rembrant nae hem selven geschildert' ('A painting, being a *tronie* by Rembrandt, painted from his own likeness'; Strauss/Van der Meulen 1979, 1658/22 [sic]; Amsterdam, Gemeentearchief, notary J. de Hué, Notarieel Archief 5528 (B), dated 1 December 1685). Harmen Becker owned 'Een manstronie van Rembrant sijnde sijn eygen conterfeytsel' ('A man's *tronie* by Rembrandt, being his own likeness'; Amsterdam, Gemeentearchief, notary S. Pelgrom, Notarieel Archief 4767, pp. 324–78, dated 19 October–23 November 1678).

3   Corson 1965, pp. 206–9. The seventeenth-century French lexicographer Antoine Furetière (1690, s.v. *Cadenette*) confirms that the *cadenette* was worn on the right: 'Cadenette: Moustache, poignée de cheveux qu'on laissoit croître autrefois du côté gauche, tandis qu'on tenoit les autres courts.' Rembrandt also wears it on the right side in the etching (cat. no. 11), which means that in this case he took account of the reversal in the print.

4   For this print by Delff after Van Miereveltsee Hollstein, vol. V, no. 14.

5   See *Corpus*, vol. II, no. A 97; vol. III, nos. B 11 and C 98.

6   See *Corpus*, vol. I, nos. A 8, A 42, B 4 and B 6; vol. II, no. A 43.

7   As can be seen, for instance, in his portrait by Jan Lievens (1607–74) of c.1628 in the Rijksmuseum, Amsterdam (on loan from the Musée de la Chartreuse, Douai; see Van Thiel 1976, p. 347, no. C 1467, ill.). See also his portrait of 1627 by Thomas de Keyser (p. 27, fig. 37) in the National Gallery, London (The Hague 1997–8, no. 15).

8   Heesakkers 1994, p. 75.

9   Compare, for instance, the self portraits of Joachim Wtewael (1566–1638) of 1601 (Utrecht, Centraal Museum; Lowenthal 1986, pp. 94–6, no. A–15, fig. 24 and frontispiece); Nicolaes Eliasz Pickenoy (1588–1650/6) of 1627 (Paris, Musée du Louvre; Raupp 1984, fig. 115), Frederik Vroom (c.1600–67; Darmstadt, Hessisches Landesmuseum; Goldschneider 1936, fig. 206) and Judith Leyster (1609–60) of c.1633 (Washington, National Gallery of Art; Wheelock 1995, pp. 154–9, no. 1949.6.1, ill.).

10 On this see the appendices to Chapter IV in *Corpus*, vol. IV. For the variations in wealth between Delft painters see Montias 1982.

11 See, for example, the inventories of the Amsterdam painters Abraham Vinck, Cornelis van der Voort, his son Pieter van der Voort, and Barent Teunisz (Appendices 3–6 to Chapter IV in *Corpus*, vol. IV).

12 Van Deursen 1991, pp. 117–18.

13 Teellinck 1620, p. 24: 'Daer sijn rijcke, ende machtige Coop-luyden, sy souden konnen gaen als Vorsten gekleed, maer sy doen wijselijcken, dat sy sich houden aen de Coop-luyden dracht. Het is niet de beurse, maer de staet welck de mate moet stellen aen de kleedinghe (There are rich and powerful merchants who could dress as princes if they chose, but wisely retained merchant's attire. It is not the purse but the station that must dictate the costume).'

14 Harte 1976.

15 J. van B. 1662, pp. 3–4; Knuttel 1892, vol. II, no. 8670.

16 According to the *Woordenboek der Nederlandsche Taal*, the word *dol*, which J. van B. uses in his description of painters, not only meant mad in the seventeenth century, but also highly exuberant, intemperate, impetuous and wild. The latter senses appear more appropriate in this context. With the word 'spirit' (*geest*), the author was probably alluding to the concept of *ingenium* or *inspiratio*, which artists were believed to possess to a higher degree than other people. It was a quality that was admired on the one hand, because it led to the inventiveness necessary for making inspired works of art, but on the other hand ensured that a painter was regarded as displaying maladjusted social behaviour (see Miedema 1989, pp. 206–8). Van Mander (1604a, fol. 3 recto, line 23) speaks in this context of 'Schilder cranck-hooft (crackpot painter)' and 'hoe Schilder hoe wilder (the more artistic, the more eccentric)'.

17 Kemp 1989, p. 39.

18 In 1645, the Amsterdam baker Jan Pietersz owned, in addition to three black and two coloured suits, 'eenige oude kleeren bij den overleden inde backerij gedragen, dewelcke met wedersijts believen voor d'arme sijn gedestineert (some old clothes worn by the deceased in the bakery which, upon mutual agreement, are destined for the poor)'. He also had 'mans linnen klederen: 18 linnen schortecleden en drij mansmutsen (men's linen clothing: eighteen linen aprons and three men's caps)', which he would also have worn in the bakery (Amsterdam, Gemeentearchief, notary J. Steur, Notarieel Archief 1861, fols. 578–585, dated 11 February 1645). The carpenter's apprentice Simon Jansz had a 'leere schootsvel (leather apron)' as well as several suits (Amsterdam, Gemeentearchief, notary J.H. van Leuven, Notarieel Archief 2738, fols. 725–728, dated 17 February 1662).

19 Paris, Institut Néerlandais, Frits Lugt Collection, inv. no. 490; The Hague/Münster 1974, pp. 222–3.

20 Chapman 1990, p. 84.

21 A few elderly gentlemen and clerics were still having themselves portrayed in this type of gown in the early seventeenth century. See De Winkel 1995 for the various seventeenth-century connotations of this outmoded garment, which was also worn in official and academic circles.

22 Bredius 1915–22, vol. IV, pp. 2019–20.

23 In 1607, for example, Gillis van Coninxloo owned a coloured, fur-lined nightgown and a coloured *tabbaard* lined with sheepskin, while in 1629 Barent Teunisz had an old, grey, cloth *tabbaard*. The seventeenth-century painters Abraham Vinck (inventory of 1621) and Dirck Hermansz (inventory of 1640) also had one. See the appendices to Chapter IV in *Corpus*, vol. IV, nos. 2–3, 6 and 7.

24 Amsterdam, Gemeentearchief, Weeskamer 948, dated 6 November 1621, sale of the estate of Gerrit Govertsen Souburch in Warmoesstraat: '1 groffgreijne tabbert ƒ 6:10:– door: Adriaen vanden Bogaert, schilder (One grograin *tabbaard*, to Adriaen vanden

Bogaert for ƒ 6:10:-).' Seven years later, an inventory was made of the possessions of Gierte Pieters, the wife of the painter Adriaen Geurtsz Bogaert, who was abroad at the time. That is probably why so little male clothing is listed, although there are entries specifying 'een blau lakense rock (one gown of blue cloth)' and 'een graeuwe rock (one grey gown)'; (Amsterdam, Gemeentearchief, notary L. Lamberti, Notarieel Archief 568, fols. 15–19, dated 20 January 1628).

25 Strauss/Van der Meulen 1979, 1656/12, no. 346: 'Op de Schilder Loos. twee bonte rocken' (incorrectly translated there as 'on the Picture Rack. two multicolored coats'). Scheller (1969) identified the 'schilder loos' as the attic where the apprentices painted.

26 This type of cylindrical hat, wrongly labelled 'prosaic' and 'middle-class' by Chapman (1990, p. 81), is first seen in portraits of 1645, one being Frans Hals's *Portrait of Willem Coymans* (Washington, National Gallery of Art; Wheelock 1995, pp. 76–9, no. 1937.1.69), and in Rembrandt's small portrait drawing of Jan Six of c.1647 (Amsterdam, Historisch Museum; Benesch 1973, vol. IV, p. 196, no. 749 verso and fig. 947). Neither was a person to whom Chapman's adjectives would apply.

27 See Bientjes 1967, pp. 218–19, and Van Strien 1989, p. 157.

28 See also Bredius/Gerson 1969, no. 40, as well as cat. nos. 67 and 70.

29 One being that of the painter Dirck Hermansz, who owned three 'roode hemtrocken (red waistcoats)' in 1640, while Simon Luttichuijsen had one of red satin (see the appendices to Chapter IV in *Corpus*, vol. IV, nos. 2–3, 6–10, 13 and 16–19).

30 Chapman 1990, pp. 95–8.

31 Raupp 1984, pp. 179–80, following Emmens (1964), who introduced the term *pictor vulgaris* as the opposite of the *pictor doctus* (learned painter). Miedema (1969, pp. 252–5) criticised the use of the former on the grounds that it was not current in the seventeenth century.

32 Houbraken 1718–21, vol. I, p. 272.

33 Baldinucci 1686, p. 79. Baldinucci got his information from Bernhard Keil (1624–87), a Danish artist who worked in Rembrandt's studio in the early 1640s. Although this appears to be a reliable source, it turns out that some of the facts do not tally, so this observation must be treated with caution (see Emmens 1964, pp. 77–8).

34 Raupp 1984, p. 180; Lomazzo 1590, p. 333. Although Lomazzo's work seems to have had only a limited influence in the Netherlands and is very rarely mentioned in the inventories of seventeenth-century libraries, it is perfectly possible that Rembrandt heard this anecdote from Jan Six, who owned a copy of the book (see Six 1706, no. 409: 'Idea del Templo [sic] della Pittura di Gio Paolo Lomazzo Pittore, Milano 1590'). As with most of the works in his library, Six probably acquired this book during his Grand Tour of Italy from 1641 to 1642. Joachim von Sandrart (1606–88), the painter and writer on art who was in Amsterdam around 1640, also knew the anecdote, and used it in his book of 1675 (Von Sandrart 1675, vol. II, p. 225).

35 Strauss/Van der Meulen 1979, 1657/2, no. 292. In the seventeenth century, the term *antyk* stood not only for classical antiquity but also for 'old' in general (see Chapter IV in *Corpus*, vol. IV).

36 Since the chains draped over the shoulders in Rembrandt's early self portraits are also worn by several figures in his history paintings, it seems that its connotation cannot be traced back solely to the badges of honour that rulers bestowed on celebrated artists. Like the bonnet, which will be discussed below, the chain appears to have been part of the historicising costume based on early sixteenth-century fashions.

37 Chains with a cross are often found in pre-Reformation portraits; see, for instance, the *Portrait of a Man* of *c*.1520 attributed to Quinten Metsys (*c*.1465–1530) in the Metropolitan Museum of Art, New York (New York 1998–9, p. 143, fig. 60).

38 For these early sixteenth-century items of apparel see De Jonge 1919, p. 166.

39 De Jonge 1918.

40 See, for instance, Randle Cotgrave's French-English dictionary of 1611, where the author lists sayings associated with the word bonnet: '*Bonnet*: Bonnet, cap. *Du temps des hauts bonnets.* In old time, when men being rude and sillie, had not the wit to apparell themselves handsomely and hence; *Langue du temps des bonnets,* an old wives tale; or a stale, obsolete, or over-worne language; a fashion of speaking thats old, and quite out of fashion' (Cotgrave 1611, s.v. *Bonnet*).

41 Heyns 1601. See, for example, his 'Vlaminck na d'oude zede (Fleming after the old style)', 'Bedaecht borger (Elderly burgher)', 'Den Hoochduyts (The high German)', 'Den Switser (The Swiss)' and 'Den Switserschen Ioncker (The Swiss Jonker)'. Under 'Den borger na d'out fatsoen (The burgher after the old fashion)', who is wearing a costume of *c*.1550, he

adds the rhyme: 'In Brabant [gaat] me[de] veel volx na d'oude wet, … [dragen] op hun hooft een klapmuts oft bonnet (In Brabant, too, many people dress according to the old order, … wearing on their heads a *klapmuts* or a bonnet).' The word *klapmuts,* which is here used as a synonym for a bonnet, has led to some confusion in art-historical literature. Bredius (1915–22) invariably interpreted it incorrectly as 'beer tankard'.

42 Amsterdam 1991, figs. 19, 22, nos. 6, 9.

43 Pels 1681, pp. 36–7; Baldinucci 1686, p. 79.

44 Scheller 1969, p. 128.

45 See especially Van Rijckevorsel 1932; Tümpel 1968; Tümpel 1971; Campbell 1971.

46 Goeree 1670, pp. 50–1 and 75–6.

47 Angel 1642, p. 47. There is an English translation of Angel's *Lof der schilder-konst* in Hoyle/Miedema 1996, with this particular passage on p. 246.

48 Lampsonius/Cock 1572; Hondius 1610. There is an analysis of this and other series of artists' portraits in Raupp 1984, pp. 18–31, where great stress is placed on the wide circulation and importance of this series.

49 Thomas Döring (in Brunswick 1997, pp. 11–12) sees a link between this etching and the portrait of Jan Gossaert (p. 43, fig. 5) in the same series of artists by Hieronymus Cock.

50 At the Jan Basse auction of 9–30 March 1637 (Strauss/Van der Meulen 1979, 1637/2) and at the sale of the collection of Gommer Spranger in February 1638 (Strauss/Van der Meulen 1979, 1638/2). Manuth and Dickey have recently established a connection between Rembrandt's

obvious interest in and purchase of graphic art, particularly Dürer's, and its effect on his own work in this period (V. Manuth, *Tradition und Ikonographie: Zum Verhältnis von Dürer und Rembrandt,* paper dedicated to Egbert Haverkamp Begemann, Kunsthistorisches Institut der Rheinischen Friedrich-Wilhelms-Universität, Bonn, 10 March 1993, and London, Warburg Institute, 31 May 1995; Dickey 1994, pp. 105–200).

51 Out of the many publications on the presumed emulation of Titian and Raphael see especially De Jongh 1969. See the essay by Manuth in the present catalogue, as well as Dickey 1994, for the theory that Rembrandt was more inclined towards Lucas van Leyden and Dürer.

52 Published by Gillis Hendricx, second edition: *Icones principum virorum doctorum, pictorum, chalcographorum, statuarum nec non amatorum …,* Antwerp 1645. Listed in Rembrandt's inventory of 1656 is 'Een boek, vol contrefijtsels soo van van Dijck, Rubens en verscheijde andere oude meesters (A book full of portraits by Van Dyck, Rubens and divers other old masters)'; (Strauss/Van der Meulen 1979, 1656/12, no. 228).

53 This is true of the portrait of Rogier van der Weyden (1399–1464) in the same series.

54 Strauss/Van der Meulen 1979, 1669/5, no. 46. In a painting by Michiel Sweerts (1618–64) of *c*.1654 (Haarlem, Frans Halsmuseum; Kultzen 1996, p. 110, no. 74 and fig. 74), depicting a group of apprentices learning to draw from the model, the master is clad in a red *tabbaard* and a similar white cap.

55 See the appendices to Chapter IV in *Corpus,* vol. IV, nos. 4, 6–7, 8, 11 and 16–20.

The Life of Rembrandt van Rijn (1606–1669)

Ben Broos

1606

Rembrandt Harmensz van Rijn is born in Leiden on 15 July. He is the ninth child of the miller Harmen Gerritsz van Rijn (1569–1630) and Neeltgen (Cornelia) Willemsdr (van) Zuytbrouck (1568–1640), whose family is quite wealthy.

c.1613–15

Rembrandt van Rijn attends the Latin School to prepare for admission to Leiden University.

1620

The earliest document to refer to Rembrandt by name dates from 20 May 1620: his enrolment at Leiden University as 'Rembrandus hermanni Leydensis studiosus litterarum annor[um] 14 apud parentes'. This indicates he is still living with his parents and he is not yet 14 years old.

1622

A document of 18 October 1622 shows that Rembrandt is still living with his parents in Leiden's Weddesteeg, together with his brothers and sisters Gerrit, Machtelt, Cornelis and Lysbeth. His brothers Willem and Adriaen have left home.

Rembrandt starts a three-year apprenticeship with the Leiden painter and burgomaster's son Jacob Isaacsz van Swanenburgh (1571–1638).

1625

The Stoning of Saint Stephen (p. 22, fig. 28) is Rembrandt's earliest dated painting. In this picture, as well as in other undated history paintings from his early career, Rembrandt gives a spectator his own features (see cat. no. 1).

1625–6

Several dated history paintings of 1625 and 1626 are signed 'R f. (Rembrandt made this)' or 'RH (Rembrandt Harmenszoon)'.

The young artist spends at least six months in Amsterdam studying with the history painter Pieter Lastman (1583–1633), probably in 1625–6.

c.1626

Rembrandt sets up as an independent painter in Leiden.

He publishes an etching in Haarlem signed with his name (S. 398). He rapidly develops into a talented graphic artist.

1628

Rembrandt is regularly mentioned as a painter from this year on. The Utrecht lawyer Arnold van Buchel (1565–1641) visits Leiden on 10 January, and notes in his diary that a miller's son is causing a sensation there as an artist, although he finds that a little premature ('sed ante tempus').

On 14 February, the 14-year-old Gerrit Dou (cat. no. 89) becomes Rembrandt's first pupil.

Rembrandt makes two etchings of an old woman, probably his mother, as well as several undated self portraits (cat. nos. 2–4 and 6).

1629

Rembrandt completes a painted self portrait (cat. no. 7) – his earliest dated picture of himself. The same year he signs and dates an etched self portrait (cat. no. 11).

After his stay in the northern Netherlands in this year, Ambassador Sir Robert Kerr (1578–1654), later the first Earl of Ancrum, gives several paintings to King Charles I, among them 'the picture done by Rembrant, being his owne picture & done by himself' (cat. no. 26).

An Amsterdam inventory of 19 October lists a painting (no longer identifiable) as 'A small *tronie* (head) by Rembrandt'.

c.1629

Constantijn Huygens (1596–1687), secretary to Stadholder Frederick Henry (p. 27, fig. 37), visits the Leiden studio shared by Rembrandt and Jan Lievens (1607–74), and compares their work. He finds them both brilliant, but too introverted. Not long afterwards, Huygens procures Rembrandt important commissions from the court in The Hague.

1630

Harmen Gerritsz is buried in Leiden on 27 April. Rembrandt draws a posthumous (?) portrait of his father.

In May and November Rembrandt signs two receipts. Each is for fifty guilders, the six-monthly tuition fee of his pupil Isaac de Jouderville (cat. no. 29b). On 29 November the following year he receives a further fifty guilders for another six-month term of apprenticeship.

In the course of the year Rembrandt makes a large number of etchings, most of them small, which he signs with his customary monogram 'RHL (Rembrandt Harmenszoon of Leiden)'. In four etchings he experiments with facial expressions, showing himself surprised, frowning with his mouth open, angry and smiling (cat. nos. 20–3).

1631

On 20 June, Rembrandt lends the sizable sum of 1,000 guilders to the Amsterdam art dealer Hendrick van Uylenburgh (1587–1661).

At the end of 1631 (probably) the painter leaves his native city for Amsterdam, where he lodges with Van Uylenburgh. The latter has a successful art gallery with an 'academy' attached, where young painters are trained. Rembrandt teaches there. His main commissions are for portraits.

The first in a long series is that of the Amsterdam merchant Nicolaas Ruts (1573–1638; New York, The Frick Collection).

Rembrandt etches his first 'formal' self portrait (cat. no. 32) after a model seemingly by Peter Paul Rubens (p. 144, fig. 32d).

1632

Rembrandt's portrait of Amalia of Solms (Paris, Musée Jacquemart-André), wife of Frederick Henry, is mentioned in an inventory of the stadholder's collection drawn up in The Hague on 16 August. This year he completes *The Anatomy Lesson of Dr Nicolaes Tulp* (The Hague, Mauritshuis), his first large group portrait. He is now 26 years old.

1633

On 4 April, Pieter Lastman is buried in Amsterdam's Oude Kerk (Old Church). Rembrandt honours his teacher's memory with drawn copies of several of his paintings.

Rembrandt is amazingly prolific as a portraitist. A painted self portrait (cat. no. 35) is his first work to bear the signature 'Rembrandt f[ecit]'. From 1633 he signs almost exclusively with his Christian name, undoubtedly in imitation of great Italian painters like Leonardo (1452–1519), Michelangelo (1475–1564), Raphael (1483–1520) and Titian (active by 1510; died 1576).

The Remonstrant preacher Johannes Wtenbogaert (1608–80) records in his notebook that he was 'painted by Rembrandt' on 13 April (p. 10, fig. 2).

On 8 June, Rembrandt makes a silverpoint drawing on vellum of Saskia van Uylenburgh (1612–42), a burgomaster's daughter from Leeuwarden and cousin of his employer, Van Uylenburgh. It emerges from the inscription that Rembrandt and Saskia are betrothed.

1634

Rembrandt becomes a citizen of Amsterdam and a member of the city's guild of painters. He is given the customary guild funeral token bearing his name: 'Rembrant Hermans [Painter]'.

On 10 June, 'Rembrant Harmanss van Rijn of Leiden, 26 years old . . . living in Bre[e]straet' registers the banns of his marriage to Saskia. On 14 June, his mother gives her consent to the match in a notarial deed.

Hendrick van Uylenburgh writes the motto 'Miedelmaet haut staet (The golden mean is best)' in the *album amicorum* of a German client, Burchard Grossman. Rembrandt contributes the age-old adage: 'Een vroom gemoet / Acht eer voor goet (The pious hold, esteem o'er gold)'.

Rembrandt marries Saskia on 22 June in the parish of St Anne in Friesland.

On 3 July, Saskia signs a document in Friesland arranging for the sale of property. Three weeks later, Rembrandt is described as a 'merchant of Amsterdam' in connection with a portrait commission in Rotterdam.

1635

On 22 February, Rembrandt and Saskia are still living with her much older cousin in Amsterdam: an annotated auction list gives his address as 'Rembrandt van Rijn at Hendrick [van] Uylenburgh's'.

Rembrandt makes a large painting (cat. no. 43), which is interpreted as a kind of self portrait of the painter and his wife.

Rembrandt's son Rumbartus, named after Saskia's father, is born on 15 December. This first child lives only two months.

c.1635

Numerous pupils come to study with Rembrandt, among them Ferdinand Bol (cat. nos. 87 and 88) and Gerbrand van den Eeckhout (cat. no. 91). Govert Flinck (cat. nos. 93 and 94) may have entered the master's studio earlier in c.1633.

1636

In February, Rembrandt writes to Huygens to tell him that he has moved. He is now living in Nieuwe Doelenstraat (present-day nos. 16 and 18), with a view across the Amstel. The painter is working on a series of Passion scenes for the Stadholder (Munich, Alte Pinakothek). He portrays himself in *The Raising of the Cross* as one of the men helping to lift the Cross (p. 22, fig. 27).

Rembrandt etches a portrait of himself holding a drawing stylus, with Saskia looking on (cat. no. 46).

1637

Rembrandt buys a large number of old prints, drawings, albums and curios at the sale of the collection of Jan Basse (c.1571–1637), which was held from 9 to 30 March.

In May, Saskia and Rembrandt move to a house called 'The Confectionary (die suijckerbackerij)' on Binnen-Amstel (now no. 41, Zwanenburgerstraat).

An inventory of the possessions of Lambert Jacobsz (c.1598–1636), Hendrick van Uylenburgh's branch manager in Leeuwarden, lists numerous copies after originals by Rembrandt.

1638

In a document drawn up by the Leeuwarden Court on 16 July, members of Saskia's family complain (to no avail) that she is squandering her inheritance.

Rembrandt's daughter Cornelia is baptised in Amsterdam's Oude Kerk on 22 July, but lives only three weeks.

1639

On 5 January, Rembrandt buys a magnificent merchant's house for 13,000 guilders in Sint-Anthonisbreestraat (now nos. 4–6, Jodenbreestraat), which is today the Rembrandthuis Museum. He retains his address in Binnen-Amstel until 1 May.

Rembrandt draws a copy of Raphael's *Portrait of Baldassare Castiglione* (p. 172, fig. 53c) belonging to the collector Don Alfonso Lopez (1572–1649), who bought the painting at auction for 3,500 guilders. This picture is one of the sources of inspiration for an etched self portrait by Rembrandt (cat. no. 53). His self portrait of 1640 (cat. no. 54) is a painted variant of the etching.

1640

On 12 August, a second daughter called Cornelia is buried in the Zuiderkerk (South Church), having lived only a few weeks.

Rembrandt's mother is buried in St Peter's in Leiden. She leaves more than 10,000 guilders.

The Englishman Peter Mundy writes in his travel journal that 'there having bin in this Country Many excellent Men in that Faculty [= Painting], some att Presentt, as Rimbrantt'.

Samuel van Hoogstraten (cat. no. 96) becomes Rembrandt's pupil.

1641

Titus is baptised in the Zuiderkerk on 22 September. The fourth child of Rembrandt and Saskia, he was the only one to reach adulthood.

On 18 October, the artist Philips Angel (c.1618–62) delivers an address to the members of the Leiden painters' guild in which he praises Rembrandt's 'keen and deep reflection'. The city chronicler Jan Jansz Orlers (1570–1646) mentions Rembrandt in the first printed biography of him as 'now one of the most celebrated painters of this century'. The artist is 35 years old.

Carel Fabritius (cat. no. 92) becomes Rembrandt's pupil.

1642

On 5 June, Saskia van Uylenburgh, 'lying sick abed', makes her second will, in which she stipulates that Rembrandt is to have the usufruct of her estate, provided he does not remarry.

Saskia dies on 14 June, according to a note written by one of her Frisian cousins in a family chronicle, and is buried five days later in a private grave in the Oude Kerk in Amsterdam.

Rembrandt buys prints by Lucas van Leyden (active 1508; died 1533) for 200 to 250 guilders each. The sixteen civic guardsmen in *The Nightwatch* (p. 32, fig. 47) pay an average of 100 guilders each for their portraits.

After Saskia's death, the widow Geertje Dircx (1610/15–after 1656) becomes Titus's dry nurse. She and the painter embark on a relationship, and she tries to persuade Rembrandt to marry her.

1643

The house abutting on the rear of Rembrandt's is sold. It turns out that it had a gallery in which he probably painted *The Nightwatch. The Three Trees* (B. 212) is the finest of the landscapes that he started etching shortly before.

1644–5

Paintings, drawings and etchings by Rembrandt are listed in inventories across the country. However, his output, even of the self portraits, now slows to a trickle.

1646

Rembrandt buys marble statues (possibly classical) in Antwerp on 13 September.

On 29 November, Stadholder Frederick Henry orders his treasurer to pay Rembrandt 2,400 guilders for two paintings that have been added to the Passion series commissioned earlier.

1647

Rembrandt's estate, including his inheritance from Saskia, is estimated at 40,750 guilders.

Hendrickje Stoffels (*c.*1625–63) begins work as Rembrandt's housekeeper.

1648

Geertje Dircx makes a will on 24 January, leaving all her possessions to Titus van Rijn.

Rembrandt etches a self portrait (cat. no. 62) showing himself at work with an etching needle.

1649

On 1 October, Hendrickje Stoffels, 'spinster aged 23', testifies in the court case brought against Rembrandt by Geertje Dircx for breaking his troth, and says that an agreement has been reached with Geertje. Hendrickje becomes the second great love of Rembrandt's life.

A document of 14 November, drawn up in connection with the court case, refers to Rembrandt as 'the honourable and widely celebrated painter'. Hendrickje secures her position as Geertje's successor in Rembrandt's household.

On 23 October, at the Town Hall, the Commissioners of Marital Affairs hear that Rembrandt has indeed slept with Geertje, but that he has made no promise to marry her. They award her an annuity of 200 guilders in alimony.

1650

On 4 July, a successful scheme is hatched to have Geertje Dircx committed to the Spinning House (house of correction) in Gouda.

Rembrandt draws himself, according to the later inscription, 'from his own likeness in the attire he wore in his studio' (cat. no. 63). He repeats the pose with his hands on his hips in a self portrait of 1652 (cat. no. 65).

c.1650

Willem Drost (cat. no. 90) becomes Rembrandt's pupil.

1652

Rembrandt's brother Adriaen (born c.1597), a miller in Leiden, is buried on 19 October.

The artist makes a drawing for the *album amicorum* of the Amsterdam patrician Jan Six (1618–1700), with the inscription: 'Rembrandt aen [to] Joanus Six. 1652'.

1653

On 1 February, Rembrandt receives a hefty bill for arrears of payment for the house he bought in Sint-Anthonisbreestraat in 1639. He borrows, in succession, 4,180 guilders from the former alderman Cornelis Witsen, 1,000 guilders from Jan Six, and 4,200 guilders from Isaack van Hertsbeeck. This appears to be sufficient to pay off his debts, but his financial problems get worse.

Rembrandt paints *Aristotle with the Bust of Homer* (New York, The Metropolitan Museum of Art) for the Sicilian nobleman Don Antonio Ruffo (1610–78).

1654

Hendrickje is summoned to appear before the council of the Reformed Congregation on 25 June, 2 July and 16 July for 'practising whoredom with the painter Rembrandt'. On 23 July she admits to her relationship with Rembrandt.

On 30 October, Cornelia, an illegitimate daughter, is baptised in the Oude Kerk. Like the two daughters who died young, she is named after Rembrandt's mother.

Rembrandt tries to buy a house in Handboogstraat, but fails to secure a loan.

Rembrandt paints the *Portrait of Jan Six* (Amsterdam, Six Collection).

1655

Geertje Dircx is released from the Gouda house of correction on 31 May.

The 14-year-old Titus van Rijn makes his father his universal heir, thereby excluding the family of his mother Saskia.

1656

On 14 July, Rembrandt applies to the High Court of Holland for *cessio bonorum* (voluntary surrender of effects to one's creditors). He attributes his financial problems to 'losses suffered in business as well as damages and losses at sea'. His art business was doing badly, in other words, and he had been speculating. The case is assigned to the Amsterdam Commissioners of Bankruptcy in the Town Hall.

An inventory is made of Rembrandt's possessions, including his impressive art collection, on 25 and 26 July. The sale of many treasures has been under way for some time. In December 1655 and January 1656, Rembrandt held sales of works from his collection in the Keizerskroon Inn in Amsterdam. He continues to borrow money.

The letter of cession is awarded on 8 August. The first public auction takes place before 12 September.

Rembrandt paints *The Anatomy Lesson of Dr Jan Deijman* (surviving fragment in Amsterdam, Amsterdams Historisch Museum).

1657

On 27 June, 'Rembrandt's likeness *à l'antique*', an unidentifiable self portrait, is valued at 150 guilders . One of his history paintings fetches ten times as much.

1658

The sale of Rembrandt's possessions continues. The house in Sint-Anthonisbreestraat is distrained and sold on 1 February.

In May, Rembrandt, Hendrickje, Titus and Cornelia move to a rented house in Rozengracht (now no. 184) in the Jordaan district of Amsterdam, opposite the Nieuwe Doolhof (the maze).

Rembrandt paints himself seated in state like a monarch (cat. no. 71).

In an etched self portrait of 1658 we see the artist at work as an etcher (cat. no. 72). It is his last self portrait in this medium.

1659
On 7 October, Rembrandt gives his son Titus power of attorney to act for him in 'petty matters'.

c.1659
Arent de Gelder (cat. no. 95) is supposed to have become Rembrandt's last pupil in or after 1659, although he may have entered the artist's studio as late as 1662 to 1664 (see cat. no. 82).

1660
On 15 December, Hendrickje and Titus transfer the 'company and trade in paintings, graphic art, engravings and woodcuts' to their names, thus relieving Rembrandt of all financial control. He can continue to paint, but must leave business matters to them.

Hendrickje Stoffels makes Titus her universal heir in her will of 7 August. Rembrandt is given the usufruct.

A document drawn up on 20 October calls Hendrickje 'the wife of Mr Rembrandt van Rijn, art painter', although they have not married.

1661
The biographer Cornelis de Bie (1627–after 1711) praises not only Rembrandt's paintings 'which enlighten every mind', but also his etchings: 'It is the very soul of life that lives therein'.

Rembrandt paints himself as the apostle Paul (cat. no. 81).

1662
Rembrandt sells Saskia's grave on 27 October.

He paints *The Sampling Officials of the Amsterdam Drapers' Guild* (Amsterdam, Rijksmuseum), and receives major commissions for portraits and other works, some from the extremely wealthy Trip family.

1663
Hendrickje Stoffels is buried in a rented grave in Amsterdam's Westerkerk (West Church) on 24 July, probably a victim of the plague.

1664
The painter Christiaen Dusart (1618–82) is appointed guardian of Cornelia van Rijn on 21 July. Her father, Rembrandt, is described as 'hale and hearty, in full use of his mind, memory and speech'.

The learned Swiss monk, Gabriel Bucelinus (1599–1681), notes in his diary that Rembrandt is 'the miracle of our age (Rimprant, nostrae aetatis miraculum)'.

1665
Titus van Rijn proudly declares to a Leiden notary on 21 March: 'Yes, my father cuts [etches] very skilfully'.

On 19 June, Titus van Rijn applies for and is awarded *veniam aetatis* (legal maturity).

1666

On 18 November, Titus is appointed Rembrandt's legal agent.

1667

On 29 December, Cosimo de' Medici (1642–1723) calls on Rembrandt, who is described as 'pittore famoso (famous painter)' in his travel journal. It later transpires that the Italian Grand Duke owns one of the painter's self portraits (cat. no. 85).

1668

Titus van Rijn marries Magdalena van Loo (1642–69) on 28 February. In 1659, her father, the silversmith Jan van Loo declared in a deposition that he and his wife 'had been very close friends of the aforesaid Rembrandt van Rijn and his late wife, Saskia van Uylenburgh'.

On 7 September, shortly before his twenty-seventh birthday, Titus is buried in the Westerkerk in Amsterdam.

1669

Titia van Rijn, Rembrandt's granddaughter and goddaughter, is baptised in the Nieuwezijds Chapel on 22 March, six months after the death of her father Titus.

Rembrandt paints three self portraits in the last year of his life (cat. nos. 84–6).

On 2 October, Rembrandt is visited by the amateur genealogist Pieter van Brederode (1631–97), who makes a record of antiquities and curios in his collection.

Rembrandt dies on 4 October. He is buried in an anonymous rented grave in Amsterdam's Westerkerk on 8 October.

For the documents on Rembrandt's life see Strauss / Van der Meulen 1979, with additional information in Broos 1981–2, Broos 1983 and Broos 1984a.

Note to the catalogue

Christopher White
Quentin Buvelot

In order to provide as complete a record as possible, the catalogue discusses and reproduces all the paintings, drawings and etchings which can reasonably be considered as self portraits by Rembrandt, whether or not they are included in the exhibition. Works not in the exhibition are marked with an asterisk (in the entries on the etchings, which are all in the exhibition, asterisks refer to the illustrated sheet, from Amsterdam or London respectively). Unless otherwise indicated, catalogued works will be exhibited in both London and The Hague. It is hoped that this unique exhibition will not only offer an opportunity to increase understanding of the role of self portraiture in Rembrandt's art, but also by the juxtaposition of one work with another achieve heightened agreement over problems of attribution and dating.

The editors have adopted an inclusive approach to what remains a contentious subject, and are aware that there is far from unanimity about a number of works listed here. The catalogue entries are arranged in chronological order, but given the difficulty of establishing the year of execution of the great number of undated works, it should be taken *cum grano salis*. Dates accompanying copies after lost self portraits (described in the catalogue as 'portraits of Rembrandt') refer to the presumed year of completion of the original composition. Facial studies by Rembrandt – in seventeenth-century Holland known as *tronies* – are strictly speaking not self portraits (for instance, cat. nos. 20–3), although they show the artist's face. In the titles of the works in question the word self portrait has been put between single quote marks. In other cases this has also been done when the identification of the work as a self portrait by Rembrandt is questionable (for instance, cat. nos. 43, 50).

The entries for the paintings by Rembrandt have been written by Edwin Buijsen (with the exception of cat. no. 34, which was written by Prof. Dr Ernst van de Wetering and cat. nos. 75–6, written by Christopher White), the etchings by Peter Schatborn, the drawings by Ben Broos, and the works by Rembrandt's pupils by Ariane van Suchtelen.

The editors would like to make grateful acknowledgement to the friendly co-operation of the Rembrandt Research Project, which has kindly made available draft entries for paintings in the fourth volume of the *Corpus* which was prepared to go to press when this publication was being written. The entries of the latter have provided essential information for the relevant entries in the catalogue.

All bibliographical references in the catalogue entries are cited in abbreviated form as in the essays – corresponding full citations are given in the bibliography. The letter 'B.' refers to A. von Bartsch, *Catalogue Raisonné de toutes les Estampes qui forment l'Oeuvre de Rembrandt, et ceux de ses principaux Imitateurs*, a catalogue of Rembrandt's etchings that was published in Vienna in 1797. All Rembrandt etchings are identified by their Bartsch number, which is identical to that in F.W.H. Hollstein, *Dutch and Flemish Etchings, Engravings and Woodcuts, ca. 1450–1700* (series in progress). Hind refers to A.M. Hind's *A Catalogue of Rembrandt's Etchings* (London 1923).

Descriptions of the works in the catalogue have been written from the eye of the beholder (i.e. 'the' left or 'the' right hand). In the case of painted and drawn self portraits, which show the mirror image of the artist, the left and right in the eye of the beholder coincide with the actual left and right in the face and body of the artist. The etchings, however, in which the original design has been printed in reverse, show Rembrandt as contemporaries saw him when they stood face to face with the artist. In some instances references have been made to 'his' left or 'his' right hand, meaning from the eye of Rembrandt himself.

Catalogue

Edwin Buijsen

Peter Schatborn

Ben Broos

1
History Piece 1626

Panel, 90.1 × 121.3 cm

Signed and dated at lower right:
Rf [or *RH* in monogram]*16(2)6*

Leiden, Stedelijk Museum De Lakenhal, inv. no. 814 (on loan from the Netherlands Institute for Cultural Heritage, Amsterdam/Rijswijk)

Bredius/Gerson 1969, no. 460; *Corpus*, vol. I, no. A 6; Chapman 1990, pp. 15–16, 20, 106, 108, 111 and fig. 7

Previous page
Self Portrait as a Young Man (cat. no. 5)

AT THE BEGINNING OF HIS career Rembrandt confined himself largely to history pieces, but he was occasionally unable to resist the urge to depict his own face. In some of his earliest works he appears among the staffage of biblical or historical scenes. His *History Piece* from 1626 shows the young painter as an eye-witness to a solemn event. A princely personage, possibly an emperor, stands on the steps of a palatial building. An army has gathered round about him. A clerk looks up enquiringly from his desk at the crowned figure with his raised sceptre. Two men kneeling before the steps make gestures of dismay, while a soldier stands taking an oath.

Scholars have still not managed to reach a consensus about what exactly is happening here.[1] All agree, however, on the identity of the young man behind and to the right of the sovereign: it is the painter himself (see fig. p. 39). Although the face is partly obscured by the sceptre, the facial features are clearly visible as those of the early, etched self portraits. Rembrandt gazes intently at the viewer, without taking any part in the events unfolding around him. The rendering of his curly head of hair is particularly striking. The hairs have been scratched into the wet paint using a sharp object, probably the back of the brush, revealing the lighter-coloured lower layer.[2] The same technique is used for the hair of a figure standing a little further to the right.

An X-radiograph of the painting shows that the painter added this self portrait at a later stage.[3] Initially, something else was painted here; Rembrandt covered this shape with a layer of paint before introducing the present head. Above the mop of curls it is still possible, with the aid of infra-red reflectography, to discern something of the original design (fig. 1a). It was probably a head placed higher up in the pictorial plane, with the point of a lance protruding above it. Whether Rembrandt decided to add himself to the scene at the last moment or was dissatisfied with an earlier rendering of his own portrait remains unclear.

The Stoning of Saint Stephen, produced one year earlier, also contains a self portrait (fig. 1b and p. 22, fig. 28).[4] Above the saint's tormented face, and below the raised arm of one of the stone-throwers, Rembrandt's head suddenly comes into view. Whereas in the *History Piece* he adopts a neutral role, here he sides with the aggressive crowd, and his face shows clear signs of excitement. A head can be made out in another early work, *David before Saul with the Head of Goliath*, from 1627, that may be a self portrait (fig. 1c).[5]

It was recently pointed out that some of the figures in *The Stoning of Saint Stephen*, including the saint himself, display facial features reminiscent of, though not identical to, Rembrandt's own.[6] In the left background of the *History Piece* is a man with a plumed hat who takes after Rembrandt (fig. 1d), and even the angel in *Balaam's Ass and the Angel* from 1626 looks like a distant relative. One possible explanation is that Rembrandt practised depicting emotions – essential for the history painter that he aspired to be – by studying his own expressions in the mirror.

The painter's inclusion in his own history pieces was a tradition rooted in classical antiquity (see p. 41). Countless artists, both renowned and obscure, had gone before Rembrandt in this practice and art-lovers delighted in detecting their portraits. One example from Rembrandt's own circle is the painting *The Surrender of Weinsberg* (fig. 1e) by the little-known Leiden portrait painter Jan Cornelisz van 't Woudt (*c.*1570–1615).[7] The painter can be identified amid the historical figures not only by his seventeenth-century dress, but above all by the palette he holds in his hand. In contrast, Rembrandt preferred to be an anonymous member of the crowd. Still, his self portraits incorporated into such scenes would have been recognisable to adepts and were one of the painting's special attractions.

fig. 1a
Computer montage of infra-red reflectogram of
a detail from cat. no. 1 (courtesy of A. Verburg,
Netherlands Institute for Art History, The Hague).

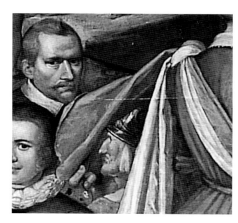

When Rembrandt made *The Stoning of Saint Stephen* and the *History Piece*, he was not yet widely known, and it seems likely that purchasers were personally acquainted with him, or at least knew him by sight.[8] Although we cannot yet name the client who commissioned the *History Piece*, we may know what he looked like. Near the centre of the piece is a man with a little beard whose face makes the impression of a portrait. He looks straight at the viewer and is the only figure clad in seventeenth-century military apparel.[9] If we could discover the identity of this man, that might well shed fresh light on the subject depicted.

In his subsequent career, Rembrandt would portray himself as a minor figure of several other history pieces. One of the most obvious examples is his *Raising of the Cross* of 1633, which was one of the pictures in the Passion series produced for Stadholder Frederick Henry (1584–1647). Rembrandt's features are recognisable in one of the executioner's assistants (fig. 1f), who is straining to raise the Cross into position. His head is carefully highlighted and he is dressed in 'antique' style – a shirt with slits and a beret. Here Rembrandt may have been expressing a belief that was common currency in Protestant circles of his day, that since Christ died for our sins, all humanity was guilty of his Crucifixion.[10]

Rembrandt's presence is suspected in numerous other history pieces, but the difference between an intentional self portrait and a chance resemblance is often hard to draw (figs. 1g). Some authors have succumbed to the temptation of identifying every wide-nosed man with a moustache as the painter. He has even been wistfully identified in '*The Night Watch*' in a single eye beneath a beret (fig. 1h and p. 32, fig. 47): 'There is no doubt that this is Rembrandt's gaze.'[11]

fig. 1g *right*
Supposed self portraits in history pieces by
Rembrandt:

top left
Musical Allegory (detail), 1626.
Panel, 63 × 48 cm. Amsterdam, Rijksmuseum
(has been identified, alternatively, as Jan Lievens).

top centre
The Deposition (detail), *c.*1632–3.
Panel, 89.5 × 65 cm. Munich, Bayerische
Staatsgemäldesammlungen, Alte Pinakothek.

top right
The Deposition (detail), *c.*1632–3.
Panel, 89.5 × 65 cm. Munich, Bayerische
Staatsgemäldesammlungen, Alte Pinakothek.

above left
The Storm on the Sea of Galilee (detail), 1633.
Canvas, 159.5 × 127.5 cm. Boston, Isabella Stewart
Gardner Museum.

above centre
John the Baptist preaching (detail), *c.*1634–5.
Canvas, 62 × 80 cm. Berlin, Staatliche Museen,
Gemäldegalerie, Preussischer Kulturbesitz.

above right
Samson threatens his Father-in-law (detail), 1635.
Canvas, 156 × 129 cm. Berlin, Staatliche Museen,
Gemäldegalerie, Preussischer Kulturbesitz.

right
The Blinding of Samson (detail), 1636.
Canvas, 236 × 302 cm. Frankfurt am Main,
Städelsches Kunstinstitut.

fig. 1h *below right*
REMBRANDT, *'The Night Watch'* (detail), 1642.
Canvas, 363 × 438 cm. Amsterdam, Rijksmuseum.

2
Small Self Portrait *c.1627–8*

Etching, 6 1/4 × 48/9 mm (from I), 43 × 40 mm
(III); three states

Amsterdam, Rijksmuseum, Rijksprentenkabinet,
inv. no. RP-P-OB–7 (III)

London, British Museum, inv. no. 1973-U–772
(III)*

B. / Hollstein 5; Hind 36; White 1969, pp. 26, 108
and fig. 7; Chapman 1990, pp. 21–2 and fig. 14

fig. 2a
REMBRANDT, *The Flight into Egypt, c.1627–8.*
Etching (first state), 146 × 122 mm, Amsterdam,
Rijksmuseum, Rijksprentenkabinet.

fig. 2b
REMBRANDT, *Joseph on the Flight into Egypt, c.1627–8.*
Etching (third state), 79 × 51 mm. Amsterdam,
Rijksmuseum, Rijksprentenkabinet.

fig. 2c
REMBRANDT, *Small Self Portrait, c.1627–8.*
Etching (first state), 6 1/4 × 48/9 mm.
Amsterdam, Rijksmuseum, Rijksprentenkabinet.

REMBRANDT MADE this, the smallest and probably the earliest of his etched self portraits, on part of an etching-plate that he had previously used for a different representation, *The Flight into Egypt* (fig. 2a).[12] The latter scene is rendered in a draughtsmanlike, sketchy style, in contrast to two even earlier biblical scenes, which are more linear in character.[13]

Only two specimens have been preserved of the first state of *The Flight into Egypt*, both of which are poor impressions.[14] Rembrandt evidently saw no point in improving the print and cut the plate down to a representation of the figure of Joseph (fig. 2b).[15] After partially cleaning the remaining piece, he made a small self portrait in the upper right section (fig. 2c). The sketchy style of *The Flight into Egypt* was his point of departure for the new image. In the first state of this self portrait, the head of Mary is still visible, albeit upside-down, above Rembrandt's own head. It has been removed in the third state.[16] In this state the plate has also been cut down to size and cleaned.

Rembrandt concentrated on the depiction of the head, adding only the contours of the shoulders. The lines of shadow under Rembrandt's face help to suggest the torso. The other visible lines in the first state are the remains of the tree from *The Flight into Egypt.*

Here, more than in any other portrait, Rembrandt – who was 21 or 22 years of age when he made this undated etching – has a boyish, almost childlike appearance. The expression with which he is inspecting himself appears anxious, but in fact it reflects the concentration with which he is recording his face on the etching-plate.

3
Self Portrait with
Wide Nose *c.*1628

Etching, 71 × 59 mm; two states

Amsterdam, Rijksmuseum, Rijksprentenkabinet,
inv. no. RP-P-OB—5 (I)*

B. / Hollstein 4; Hind 2A; Münz 1, fig. 1;
Sternberg 1977, p. 143, figs. 1 and 2; Chapman
1990, pp. 22, 131 and fig. 115

THIS RARE self portrait is comparable, both stylistically and in terms of character,
to another etched self portrait (cat. no. 4), although the two pieces are of slightly
different sizes. They may be dated around the same time and have survived in only
a few impressions. In both etchings, the figure is viewed from close by and almost fills
the pictorial plane, however more space has been left around the frontal portrait
described here. Rembrandt has depicted himself in historical attire, wearing a sleeveless
and collarless cloak and a sixteenth-century shirt decorated with smocking and a jerkin.
The shadows in the face are indicated with fine hatching and the eyes are denoted
by dark dots.

4
Self Portrait, Leaning Forward *c.1628*

Etching, 66 × 53 mm; one state

Amsterdam, Rijksmuseum, Rijksprentenkabinet, inv. no. RP-P-OB–19*

London, British Museum, inv. no. 1848–9–11–13

B. / Hollstein 9; Hind 35

fig. 4a
REMBRANDT, *Old Man with Cap*, 1630.
Etching (first state), 97 × 73 mm.
Amsterdam, Rijksmuseum, Rijksprentenkabinet.

WHEREAS IN the *Self Portrait with Wide Nose* Rembrandt looks directly at the viewer (cat. no. 3), here he is looking away. For this reason, the impression made by this little etching is less than a self portrait; it was probably executed partly from memory. While the shadow of the figure in the frontal portrait referred to above is indicated by a small triangle of lines – Rembrandt's usual practice – here the shadow extends behind and above the head: the shoulder and face are brightly illuminated by the light from the lower right.

At first sight, it is not immediately apparent that there is a small partition of some kind in the lower right corner of this etching, rendered by criss-cross hatching. It would appear to be a rocky wall or embankment. This element appears in certain other prints with greater emphasis, for instance in *Old Man with Cap* (fig. 4a).[17] A partition of this kind creates depth and distance, although it is scarcely noticeable in the little self portrait described here.

5
Self Portrait as a Young Man

*c.*1628

Panel, 22.5 × 18.6 cm

Amsterdam, Rijksmuseum, inv. no. A 4691

Corpus, vol. I, no. A 14; Chapman 1990, pp. 22–4, 34, 37–8, 46, 71 and fig. I

REMBRANDT HAD already included himself in the staffage of several history pieces when he painted his first full-fledged self portraits around 1628–9. Although there is no year on this small, glowing panel from the Rijksmuseum, it can be dated on stylistic grounds before the painting from Munich, dated 1629 (cat. no. 7). Whereas most of the etched self portraits from this period emphasise facial expression (see cat. nos. 2–4), in this piece the face is largely in the shadows. The subject's features are hard to make out. Only the large ear lobe – a striking element of virtually all Rembrandt's painted self portraits – catches the full light. Here, as in the *History Piece* (cat. no. 1), the painter has depicted himself with a tousled head of hair, with curls scratched into the wet paint. Using this technique, he has exposed the ground layer in certain strategically chosen spots. In the forehead, this lower layer is yellowish-brown, which convincingly suggests the effect of hair catching the light. Through the scratches around the hair on the neck a darker colour emerges that makes a sharp contrast with the light background. In some places, by the white collar for instance, the paint has been applied thickly. The background is painted in loose brushstrokes that create the impression of a plastered wall.

Rembrandt wears a simple white shirt and some barely defined dark overgarment. That much of his face is in the shadows, in particular the eyes, which seventeenth-century art theory viewed as the windows of the soul, has been interpreted by some scholars as an expression of a melancholic temperament.[18] A more likely explanation, however, is that Rembrandt used his own face to experiment with chiaroscuro, a dominant preoccupation of his in this period. Furthermore, we are dealing here not with a portrait in the strict sense of the word but a *tronie*.[19] This is a seventeenth-century Dutch term for a type of picture intermediate between a portrait and a history piece. The sitter is portrayed in a particular role, sometimes complete with the appropriate clothing and attributes, and his identity is irrelevant. For a *tronie* the choice of model was arbitrary; the artist himself or anyone from his immediate circle would do. Rembrandt and his associate Jan Lievens (1607–74) painted numerous *tronies*

fig. 5a   *(reproduced in mirror image)*
JAN VAN VLIET AFTER REMBRANDT,
Tronie (Portrait of Rembrandt), 1634.
Etching (second state), 225 × 190 mm.
Amsterdam, Museum
Het Rembrandthuis.

fig. 5b
ANONYMOUS AFTER REMBRANDT,
Portrait of Rembrandt, Panel, 23.4 × 17.2 cm.
Cassel, Staatliche Museen,
Gemäldegalerie Alte Meister,
Schloss Wilhelmshöhe.

in their Leiden years, ranging from credulous youths and smug soldiers to wrinkled old men and women.

That there was a demand for pictures of this kind is clear from the print series depicting *tronies* after designs by Rembrandt that was marketed by the Leiden engraver Jan van Vliet (*c.*1600/10–68) in 1633–4. The painting described here was one of the pieces that served as an example for these prints (fig. 5a).[20] While the other heads in the series represent certain easily identifiable stereotypes, it is not immediately apparent what kind of person this beardless youth is intended to portray. However, this was no obstacle to an imaginative mind; when the French publisher François Langlois (1588–1647) reissued the print series, he identified the head in the shadows as the Ethiopian eunuch who was baptised by the apostle Philip (New Testament, Acts 8: 26–40).

The museum of Cassel possesses a panel with a virtually identical depiction (fig. 5b). Until the discovery of the painting discussed here, in 1959, it was regarded as an original by Rembrandt and enjoyed considerable renown. Comparison of the two versions has proved the Cassel piece, however, to be a copy.[21] The copier has tried to imitate Rembrandt's vigorous style of painting, but he was far less adept at it. The curls, for instance, are rendered roughly and with near-mechanical brushwork. The swollen ear lobe, for which Rembrandt used a subtle mixture of hues, is depicted with thick daubs of paint placed alongside one another. The mouth, nose and eyes are enlarged, an accentuation that disturbs the balance of the face. The Cassel copy was probably made not long after the original but it has not, as yet, been convincingly linked to any painter in Rembrandt's circle.

6
Self Portrait with Curly Hair *c.*1628–9

Etching, 91 × 72 mm; one state

Haarlem, Teylers Museum, inv. no. KG 3557
(cut off at the bottom)

London, British Museum, inv. no. 1848–9–11–17*

B. / Hollstein 27; Hind 3; Chapman 1990, pp. 22,
30, 71 and fig. 18

fig. 6a
REMBRANDT, *Man leaning on a Table*, *c.*1629–30.
Pen and brown ink, 97 × 100 mm.
London, British Museum.

REMBRANDT EXECUTED this self portrait very much in the manner of a sketch, devoting little attention to detail: he shaped the body with diagonal hatching, which is overlaid in a criss-cross manner in the dark portions, and applied curly lines to denote the hair. There is more diagonal hatching to the left and right of the figure. The nose, cheeks and chin stand out against the shaded areas, and the collar too has been left largely untouched. The face, in which the eyes are almost totally obscured, is bounded by dark shadows.

The sketchy quality of this etching greatly resembles Rembrandt's style of draughtsmanship at the time when it was made. A drawing in London has a similarly loose, rough style, which likewise contains dark accents that give the forms their plasticity (fig. 6a).[22] Rembrandt was the first artist to produce etchings as if they were drawings. *The Flight into Egypt* (p. 90, fig. 2a) and *Small Self Portrait* (cat. no. 2) are among the earliest examples of this type of etching.

The concealment of the eyes in the semi-darkness also characterises two painted self portraits in Amsterdam (*c.*1628; cat. no. 5) and Munich (1629; cat. no. 7). Like these paintings, this etching shows that Rembrandt created forms and space largely by manipulating light and dark effects.

The scratches in the open space at the bottom have been misread as Rembrandt's monogram and the year 1630. The etching must have been made around the same time as the paintings referred to above, in 1628–9. It may be noted that in some of the prints in which he left an open section at the bottom in this way, Rembrandt cut the plate to a smaller size in a later state (cat. nos. 9 and 19). Only one state is known of the *Self Portrait with Curly Hair*, and of this only three impressions are known: aside from those in Haarlem and London, there is a third in the Albertina in Vienna.

7
Self Portrait as a Young Man

1629

Panel, 15.5 × 12.7 cm

Monogrammed and dated at lower right: *RHL 1629*

Munich, Bayerische Staatsgemäldesammlungen, Alte Pinakothek, inv. no. 11427

Bredius/Gerson 1969, no. 2; *Corpus*, vol. I, no. A 19; Chapman 1990, pp. 23–4, 30, 34, 37–8, 46, 71 and fig. 23

F OR THIS SELF PORTRAIT, Rembrandt adopted a compositional scheme that largely corresponds to the previous painting (cat. no. 5). One major difference, however, is that in this piece he is leaning further forward, so that the head is more sharply angled. This movement is emphasised by the tangled lock of hair that falls casually over the forehead. As the slanting light is more diffuse, the facial features stand out more clearly from the semi-darkness. Thus we can see that the eyebrows are raised and the mouth slightly open. The surprised expression and turned head create the suggestion that the painter has caught himself looking in the mirror.

The loose brushwork contributes a great deal to the spontaneous impression of this piece. Rembrandt has depicted the hanging fringes of the collar with short, vigorous strokes and in the background the wide sweeps of the brush can easily be traced. Here too, Rembrandt has scratched the curly hair into the wet paint, exposing the ground layer. In the shadowy parts of the face, also, he has exposed the reddish-brown underpainting and thus it plays an important role in the colouring. He has indeed succeeded masterfully in creating a great range of hues with a minimum of colours.

In its evocative expression as well as its modest dimensions, this painting greatly resembles the etched self portraits. At a later time the panel was enlarged along the left and lower edges (fig. 7a), which partly undermined the initial snapshot effect. Between 1956 and 1967 the additional pieces were removed and the painting regained its original format.

fig. 7a
Cat. no. 7 with added sections.

8

Attributed to Rembrandt

Self Portrait with Gorget and Beret *c.1629*

Panel, 42.8 × 33 cm

Monogrammed at lower right: *RHL*

Indianapolis, Museum of Art,
The Clowes Fund Collection

Bredius/Gerson 1969, no. 3; *Corpus*, vol. I,
no. A 22 (copy 1); Chapman 1990, pp. 146–7,
note 14

ᴇᴀʀʟʏ ᴏɴ ɪɴ ʜɪs career, Rembrandt started having pupils copy his self portraits as part of their training. The composition of the panel shown here was evidently ideal for teaching purposes, as several virtually identical versions are known.[23] The gorget, a favourite attribute in Rembrandt's *tronies*, identifies the subject as a soldier. The position of the head somewhat resembles that in the Munich self portrait (cat. no. 7), but here the lips are parted more and teeth are exposed. This, together with the lopsided beret, gives the *tronie* discussed here a more expressive quality.

Of all the versions of this painting that are currently known, this one from Indianapolis is closest to Rembrandt's style of execution. The face is painted in short, varied strokes, the handling of the brush displaying a certain deftness and spontaneity. Even so, in overall quality the piece is somewhat inferior to the self portraits in Amsterdam (cat. no. 5) and Munich. A striking feature is the cracked lips, which are less pronounced in the other versions of the painting. The curls in the hair and the beard growth on the chin have been scratched into the paint in Rembrandt's characteristic style, exposing a red layer of underpainting. The X-radiograph reveals that the beret ended up much smaller than originally planned.[24] A change of this kind in the course of painting may indicate that this was the prototype of the composition.[25]

Another example, now in Japan (fig. 8a), was until recently regarded as Rembrandt's own work.[26] However, the manner of painting is far smoother than in this panel and is therefore further removed from Rembrandt. The relationship between the two works, which are qualitatively far superior to the other copies, is comparable to that between the self portrait as a young man in Nuremberg and its variant in The Hague (cat. nos. 14a-b).

fig. 8a
Sᴛᴜᴅɪᴏ ᴏꜰ Rᴇᴍʙʀᴀɴᴅᴛ, *Portrait of Rembrandt with Gorget and Beret*, *c.*1629. Panel, 19.7 × 37.3 cm. Atami, MOA Museum of Art.

9
Self Portrait in a High Cap, Framed in an Oval

*c.*1629

Etching, 90 × 54 mm; one state

Amsterdam, Rijksmuseum, Rijksprentenkabinet, inv. no. RP-P-OB–23 (reduced in size)

London, British Museum, inv. no. 1848–9–11–14*

B. / Hollstein 12; Hind 59; Chapman 1990, pp. 22, 30, 71 and fig. 17

MANY OF REMBRANDT's self portraits testify to his fascination with the rendering of light and dark. In this portrait the eyes are scarcely distinguishable in the deep shadows below the cap, which is made of a loose-woven material, or possibly fur. Rembrandt left small dots of light, however, just as in his drawings he always kept the washes he applied with the brush transparent and open.

The oval frame was added at a later stage, as is apparent from the fact that the contour of the shoulder on the left clearly carries on through it. This frame consists of a succession of tiny leaflike motifs, which may have been applied by some mechanical means.[27] Few impressions of this plate have been preserved. The example from London shown here and the sheet in the Institut Néerlandais in Paris are the only impressions that have not been cut on all sides, as were an impression in Amsterdam (fig. 9a) and another one in London.

Rembrandt worked on a small scale in paintings as well as etchings. As early as 1630 or thereabouts, Constantijn Huygens (1596–1687; p. 27, fig. 37) commented that Rembrandt differed from his associate Jan Lievens (1607–74) in preferring small paintings.[28] Diminutive portrait prints had been produced before, notably by Hendrick Goltzius (1558–1617) and Jacob de Gheyn (*c.*1596–1641), but these were not self portraits. They were often circular and furnished with an inscription and a marginal legend. Several of Rembrandt's portraits have an open space at the bottom, as this one does, but it would generally be removed at a later stage.

The type of portrait that was produced by Goltzius and De Gheyn is also familiar to us from a tiny drawing by none other than Rembrandt's master, Pieter Lastman (1583–1633), of his brother Nicolaes (fig. 9b).[29] It is reasonable to assume that Lastman made other little portraits of this kind, which his pupil must have seen. In later years Rembrandt portrayed the clergyman Jan Cornelis Sylvius similarly framed within an oval, and furnished with a caption (fig. 9c).[30]

fig. 9a
REMBRANDT, *Self Portrait in a High Cap, Framed in an Oval, c.*1629. Etching (first state, reduced in size), 62 × 50 mm. Amsterdam, Rijksmuseum, Rijksprentenkabinet.

fig. 9b
PIETER LASTMAN, *Portrait of Nicolaes Lastman*, 1613. Pen and brown ink, 45 × 45 mm. Paris, Institut Néerlandais, Frits Lugt Collection.

fig. 9c
REMBRANDT, *Portrait of Jan Cornelis Sylvius*, 1646. Etching (second state), 278 × 188 mm. Amsterdam, Rijksmuseum, Rijksprentenkabinet.

10

Self Portrait with Plumed Beret 1629

Panel, 89.5 × 73.5 cm

Monogrammed and dated at lower right:
RHL . . . 9

Boston, Isabella Stewart Gardner Museum,
inv. no. P 21 N6

Bredius/Gerson 1969, no. 8; *Corpus*, vol. I,
no. A 20; Chapman 1990, pp. 34, 46, 48, 131
and fig. II

IN ADDITION TO facial expression, costume was generally another important aspect of the *tronie*. In the self portraits in Amsterdam (cat. no. 5) and Munich (cat. no. 7) clothing scarcely played a role because Rembrandt depicted himself small, giving a close-up of the face. In this appreciably larger painting, though, Rembrandt has given himself more space and adopted a distinguished pose. As he is further away from the viewer, we glimpse his imaginative attire: hanging over a mustard-coloured cloak is a gold chain and locket, around his neck he wears a silk scarf, and on his head is a jewelled beret surmounted by an elegant plume.

The costume and beret clearly diverge from the prevailing fashion and are based on sixteenth-century examples, while the gold-striped scarf confers an oriental touch (see p. 61). Some authors have interpreted the chain, a common object in self portraits of Rembrandt, as a reference to the gold chains that sovereigns presented to painters in acknowledgement of their services, implying that the young Rembrandt was publicising his artistic aspirations.[31] However, the same decoration occurs in other *tronies* and history pieces by Rembrandt depicting figures who have nothing to do with the painting profession.[32] The decorations with which famous court painters such as Peter Paul Rubens (1577–1640) and Anthony van Dyck (1599–1641) immortalised themselves, moreover, vary in shape and were worn differently. Thus a self portrait of Van Dyck displays a chain with circular links worn diagonally over the shoulder (fig. 10a). To Rembrandt, gold chains were probably nothing more than attributes intended to emphasise that a picture was not a depiction of everyday life.

The plume on the beret should likewise be interpreted with caution. On the basis of what is in fact a fairly superficial similarity to an engraving by Lucas van Leyden (active 1508; died 1533), this feather has been interpreted as a *vanitas* symbol (fig. 10b).[33] The figure in the print, who in Rembrandt's time was taken to be a self portrait of the renowned sixteenth-century artist from Leiden, sports an over-sized bunch of feathers and points expressively to a skull he is clasping under his cloak. Rembrandt's painting contains no such unadorned allusion to death. The plume appears in other *tronies* by Rembrandt and,

fig. 10a
ANTHONY VAN DYCK, *Self Portrait with Sunflower*, *c.*1635–6. Canvas, 60.3 × 73 cm. By kind permission of His Grace The Duke of Westminster OBE TD DL.

fig. 10b
LUCAS VAN LEYDEN, *Youth with Plumed Cap and Skull*, *c.*1519. Engraving, 184 × 144 mm. Amsterdam, Rijksmuseum, Rijksprentenkabinet.

like the garments, it can best be seen as part of an old-fashioned suit of clothing, based on sixteenth-century fashion. By dressing himself in clothes evocative of a bygone age, Rembrandt has placed himself outside his own time and surroundings.

The light from the left shines on a large part of the face, but here too the eyes remain in the shade. Around the mouth and chin the first signs of beard growth can be seen. In comparison to other early self portraits, the face is more elongated and the eyes closer together.[34] It is possible to explain such disparities, perhaps, by pointing out that achieving a perfect likeness was not the main priority when painting a *tronie*. Variations in the facial features are also sometimes noticeable in the etched self portraits.

The style of painting varies from fine (in the scarf and beret) to somewhat coarser (in the barbs of the feather and the links of the gold chain). In each case, however, the attempt was to achieve the most realistic possible rendering of the material. As the paint has suffered a certain amount of wear, especially in the face and hair, some of the original radiance and detail has been lost. In the background, an underlying figure is dimly visible to the left and right of the shoulders. Analysis of the X-radiograph of the painting reveals that this is the silhouette of a larger figure, placed higher in the pictorial plane, which was initially depicted on the panel and later painted over (fig. 10c). This recycling of panels occurs elsewhere in Rembrandt's oeuvre and is especially common in his self portraits (see cat. no. 26).

fig. 10c
X-radiograph of cat. no. 10.

II
Self Portrait, Bareheaded

1629

Etching, 174 × 155 mm; one state

Monogrammed and dated at upper left, in
mirror image: *RHL 1629*

Amsterdam, Rijksmuseum, Rijksprentenkabinet,
inv. no. RP-P-OB—723*

London, British Museum, inv. no. 1848—9—11—19

B. / Hollstein 338; Hind 4; White 1969, pp. 13, 27,
28, 107—8 and fig. 131; Chapman 1990, pp. 11, 22,
24, 34 and fig. 1

IN CONTRAST TO most of the early etched self portraits, this sheet is of a fairly large size. The monogram and the year are also clearly recorded (albeit in reverse), and are comparable to the way in which Rembrandt signed and dated his paintings. Although only two impressions of the print are known, preserved in Amsterdam and London, it seems likely that Rembrandt initially intended to print a substantial edition of this handsome portrait.[35] That this was never done may have had something to do with the quality of the printing.

The print is unlike just about everything that had been done in the way of etching before then and it is a unique piece in Rembrandt's etched oeuvre. This is because Rembrandt worked not with a fine etching needle but with a feather quill or reed pen, which produces a double line if pressure is increased. He also left the plate in the acid for a long time and applied a great quantity of ink to the etching-plate, creating dark areas and sharp contrasts. The self portrait is in any case an extreme example of Rembrandt's efforts to make etchings in the manner and style of drawings, whereby, here, he even went so far as to use a draughtsman's pen. It almost seems as if in an unguarded moment he actually forgot that he was making an etching, as the signature was not etched into the plate in reverse: there would appear to be no other explanation for the fact that the monogram and year appear in mirror image.

The print bears a close resemblance to the drawn self portrait in Amsterdam from the same period (cat. no. 12). This drawing is not a real study for it, however, since it shows how Rembrandt saw himself, whereas the etching shows how he wanted others to see him: he sports a lock of hair that falls over his shoulder in a fashion favoured by the aristocracy of the day, though it was probably not worn in this way by Rembrandt himself (on this hairstyle, see p. 62). The significance of this lock of hair that he added from memory underscores the ambition he cherished as he produced this smart self portrait. For the rest he wears the same clothes as in the drawing: a white collar over a coat with frogging down the front, a mode of dress that conjures up associations with military uniform.

12

Self Portrait with
Tousled Hair c.1629

Pen and brown ink, brush and grey paint, 127 × 94 mm

Amsterdam, Rijksmuseum, Rijksprentenkabinet, inv. no. 1961:75

Benesch 1973, vol. I, no. 54; Schatborn 1985, no. 1; Chapman 1990, p. 24 and fig. 24

THE SAME EARNEST expression that characterises this sheet is seen in the etching dated 1629 (cat. no. 11). The drawing-like quality of the print is emphasised by the use of a pen instead of an etching needle. This drawing seems to have arisen at more or less the same time, and so probably also dates from 1629. Rembrandt was about 23 years of age at the time, and sported the beginnings of a beard and a small moustache.

Here, as in the self portrait that was made probably a little later (cat. no. 13), the face and collar were indicated somewhat schematically using the pen, with hatching in the unlit areas. Then the hair and upper body were styled in grey paint, using the brush. Darker sections of the figure enhance the chiaroscuro effect and brisk hatching with the brush on the right provides a certain monumentality. The most expressive element is the eyes, a characteristic feature of most of Rembrandt's self portraits. The penetrating gaze is combined with a critical frown, suggested by a single stroke of the pen in the eyebrows. It is unclear whether the wild crop of hair is intended to convey something about the subject's nature or constitution.

Rembrandt's gaze in this study corresponds to that in the painted self portrait in Nuremberg (cat. no. 14a). The strong use of light in the painting, on the other hand, seems rather to derive from the study in London. In all three works, though, the subject's clothing has military connotations. Whereas in the two studies this is only implied by the frogging down the front of the cloak, which contemporary viewers will have associated with military uniform, the gorget in the painted self portrait is a specifically military attribute (see p. 62).

13
Self Portrait, Open-Mouthed *c.*1629

Pen and brown ink, brush and grey paint,
127 × 95 mm

London, British Museum, inv. no. GG. 2–253

Benesch 1973, vol. I, no. 53; Chapman 1990,
pp. 24, 30 and fig. 25; Royalton-Kisch 1992, no. 1

I<small>N THIS STUDY</small> the face and the collar were laid in with a fine pen and brown ink in vigorous, fluid contours. The portrait was then elaborated with wide sweeps of the brush and grey paint in the hair, the unlit part of the face and the coat. The combination of brown ink and grey washes is quite rare in Rembrandt's work.[36] In its execution the piece displays a marked similarity to the somewhat earlier drawn self portrait in Amsterdam (cat. no. 12), in which the artist depicted himself from a more frontal perspective.

The suggestion of a concentrated beam of light from the left, casting deep shadows over the right half of the figure, creates a masterful illusion of depth. Lamplight or candlelight may have been used to achieve this special effect.[37] In this regard, the piece greatly resembles the self portrait in Nuremberg (cat. no. 14a), in which the reflections on the gorget provide added chiaroscuro effects (for the military connotations of the dress in the sheet described here, see cat. no. 12).

The open mouth gives the self portrait an eloquent quality that is truly arresting. This expressiveness is hence the true subject of the drawing and the portrait aspect seems to be of secondary importance. In an etching from 1630 (cat. no. 23), Rembrandt emphasised this more strongly and we see the artist with gaping mouth and bared teeth, almost screaming. This is apparently how Rembrandt liked to view himself in the mirror in etchings from 1629 to 1630: listening, frowning or tormented (cat. nos. 4, 21 and 23). In his day, these studies of facial expressions were called *tronies* and were regarded as a separate genre. He also depicted a grimace of this kind in his '*Self Portrait' as a Beggar* from 1630 (cat. no. 24). The drawing described here was probably made shortly after the Amsterdam sheet, which does not reveal any sign of experimental expressiveness.

This drawing may have been the point of departure for a painted self portrait. There is the panel in Munich, for instance (cat. no. 7), in which Rembrandt also fixes the viewer with an open-mouthed gaze and in which the shadows on the face cast by the tousled hair, in particular, are rather similar. However, the eyes in the painting – unlike in this the drawn self portrait – are hidden in the shadows. The self portrait in Indianapolis (cat. no. 8) also has similarities: the light coming from the left is the main effect. For this painting the artist donned a beret and gorget, but the open mouth and visible lower teeth appear to have been taken from this drawing. On the basis of contemporary copies of the Indianapolis painting, one might conclude that eloquent studies of the face were greatly admired at the time.

14a
Self Portrait with Gorget

*c.*1629

Panel, 38.2 × 31 cm

Remains of signature with monogram at lower right: *RHL f*

Nuremberg, Germanisches Nationalmuseum, inv. no. GM 391

Corpus, vol. I, no. A 21 (copy 1); Chapman 1990, p. 147, note 18 (as copy)

14b
Anonymous artist after Rembrandt
Portrait of Rembrandt with Gorget

Panel, 37.9 × 28.9 cm

The Hague, Royal Cabinet of Paintings Mauritshuis, inv. no. 148

Bredius/Gerson 1969, no. 6; *Corpus*, vol. I, no. A 21; Chapman 1990, pp. 34, 36, 38–9, 40, 46, 131 and fig. 41

FOR MANY YEARS, the painting in The Hague (cat. no. 14b) was regarded as one of the high points of Rembrandt's oeuvre.[38] Stylistically it occupied rather an isolated position among the early works, but given its outstanding quality, no-one saw any reason to question its authenticity. The meticulous style of painting, so different from the free handling of the brush in other early self portraits (see cat. nos. 5 and 7), was explained by positing that Rembrandt experimented with various styles in his early years.[39] At the same time, the status of the work appeared to be confirmed by its provenance from the renowned collection of Govert van Slingelandt (1694–1767), who is known to have confined himself to acquiring masterpieces. In the catalogue of his paintings it was called 'Head of a Youth', but from the second half of the nineteenth century similarities with Rembrandt's facial features in drawn and etched self portraits were noticed, which enhanced the painting's aura of authenticity.

It therefore aroused considerable surprise when Claus Grimm demoted the much-praised 'self portrait' in 1991 – the year of its inclusion in the major Rembrandt exhibition – to a copy, identifying a relatively obscure panel from the Germanisches Nationalmuseum in Nuremberg (cat. no. 14a) as the original.[40] In the second half of the nineteenth century, some experts had still regarded the Nuremberg painting as a replica of The Hague piece, but it had passed into obscurity once it had been generally accepted as an old copy.[41] Grimm based his controversial position on a critical stylistic comparison using photographs of details. During the preparations for the present exhibition, it became possible to place the two paintings side by side for the first time, and to submit them both to a thorough scientific examination.[42] The findings confirm that the panel from Nuremberg is the original by Rembrandt, and that it served as the example for The Hague version, painted by a different hand.

The underdrawing on The Hague panel (figs. 14a and b), discovered in 1998 in the conservation studio of the Mauritshuis using infra-red reflectography, provided fresh insight into the relationship between the two works.[43] A preliminary sketch of this kind, applied on the ground before painting commenced, has never before been found in a work by Rembrandt, and indeed there is nothing of the kind in the infra-red reflectograph of the painting from Nuremberg (fig. 14c).[44] The underdrawing is executed in a dry medium, possibly charcoal or black chalk, in a different style of draughtsmanship from that displayed in Rembrandt's drawings on paper.[45] The hair is sketched loosely, with long, elegant flourishes designating the place of the curls and the hairline. The contours of the eyes, nose and mouth are indicated with thin construction lines and thicker stripes. Occasional use is made of double lines – as around the upper lip and the line of the jaw – possibly to denote an area of shadow. The contours of the gorget and the torso have been drawn several times over, revealing an effort to find the correct position for these elements.

Further study of the infra-red reflectograph of The Hague painting reveals a second pair of eyes, lower and more to the right (fig. 14b). This is probably an earlier, less well-elaborated design of the composition, in which the head occupied a slightly different place in the pictorial plane. A few thin, vertical lines in the illuminated half of the face, which bear no relation to the painted image, suggest that the hairline too was initially planned further to the right. If this first stage of the underdrawing is compared with the Nuremberg painting, the position of both eyes and hairline proves identical in the two pieces (fig. 14d). Thus the composition was initially exactly the same as that of the Nuremberg piece, but in the further elaboration of the underdrawing the subject's head was tilted up a little. The search for the right shape, too, as revealed in the case of the

fig. 14a
Computer montage of infra-red reflectographs of cat. no. 14b (courtesy of A. Verburg / RKD).

fig. 14b
Detail of fig. 14a.

gorget, shows that the maker of the underdrawing did not follow the example exactly, but adapted it as he saw fit.

It therefore appears from the underdrawing that the composition of The Hague painting was based on that of the Nuremberg painting and not the other way around. This does not automatically imply, however, that the latter work was made by Rembrandt himself. Theoretically speaking, both pieces could have been copied from an original that has since been lost.[46] That this is unlikely, however, is clear from a comparative analysis of the style of painting in the two works.[47] The Nuremberg panel renders the face in a brisk impasto, with brushstrokes applied in various directions. Particularly in the light parts we can see where the painter twisted his brush, as if he had difficulty forcing the paint out. A similar method is seen in Rembrandt's self portraits in Amsterdam and Munich (cat. nos. 5 and 7). The flared hair is painted in loose brushstrokes, with the paint being applied somewhat less thickly than in the face. There are no curls scratched into the wet paint, but because of the use of thin, transparent brushstrokes, the brown-coloured ground glimmers through in places. This dark colour has remained visible in various other places too, as in the shadowed side of the face.

The execution of The Hague piece displays remarkable differences. The face is painted with the utmost control, in a regular pattern of short brushstrokes that follow the curves of the face. Because of the thinner, more liquid paint, the painted surface makes a predominantly smooth and unbroken impression. True, the lock of hair hanging down over the forehead and the white collar are laid in somewhat more thickly, but even there the paint has been applied with great caution. The highlight on the nose is made of small dots of paint placed close together; in the Nuremberg panel this reflection consists of a white brushstroke that was deposited in a single movement and then spread out.

Because of the meticulous care with which the painter of The Hague piece went to work, each element of the image appears almost self-contained. While the other painting displays near-imperceptible transitions between the facial features, in this piece the heightened light and dark contrasts create boundaries that seem unnatural in places.[48] One example is the area around the left eyelid: the transition to the shaded part is so abrupt that it gives the eyelid an oddly angular shape. In the hair, which is depicted with greater care, it almost appears as if each hair has been painted separately and reflects its own light. The even distribution of light on the elegant coiffure is absent from the painting in Nuremberg, where the hair is conceived more as a single entity. The background is also quite different: rather than varied brushstrokes, set down wet-in-wet with ostensible nonchalance, The Hague piece displays a virtually even surface.

The stylistic comparison clearly attests to two different styles of painting. The meticulous painting technique of The Hague panel contrasts with the ease and spontaneity of the Nuremberg piece. The execution of the latter bears a strong similarity to Rembrandt's early work. However, certain details are hard to assess because of abrasion or later retouching. Also, as a result of blanching (whereby the binding medium in the paint becomes opaque), greyish-white spots have arisen, for instance in the shadowed part of the face. Even so, there are enough indications of Rembrandt's style to attribute the painting to him. The remains of a signature, found at lower right, appear to belong to the initial paint layer and may therefore be original.[49]

The notion that the painting in The Hague may have been a replica by Rembrandt himself, as assumed in the nineteenth century, can be ruled out. Not only does the style of painting clearly point to a different hand, but Rembrandt also never repeated a composition in this way. Furthermore, it appears from the rendering of certain details

cat. no. 14b

fig. 14c
Computer montage of infra-red reflectographs of cat. no. 14a (courtesy of A. Verburg / RKD).

fig. 14d
Photograph of cat. no. 14a indicating the contours of the first phase of the underdrawing of cat. no. 14b (courtesy of Jørgen Wadum, Mauritshuis).

that the maker of The Hague piece did not have complete mastery of all the finesses in his example.[50] Thus the reflection on the left of the lower lip is not quite right; given the direction of the light it should be set a little higher, as in Rembrandt's original. The iris of the eye is a dark 'hole' with a tiny point of light, while the Nuremberg panel renders it more convincingly, in various shades of grey. Finally, the somewhat elongated face and close-set eyes diminish the resemblance to Rembrandt's features.

As has already become clear from the discussion of the underdrawing, The Hague painting is not a slavish copy but a variant. Not only did the artist deliberately alter the composition by placing the face higher in the pictorial plane, he also adopted a different style, one characterised by accuracy and deliberation. In this personal interpretation of the original, he differed from the copyist of the early Amsterdam self portrait (p. 95, fig. 5b), who tried to imitate Rembrandt's vigorous handling of the paint. This raises the question of who was responsible for this variant, which is of such high quality that for centuries it was believed to be an original work by Rembrandt. Since Rembrandt regularly had pupils copy his self portraits (see cat. no. 8), it seems logical to seek the painter in his Leiden workshop.[51] The number of suitable candidates is limited, however. Grimm suggested Isaac de Jouderville (cat. no. 29b), a pupil of Rembrandt around 1630. The few paintings that can be confidently attributed to him are greatly inferior in quality to this piece and exhibit a hard, relatively unconvincing rendering of textures (fig. 14e).[52]

A more plausible candidate, given the quality of his work, is Jan Lievens (1607–74; p. 14, fig. 13). He may have shared a workshop with Rembrandt in Leiden, but he was already a proficient master by then, at least as accomplished as his associate. Constantijn Huygens (1596–1687; p. 27, fig. 37), a great admirer of the two young painters, thought him in some respects the greater artist. In their Leiden years the two made a sport of artistic rivalry: they frequently chose the same subject, each depicting it in his own way. Thus a painting by Lievens from c.1629 (fig. 14f), which is believed to portray Rembrandt, can be regarded as a response to – or possibly the piece that prompted – the self portrait discussed here.[53] Although the composition also shows the half figure of a young man with a head of curls and a gorget, the result is clearly different. Lievens would probably have had too much professional pride to keep as close to Rembrandt's example as the maker of The Hague copy. What is more, Lievens's work from this period exhibits a freer handling of paint and more impasto than The Hague painting.[54]

Gerrit Dou (cat. no. 89), on the other hand, the first of Rembrandt's pupils to have worked in his Leiden studio between 1628 and c.1632, is known for his meticulous style of painting. His earliest pieces are similar in composition to Rembrandt's, but already display a recognisably individual style and mature skill. A good example is Old Woman reading a Lectionary of c.1631 (fig. 14g), which portrays a woman who also sat for Rembrandt and is traditionally identified as his mother.[55] The style of painting is not as smooth here as in Dou's later work, but already it is distinct from Rembrandt's with its controlled brushstrokes, precise rendering of textures and attention to detail. Here, as in The Hague painting, no vague transitions are seen; each element of the picture has clearly defined contours. The paint is applied evenly almost throughout, even in the hand, where the aging skin is suggested by a regular pattern of wrinkles. The reflected light on the fur of the cap is rendered in much the same way as on the hair in The Hague piece (figs. 14h and i). Dou's painting too has an underdrawing that shows up partly under infra-red reflectography.[56] In certain parts such as the cap, long parallel lines serve to indicate the contours (fig. 14j). The way in which these lines have been redrawn several times and cross in places, resembles the underdrawing in The Hague painting.

If the young Dou was indeed responsible for this freely painted copy after Rembrandt's self portrait, which further research must determine, this work represents an important stage in his early development. Though the painter was evidently not independent enough to conceive a composition of his own, he revealed his burgeoning mastery of his art by making subtle changes and by choosing a style of painting that suited him particularly well. The character of this *tronie* is indeed expressed slightly better in the copy than in Rembrandt's original. Although the gorget identifies the subject as a military man, as in the case of several other *tronies* (see cat. no. 8), the lock of hair hanging to the right of the face also points to the man's noble lineage. This pigtail, known variously as a *cadenette* or lovelock, was an international hairstyle at the time that was sported chiefly by courtiers and senior army officers (see also p. 62). By raising the head at a wider angle, closing the slightly parted lips of the original and replacing the wild curls with a well-groomed hairstyle, the copyist has given his portrait a distinguished air that is perfectly attuned to the aristocratic soldier.

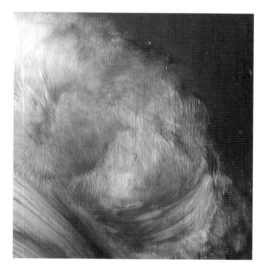

fig. 14e *top*
Isaac de Jouderville, 'Tronie' of a Young Man.
Panel, 48 × 37 cm (oval).
Dublin, National Gallery of Ireland.

fig. 14f *above left*
Jan Lievens, 'Tronie' of a Young Man with Gorget
(Portrait of Rembrandt?), c.1629.
Panel, 57 × 44 cm. Amsterdam, Rijksmuseum
(on loan from a private collector).

fig. 14g *above middle*
Gerrit Dou, Old Woman reading a Lectionary, c.1631.
Panel, 71 × 55.5 cm. Amsterdam, Rijksmuseum.

fig. 14h *bottom left*
Detail of fig. 14g.

fig. 14i *bottom right*
Detail of cat. no. 14b.

fig. 14j *above right*
Computer montage of infra-red reflectographs
of fig. 14g (courtesy of A. Verburg / RKD).

15
Self Portrait
with Curly Hair and White
Collar *c.*1629

Etching, 58 × 50 mm (I), 56 × 49 mm (II);
two states

Monogrammed at centre right: *RHL*

Amsterdam, Rijksmuseum, Rijksprentenkabinet,
inv. no. RP-P-OB 2 (II)

London, British Museum,
inv. no. 1973-U—770 (II)*

B. / Hollstein 1; Hind 33

IN THIS AND two other self portraits that Rembrandt etched in the same period (cat. nos. 25 and 27), he focused not on capturing specific facial expressions, as in the four sheets from 1630 (cat. nos. 20–3), but on the rendering of physical details and the effect of light. He achieved this with great precision and effectiveness, especially in the faces, but also in the depiction of the hair and clothing. In contrast to the two etchings referred to above, all later states of which were elaborated by another hand, both states of this monogrammed self portrait were executed wholly by Rembrandt.

This etching is compositionally very similar to other self portraits from around 1629, the year in which it must have been made. In the London drawing (cat. no. 13) the right half of the face is likewise in the shadow and the curly hair too is much the same. The frogging down the front of the coat in the drawn self portrait, a detail that also seems to appear in this etching, has connotations with military dress, in which Rembrandt portrayed himself explicitly in the Nuremberg painting (cat. no. 14a). In terms of composition, the latter self portrait bears many similarities to the one discussed here, both in the position of the head and torso, and in the shadowed right half of the face. Whether Rembrandt intended his wild hairstyle in this etched self portrait to express his mood is unclear.

16

Anonymous artist after Rembrandt (?)

Portrait of Rembrandt with Gold Chain

Panel, 61.4 × 46.9 cm

Private Collection

Bredius/Gerson 1969, no. 7;
Corpus, vol. I, no. C 36

I N TERMS OF composition, this painting may be regarded as a combination of the self portraits in Boston (cat. no. 10) and Nuremberg (cat. no. 14a). In execution, however, it departs markedly from Rembrandt's style of painting, and it is therefore probably a workshop copy produced after a lost self portrait from *c.*1629.

17
The Painter in his Studio

*c.*1629

Panel, 25.1 × 31.9 cm

Boston, Museum of Fine Arts, Zoë Oliver
Sherman Collection, Given in Memory of
Lillie Oliver Poor, inv. no. 38.1838

Bredius/Gerson 1969, no. 419; *Corpus*, vol. I,
no. A 18; Chapman 1990, pp. 13, 34, 49, 84–5, 95,
97, 98, 99, 124 and fig. 117

fig. 17a
GERRIT DOU, *A Painter in his Studio, c.*1630–2.
Panel, 59 × 43.5 cm.
New York, Newhouse Galleries Inc.

A YOUNG PAINTER cloaked in the shadows gazes intently at an easel that dominates the foreground and forms the main subject of this workshop scene. We cannot see the painting in progress, which arouses our curiosity. The considerable distance between the master and his work is emphasised by the slanting light, which is reflected by the floorboards, the plastered walls and the side of the wooden panel on the easel. There is nothing in the soberly furnished interior that would distract the viewer's attention from the painter. All the objects it contains are in some way related to his profession. Thus the large whetstone lying on a tree-trunk against the back wall is used in the preparation of paint. On the left of the table stand bottles, possibly containing oil and varnish, while two unused palettes of different sizes hang from a nail. The painter holds a third palette, together with a bundle of paintbrushes, and with the little finger of the same hand he grasps a maulstick. In his other hand he holds a single brush poised for action. At first sight his long robe looks like fancy dress, but on further inspection it proves to be a realistic rendering of working clothes (see ill. p. 59 and p. 66). In contrast to other works made by Rembrandt in his Leiden period, with their vaguely delineated interiors, this room has a clear structure, and it would even be possible to draw its floor plan.[57]

All the evidence suggests that Rembrandt depicted an existing situation in this picture, and the most obvious conclusion is that it was his own studio. This brings us to the question of the identity of the young painter, who has been identified variously as Rembrandt himself and his first pupil Gerrit Dou (cat. no. 89). The idea that it could be Dou, who arrived in Rembrandt's workshop at 14 years of age, is largely based on the apparently childlike stature of the figure.[58] A reconstruction of the scheme of perspective used in this piece, however, reveals that appearances are deceptive and the man's height is normal for the time.[59] So it is more likely that the person depicted is in fact Rembrandt, and the facial features indeed display a resemblance – which careful study makes clear – to his painted and etched self portraits.[60] The same questioning look with the raised eyebrows occurs in the Munich painting from 1629 (cat. no. 7). Here, however, the face is rendered more sketchily, and the painter is placed literally and symbolically in the shadows. This indicates that his identity is not of prime importance; rather, Rembrandt has used his own situation to present a general picture of 'the painter in his studio'.

What is remarkable about this studio scene is that the artist is not actually painting. This is clear not only from his great distance from the panel, but also from the fact that he is standing. Seventeenth-century artists generally painted in a sitting position. This allowed them to rest their feet on the lowest horizontal bar of the easel, as evidenced by the clear patches of wear on the easel in this painting.[61] The late self portraits too, in which Rembrandt depicts himself at work (cat. nos. 79 and 83), testify to his reluctance to record the act of painting itself, as if he was afraid to divulge his secret.

As the panel on the easel faces away from us, we have no way of knowing what stage it is in. Perhaps it is finished and the painter is inspecting it with a final gaze of approval. Or perhaps he is taking a break to view his progress from a distance. It is even possible that he has not yet begun and that he is formulating his ideas while staring at a blank panel. In the latter case, Rembrandt would have been illustrating a common view in the art theory of his age, namely that the artist first had to formulate the overall conception of a painting before he could actually start work on it.[62]

Possibly inspired by Rembrandt, Gerrit Dou adopted the painter's studio as a subject too. A piece from 1630 to 1632 may have been produced under his master's watchful eye (fig. 17a).[63] However, this picture is different in character from Rembrandt's painting. The easel has been relegated to the background, with the artist occupying the central position.

Scattered around the studio is a motley collection of objects, including a book, an emperor's bust, a globe, musical instruments, a skull and a sword. Not only can they be classified as the attributes of a painter, in this case a still life painter, but some also allude to the ephemeral nature of earthly life. Other pictures of artists' studios by Dou are similarly crowded with objects with double meanings (p. 29, fig. 42).[64] The richness of the studios painted by Dou emphasises the bareness and simplicity of Rembrandt's own workshop. These Spartan surroundings, in which everything is related to painting, correspond in every respect to the account of Constantijn Huygens (1596–1687), who visited Rembrandt and Jan Lievens (1607–74) at their shared studio in or around 1629. In his memoirs Huygens (p. 27, fig. 37) expressed his admiration for the single-mindedness with which these young painters approached their work: 'I feel obliged to declare that I have never before witnessed such dedication and determination in any group of people of any age, involved in any activity. For truly, they use their time to good effect. This is all that counts for them. The most astonishing thing is that they dismiss even the most innocent pleasures of youth as a waste of time ... This indefatigable perseverance in diligent labours may soon yield great results, and yet I have often wished that the excellent youths would exercise a little moderation in this regard and think of their constitution, which, because of their sedentary lives, is even now lacking in strength and vitality.'[65]

18
Self Portrait 1630

Copper, 15 × 12.2 cm

Signed and dated at upper left: *R... 1630*

Stockholm, Nationalmuseum, inv. no. 5324

Bredius/Gerson 1969, no. 11; *Corpus*, vol. I, no. B 5;
on the provenance of the painting see p. 53

THIS SELF PORTRAIT is roughly the same size as two other small paintings by Rembrandt: *The Laughing Soldier* (fig. 18a), which was once identified, though hardly convincingly, as the painter himself, and *Old Woman at Prayer* (fig. 18b). Aside from the size and subject-matter – all three are characteristic examples of *tronies* – these works share another feature: their support is thin copperplate, covered with a scant layer of gold leaf.[66] Painting on copper was not in itself uncommon in the seventeenth century, but the gold leaf overlay was an unusual addition.[67] The aim may have been to give more radiance to the colours. Rembrandt did not use this expensive material on any other occasion: these pieces probably represent experiments that he decided did not merit repetition.

Given the similarities between the three small paintings, it is all the more striking that each is executed in a different style. Whereas in the wrinkled old woman Rembrandt has worked with great precision, the head of the laughing soldier is modelled in wide sweeps of the brush. The self portrait has been executed in a style intermediate between these extremes: the face is meticulously painted in an even pattern of small brushstrokes, whereas the folds of the shirt are conveyed with vigorous zigzag lines.

The remarkable differences in execution have even prompted some to question the authenticity of two of the three pieces – the *Self Portrait* and *The Laughing Soldier*.[68] A better explanation for the emphatic variations in painting style is that Rembrandt deliberately set out here to display his versatility. In his didactic poem *Den grondt der edel vry schilder-const* (1604) the art theorist Karel van Mander (1548-1606) distinguished 'smooth' and 'coarse' painting as two different techniques.[69] The three small paintings demonstrate not only that Rembrandt had mastered both methods, but also that he was able to combine them. His choice of copperplate, which he did not use very often, may have been partly motivated by the knowledge that the brushstrokes would be clearly visible on this hard, smooth material. It is entirely possible that these three pieces, which run the gamut of Rembrandt's technical skills, were used in the workshop as examples for his pupils.[70] By studying and copying these works by the master, a fixed part of the learning process, they could become acquainted not only with different styles of painting, but also with three quite different types of *tronie*: the old woman, the soldier and the youth.

This is the first of Rembrandt's painted self portraits in which he has represented a definite mood. The morose expression and plain garments can also be seen in some of his early etchings (cat. nos. 9 and 25).[71] The pleated shirt is not contemporary, but is based on a sixteenth-century model and hence contains a subtle allusion to another age.

fig. 18a
REMBRANDT, *The Laughing Soldier*, c.1629–30.
Copper, 15.4 × 12.2 cm.
The Hague, Mauritshuis.

fig. 18b
REMBRANDT, *Old Woman at Prayer*, c.1629–30.
Copper, 15.5 × 12.2 cm.
Salzburg, Residenzgalerie.

19
Self Portrait with Fur Hat and Light-Coloured Coat

1630

Etching, 92 × 69 mm (I), 62 × 52 mm (from II); four states

Monogrammed and dated at lower centre: *RHL 1630* (moved to the upper left in the second state)

Amsterdam, Rijksmuseum, Rijksprentenkabinet, inv. no. RP-P-OB—45 (I)*

London, British Museum, inv. no. 1853—12—10—311 (II)

B. / Hollstein 24; Hind 29

fig. 19a
REMBRANDT, *Self Portrait with Fur Hat and Light-Coloured Coat*, 1630.
Etching (fourth state), 62 × 52 mm.
Amsterdam, Rijksmuseum, Rijksprentenkabinet.

BOTH IN 1630 AND 1631 Rembrandt made etchings of himself dressed in a coat with a fur-trimmed collar over a white shirt, and wearing what most authors agree is a fur hat.[72] In this etching from 1630, only the right section of the coat is shaded, whereas in the 1631 print the whole coat is dark (cat. no. 28).

Coats or gowns with fur-trimmed collars were in origin a sixteenth-century mode of dress.[73] However, they were sometimes worn in the seventeenth century as house-robes, and painters and others with a sedentary profession found that they afforded excellent protection from the cold (see also p. 66). Thus, this print from 1630 and the print from 1631 show Rembrandt wearing old-fashioned apparel that few would have worn in his day.[74]

The copperplate used for this print was reduced in size in the second state, as a result of which the figure was cut off from the lower edge of the plate. This operation removed Rembrandt's signature from the bottom, so he therefore added his monogram and the year at the upper left. In the third and fourth states of the etching, shadows were added, in particular above the eyes. As a result, the eyelids were straightened somewhat and the stare of the earlier states was corrected (fig. 19a).

20

'Self Portrait', Wide-Eyed

1630

Etching and burin, 51 × 46 mm; one state

Monogrammed and dated at the lower centre:
RHL 1630

Amsterdam, Rijksmuseum, Rijksprentenkabinet,
inv. no. RP-P-OB–697*

London, British Museum, inv. no. 1973-U–769

B. / Hollstein 320; Hind 32; White 1969,
pp. 108–9; Chapman 1990, pp. 19, 21 and fig. 10

fig. 20a
REMBRANDT, *The Raising of Lazarus* (detail), *c.*1632.
Etching (eighth state), 366 × 258 mm.
Amsterdam, Rijksmuseum, Rijksprentenkabinet.

THE DEPICTION OF feelings and emotions played a particularly important role in biblical, mythological and allegorical scenes. It was of course in the face that such feelings were expected to be expressed most eloquently. One way of mastering this skill was proposed by Samuel van Hoogstraten (cat. no. 96) in his *Inleyding tot de hooge schoole der schilderkonst* (Introduction to the Art of Painting), published in 1678 (see p. 26, fig. 36): 'You will benefit from depicting your passions as you see them before you, especially before a mirror, where you are at once subject and beholder.'[75] Van Hoogstraten was a pupil of Rembrandt in the early 1640s, and may have been given this advice by his master. It is possible that recording 'passions' in front of the mirror was a more or less common practice (see also p. 11, fig. 4). The artists' biographer Arnold Houbraken (1660–1719) wrote as early as 1718 of Rembrandt's 'heedful reflections on all manner of Passions', and it is precisely this true-to-life rendering of emotions for which Rembrandt continued to be celebrated through the ages.[76]

The *'Self Portrait', Wide-Eyed* is one of a group of four studies of different facial expressions that the artist produced in 1630 (cat. nos. 21–3). Rembrandt's face fills almost the entire pictorial plane and the composition, in which the head is cut off by the upper edge, appears to contribute to the emotion depicted, as if the artist's head, which we see from a fairly low perspective, has jerked up and back in wonder and astonishment.

The expression on the face in this print puts in other appearances in Rembrandt's work, for instance in the surprised figure on the right in *The Raising of Lazarus* from *c.*1632, although in the latter case the mouth is open wider (fig. 20a).[77] The same kind of amazement appears in the print after a drawing by Rembrandt that Houbraken included as an illustration to accompany his biography of the artist: one of the men of Emmaus opens his eyes wide as Christ disappears from sight.[78]

21

'Self Portrait' with Angry Expression 1630

Etching, 75 × 75 mm (I), 72 × 60 mm (from II); four states

Monogrammed and dated at upper left: *RHL 1630* (in the first state only)

Amsterdam, Rijksmuseum, Rijksprentenkabinet, inv. no. RP-P-1961–978 (II)

London, British Museum, inv. no. 1973-U–765 (II)*

B. / Hollstein 10; Hind 30; White 1969, p. 108; Chapman 1990, pp. 19, 21 and fig. 11

fig. 21a
REMBRANDT, '*Self Portrait' with Angry Expression*, 1630. Etching (first state), 75 × 75 mm. Amsterdam, Rijksmuseum, Rijksprentenkabinet.

THIS ETCHING belongs to a group of four prints from 1630 in which Rembrandt recorded his face exhibiting a variety of expressions (cat. nos. 20 and 22–3). In this one Rembrandt glares furiously at the viewer. His anger is conveyed most eloquently by the straight lines of his mouth, the round, dark eyes and his knotted brow. The artist is bare-headed and his unruly hair adds to the drama of the picture. The same applies to the straight line of the shadow on the left of the face, which enhances the expression's intensity. Because of the simplicity of the clothing – Rembrandt wears a cloak with a fur collar, under which we glimpse a white shirt – all attention is focused on the face.[79]

Rembrandt heightened the effect of anger by making compositional changes. In the first state, the head is right of centre (fig. 21a). To intensify the portrait's directness, Rembrandt then cut the plate along the left edge, bringing the figure to the centre of the composition. In an example of a state that was formerly unknown, which is preserved in Berlin, Rembrandt traced a new outline for the left shoulder, shaped as a mirror image of the right.[80] This symmetry evidently failed to appeal to him: by the following state the outline had been removed again.

22

'Self Portrait', Smiling 1630

Etching, 50 × 44 mm, 48 × 43 mm (from IV);
six states[81]

Monogrammed and dated at upper left:
RHL 1630

Amsterdam, Rijksmuseum, Rijksprentenkabinet,
inv. no. RP-P-1961–1181 (III)

London, British Museum,
inv. no. 1848–9–11–18 (II)*

B. / Hollstein 316; Hind 34; White 1969, p. 108;
Chapman 1990, pp. 17, 19 and fig. 9

fig. 22a
ANONYMOUS PUPIL OF REMBRANDT,
The Smiling Young Man, c.1630. Panel, 41.2 × 33.8 cm.
Amsterdam, Rijksmuseum.

THIS SELF PORTRAIT in which Rembrandt smiles at us, wearing a cap on his head and a scarf around his neck, is one of a group of four etchings produced in the same year, in which he used his own face to record a variety of expressions (cat. nos. 20–1 and 23). Thus his aim in making this etching was not so much to make a portrait of himself as to depict a cheerful expression.

Prints of this kind could be used as examples by Rembrandt himself or by his pupils and other artists. The lines in these small etchings are drawn in the most delicate and meticulous manner, and are at the same time very lively. Both the angle of the head and the play of light do much to create the lifelike characterisation. Thus the left eye just catching the light and the glimpse of a few teeth are both features that serve to emphasise the subject's merry mood.

Karel van Mander's *Schilder-Boeck* from 1604, a publication with which Rembrandt certainly became acquainted either during or after his apprenticeship, has a chapter on the rendering of the 'affects' (emotions), including merriment: 'we must make the eyes half-closed, the mouth slightly open in a pleasant, cheerful smile ... a glad brow, which is smooth and sincere, and not furrowed with numerous wrinkles.'[82] Van Mander continues: 'But if we study life [after nature or a model] we shall see that smiling makes the mouth and cheeks wider and causes them to rise, while the brow is lowered, and between the two the eyes are slightly narrowed, creating small creases right up to the ears.'[83] Rembrandt would not have had these guidelines at hand when he made this print, but Van Mander's description corresponds roughly to what we see in this etching. This and the other images of 'affects' are the result of Rembrandt's observation and registration of reality, or of 'life', to use Van Mander's word.

Some of the heads in the series may be compared with figures in biblical or other narrative scenes. Rembrandt also tackled the subject of this etching in *The Laughing Soldier*, a small painting from the same period (p. 122, fig. 18a).[84] Aside from this, one of his pupils painted *The Smiling Young Man* (fig. 22a).[85] This piece, which was inspired by Rembrandt, used to be regarded as a self portrait of the master.

23
'Self Portrait', Open-Mouthed 1630

Etching, 81 × 72 mm (I), 73 × 62 mm (from II); three states

Monogrammed and dated at upper left: *RHL 1630* (partly lost in second state)

Amsterdam, Rijksmuseum, Rijksprentenkabinet, inv. no. RP-P—1961—979 (II)

London, British Museum, inv. no. 1973-U—768 (II)*

B. / Hollstein 13; Hind 31; White 1969, pp. 108—9, fig. 133; Chapman 1990, pp. 19, 21 and fig. 12

fig. 23a
REMBRANDT, *Christ on the Cross*, 1631.
Canvas on panel, 99.9 × 72.6 cm.
Le Mas d'Agenais, Parish Church.

THIS IS ONE of the four prints from 1630 in which Rembrandt recorded his face exhibiting a variety of expressions (cat. nos. 20–2). In this etching, the open mouth and furrowed brow give the face a dramatic appearance, while the strong contrasts between light and dark accentuate the impression of suffering. Just as in Rembrandt's *'Self Portrait' with Angry Expression* (cat. no. 21), the loose hair adds to the dramatic effect.

In the chapter on the 'affects' in *Den grondt der edel vry schilder-const* (1604), Karel van Mander (1548–1606) writes that 'wrinkles and furrows there [in the forehead] show that a melancholy spirit is concealed within us, entrapped and care-worn'.[86] Van Mander's description of the rendering of pain certainly corresponds to this etching, but the passage as a whole is perhaps even more applicable to the head of Christ in a painting by Rembrandt from 1631 (fig. 23a):[87] 'the eyebrows must be somewhat raised on the left, with the eye half-closed, and the crease that leads from the nose to the cheek [also] drawn to that point and shortened.'[88] Although Van Mander's text is unlikely to have been used by Rembrandt as a practical set of guidelines, his description of the rendering of 'affects' may have been common currency among the artists of his day.

Besides the painting of the head of Christ, a similar expression is also seen in Rembrandt's etched *'Self Portrait' as a Beggar* (cat. no. 24), which dates from the same year as the etching described here. This etching with the pained expression was probably an exercise and a direct example for the latter piece.

24

'Self Portrait' as a Beggar

1630

Etching, 116 × 70 mm; one state

Monogrammed and dated at lower centre: *RHL 1630*

Amsterdam, Rijksmuseum, Rijksprentenkabinet, inv. no. RP-P-OB—411*

London, British Museum, inv. no. 1973-U—742

B. / Hollstein 174; Hind 11; Chapman 1990, p. 33 and fig. 38

THIS BEGGAR HAS the facial features of Rembrandt in his etched self portrait from the same year (cat. no. 23). In both prints, the figure's forehead is puckered into a frown, he has an open mouth revealing several teeth and a beam of light falls across the tongue. In this etching, however, Rembrandt added a beard and a small hat. His cloak is fastened with a single button.

The figure sits at the foot of a rugged hill. Rembrandt probably derived this motif from an engraving by Lucas van Leyden (active 1508; died 1533) depicting a beggar and his wife seated on an almost barren rock (fig. 24a).[89] Their poverty is emphasised still more by a leafless tree, though they are not clad in the pitiful rags of Rembrandt's figure.[90] It was above all the etchings by the French artist Jacques Callot (1592–1635) that served as Rembrandt's example here, as was often the case in his prints and drawings with this theme.[91] The open-mouthed face and begging gesture of the hand in the self portrait described here occurs in Callot's print of a standing beggar (fig. 24b).[92]

In Rembrandt's oeuvre it is largely in the period from the late 1620s to the mid-1630s that beggars and cripples occur in his prints and drawings. The satirical overtone that had accompanied this subject ever since it first began to be depicted in the Middle Ages gradually disappeared in the course of the seventeenth century.[93] In the etching depicted here, the beggar's clothing, especially his beret, recalls a past era, while Rembrandt's later renderings of the subject have a more contemporary flavour.[94]

Rembrandt is unlikely to have intended to portray himself as a beggar.[95] His concern was rather to depict the subject of wretchedness, as he had depicted it in his '*Self Portrait*', *Open-Mouthed* (cat. no. 23). In a print from 1634, the face of the larger figure displays only the barest resemblance to Rembrandt (fig. 24c).[96] Evidently the artist gave the figure his grim facial features without looking in the mirror.

fig. 24a
LUCAS VAN LEYDEN, *Beggars*, c.1509.
Engraving, 108 × 77 mm.
Amsterdam, Rijksmuseum, Rijksprentenkabinet.

fig. 24b
JACQUES CALLOT, *The Standing Beggar*, c.1620–3.
Etching, 137 × 82 mm.
Amsterdam, Rijksmuseum, Rijksprentenkabinet.

fig. 24c
REMBRANDT, '*Tis Bitterly Cold*', 1634.
Etching, 112 × 43 mm.
Amsterdam, Rijksmuseum, Rijksprentenkabinet.

25

Self Portrait in a Cloak 1630/1

Etching, 64 × 54 mm; five states

Monogrammed and dated at upper left:
RHL 1630 (altered in the second state into: *1631*)

Amsterdam, Rijksmuseum, Rijksprentenkabinet,
inv. no. RP-P-1961–984 (II)

London, British Museum,
inv. no. 1843–6–7–7 (I)*

B. / Hollstein 15; Hind 63

fig. 25a
REMBRANDT AND JAN VAN VLIET,
Self Portrait in a Cloak, 1631.
Etching (fourth state), 64 × 54 mm.
Amsterdam, Rijksmuseum, Rijksprentenkabinet.

A NUMBER OF Rembrandt's early prints were not completed by himself. Several plates were elaborated by Jan van Vliet (*c.*1600/10–68) and published in large numbers, probably in collaboration with the artist and on his instructions. These prints were initially experimental in nature; Rembrandt often had only a few impressions made. In some cases, not a single impression by the master is known, as in the case with the etching described here. In the earliest known example bearing the year 1630, the face was probably developed by Van Vliet, especially where the contours of the eyes and mouth are concerned.[97] In the fourth state, the face has been given a different expression (fig. 25a). The year 1630 had already been changed to 1631 in the second state.

26
Self Portrait with Beret and Gold Chain *c.*1630–1

Panel, 69.7 × 57 cm

Signed and dated at upper left: *Rembrant. f* (not autograph)

Liverpool, Walker Art Gallery, inv. no. 1011

Bredius/Gerson 1969, no. 12; *Corpus*, vol. I, no. A 33; Chapman 1990, pp. 46–8, 53–4, 55, 58, 63, 149 and fig. 70

Aⁿᶜᶜᵒʳᴅɪɴɢ ᴛᴏ ᴛʜᴇ inventory of the collection of the English royal family, compiled around 1639 by the curator Abraham van der Doort (1575/80–1640), Charles I (1600–49) possessed a self portrait by Rembrandt: 'being his owne picture & done by himself in a Black capp and furrd habbitt with a lit[t]le goulden chaine upon both his Shouldʳˢ In an Ovall and a square black frame.'⁹⁸ After the beheading of the king in 1649, his collection was sold at auction and the painting came into the hands of one Major Edward Bass. What happened to it afterwards is unknown. It was not until 1935 that the self portrait could be convincingly identified, on the basis of the description in Van der Doort's inventory and the dimensions it records, with the panel described here.⁹⁹

In the chronology of Rembrandt's self portraits, this painting can be classified as a transitional work. In terms of composition and clothing it fits perfectly into the tradition of the *tronie*, particularly as Rembrandt has used his own face to experiment with the play of light too. The angle of the head would appear to derive from the 1630 self portrait in Stockholm (cat. no. 18). But in contrast to earlier pieces, the painter has taken pains here to depict himself recognisably. The description in the 1639 royal inventory – 'his owne picture & done by himself' – proves that Rembrandt succeeded in this objective. Even so, this painting lacks the personal quality that characterises his later self portraits. This is mainly because of an almost total lack of accents in the face, creating the effect of a rather vacuous expression.

Judging by the style in which it was painted, the self portrait dates from 1630 or 1631. It must have been shipped to England shortly after it was made, since it was already in the Royal Collection in 1633.¹⁰⁰ Together with two other works attributed to Rembrandt, the painting was presented as a gift from Sir Robert Kerr (1578–1654), the first Earl of Ancrum, who, as 'Lord of the Bedchamber' and 'Master of the Privy Purse' belonged to the royal household. In 1629 Charles I had sent him on a diplomatic mission to The Hague and it was probably on this occasion that he made Rembrandt's acquaintance. It seems logical to assume that they were introduced by Constantijn Huygens (1596–1687; p. 27, fig. 37), secretary to the stadholder Frederick Henry (1584–1647), who prided himself on having 'discovered' the young painter from Leiden (see also cat. no. 17). Unfortunately we do not know whether Kerr ordered the painting from Rembrandt during the 1629 visit or later. It could have been the painter himself who suggested supplying a self portrait for the Royal Collection. It is not impossible that Rembrandt knew about Charles I's collection of artists' portraits (see also p. 47) and it would have been an honour for him to add his own face to it.

Alternatively, the painting may have been a gift from Frederick Henry, intended to further his relations with the king. We know from a contemporary source that the stadholder gave one of the other two 'Rembrandts' that Kerr presented to Charles I – a young scholar, reading by the fireside – to the English ambassador, 'who in turn presented it to his Majesty the King'.¹⁰¹ This same source reveals that this painting, now lost, was made by Jan Lievens (1607–74) and not by Rembrandt. In their Leiden years, Rembrandt and Lievens followed one another's artistic development closely, and they probably shared a workshop. This may explain why even their contemporaries had difficulty telling their work apart. Van der Doort was probably mistaken about the third 'Rembrandt' in the inventory he drew up: 'an old woeman with a great Scarfe upon her heade.' This painting, which is still in the possession of the royal family (fig. 26a), was long regarded as an undisputed work by Rembrandt, but is now attributed to Lievens.¹⁰² The X-radiograph of the painting in Liverpool (fig. 26b) reveals the contours of a standing figure, whose pose corresponds to the *Self Portrait in Oriental Clothing* from 1631

Attributed to Jan Lievens, *An Old Woman*.
Panel, 61 × 47.4 cm. London, The Royal
Collection.

(cat. no. 29a). Before executing the final picture, the original composition was partly
scratched away. Rembrandt probably removed only the wet part of the representation, so
that the phantom of a figure was left behind. It must have been during this scratching
process that the curious triangular shape came into being that can now be seen through
the present layer of paint above Rembrandt's head.

A reused panel is referred to as a palimpsest, a term from literary studies derived
from the Greek *palin-psestos*, meaning 'scratched off again'.[103] Rembrandt applied this
method in a number of the self portraits now known to us (cat. nos. 10, 33, 48, 51, 57,
60, 66, 68), whereas it occurs only sporadically in his other pieces. Some have concluded
from this that he did not particularly intend to sell his self portraits, otherwise he would
not have painted on used material.[104] But the client could not see the previous effort
concealed beneath his purchase, and elsewhere in this catalogue it is argued that there
was indeed a market for Rembrandt's self portraits (see pp. 28–36). This latter point
is confirmed by the presence of the painting discussed here – a reused panel – in the
collection of Charles I, only a short time after it was painted.[105] This means that another
explanation must be sought for the numerous palimpsests. Like *tronies*, self portraits
would not, as a rule, have been commissioned. The artist could choose the moment that
suited him best, especially since he functioned as his own model. So self portraits were
an excellent way of putting surplus material to good use, particularly at a time when new
panels were quite expensive. This reasoning does not appear to apply, however, to this self
portrait, at least not if it is assumed to have been commissioned. But, if the painting was
indeed a gift from Frederick Henry, or from Rembrandt himself, it is not inconceivable
that it was chosen from the available stock in his studio.

fig. 26b
X-radiograph of cat. no. 26.

27
Self Portrait
with Cap Pulled Forward

*c.*1631

Etching, 56 × 45 mm (I), 50 × 42 mm (from III);
six states

Amsterdam, Rijksmuseum, Rijksprentenkabinet,
inv. no. RP-P—1961—1184 (IV)

London, British Museum,
inv. no. 1973-U—973 (I)*

B. / Hollstein 319; Hind 58

THIS SELF PORTRAIT is only autographed in the first state. The five later states were
elaborated by Jan van Vliet (*c.*1600/10—68).[106] In contrast to other prints elaborated
by Van Vliet, including the *Self Portrait in a Cloak* from 1630/1 (cat. no. 25), Rembrandt's
facial features remained the same here, despite all the additions. As far as is known,
contemporary viewers did not find the difference in style between Rembrandt and Van
Vliet disturbing; they were probably more interested in the image as a whole.

28
Self Portrait with Fur Hat and Dark Coat 1631

Etching, 63 × 57 mm; one state

Monogrammed and dated at upper left: *RHL 1631*

Amsterdam, Rijksmuseum, Rijksprentenkabinet, inv. no. RP-P-OB–30*

London, British Museum, inv. no. 1835–6–13–1

B. / Hollstein 16; Hind 56

fig. 28a
REMBRANDT, *Old Man with Fur Hat*, 1631.
Etching (second state), 145 × 129 mm.
Amsterdam, Rijksmuseum, Rijksprentenkabinet.

IN THIS SELF PORTRAIT from 1631 Rembrandt has once again depicted himself in a coat with a fur-trimmed collar and a fur hat on his head, as he had done the year before (see cat. no. 19). It is not certain, however, whether Rembrandt actually wore a fur hat while producing this portrait before the mirror. We can clearly see in this print that the head and the hair under the hat were elaborated almost completely. Rembrandt did not add the hat until later, probably from his imagination. The fur-trimmed collar, too, was a later addition.

Fur hats put in several other appearances in Rembrandt's work from the early 1630s. One of the models in his two etchings of old men with fur hats (fig. 28a) reappears in a painting in which the master portrayed him wearing a fur hat and a coat with a fur-trimmed collar.[107]

29a
Self Portrait in
Oriental Attire   1631

Panel, 66.5 × 52 cm

Signed and dated at lower right: *Rembrant.f 1631*
(autograph?)

Paris, Musée du Petit Palais, inv. no. 925

Bredius/Gerson 1969, no. 16; *Corpus*, vol. I,
no. A 40; vol. II, p. 840; Chapman 1990, pp. 40,
64, 92 and fig. 50

29b
Attributed to Isaac de Jouderville
(Leiden 1613–1645/8 Amsterdam)
Portrait of Rembrandt
in Oriental Attire

Panel, 70.4 × 50.2 cm

Amsterdam, Museum Het Rembrandthuis,
inv. no. 276

Corpus, vol. I, p. 381, fig. 7, under no. A 40 (copy 1);
vol. II, p. 840; vol. III, p. 17, fig. 4; E. van de
Wetering in Amsterdam/Groningen 1983, p. 66
and fig. 9; Sumowski 1983–95, vol. II, no. 948

REMBRANDT AND the artists of his circle were fond of depicting figures in oriental attire. They sometimes represent characters from biblical tales, which are set, of course, in the Middle East.[108] But in general the main effect of pictures of this kind was to evoke the atmosphere of remote, exotic regions, for which there was a growing interest in the Dutch Republic. It can be inferred from a comment by Constantijn Huygens (1596–1687; p. 27, fig. 37) that the subjects were not true Orientals, but Dutchmen in fancy dress. In his memoirs, Huygens described a painting by Jan Lievens (1607–74) in the collection of the stadholder Frederick Henry (1584–1647) as portraying 'a sort of Turkish potentate with a Dutch head'.[109] That Rembrandt too had people in his surroundings pose in outlandish costumes is clear from a reference in a 1637 inventory: 'a small oriental woman's *tronie*, being the likeness of H. Uylenburgh's wife after Rembrandt' (Hendrick van Uylenburgh was Rembrandt's Amsterdam employer).[110]

In this painting from the Petit Palais, Rembrandt has depicted himself as an Eastern potentate, an exercise he would later repeat in an etching (cat. no. 41). Under a heavy cloak he wears a coat of some shiny material, with a gold-striped sash tied around his waist. Striped material was regarded as typically oriental (see p. 61), as was the plumed turban on his head. With his gloved right hand he leans at ease on a stick, while his left hand rests on his hip. Both the self-assured pose and the clothing were derived from one of the three kings in a print after a painting by Peter Paul Rubens (1577–1640) in the Musée des Beaux-Arts in Lyon (fig. 29a). The diagonal line in which the cloak falls, however, gives the composition a dynamic thrust. A large poodle sits at Rembrandt's feet, and against the back wall a variety of objects are displayed, including a helmet and a goblet. The horizontal and diagonal stripes to the right of the head – roughly level with the eyes – could denote the upper section of a column, but apart from this the space is scarcely defined. The vigorously painted floor and background make a sharp contrast with the meticulous rendering of some of the garments.

As far as is known, this is the only occasion on which Rembrandt painted a full-length portrait of himself. That he found it no easy task is revealed by the X-radiograph of the painting (fig. 29b), which shows that he initially depicted his feet in full. Evidently he was dissatisfied with this part of his painting, as he later decided to shorten the legs. This was probably an afterthought, changed after the painting was completed, since a near-literal copy from Rembrandt's workshop (cat. no. 29b), attributed to his pupil Isaac de Jouderville, shows the legs in their original position.[111] In the end, Rembrandt decided to leave out the feet altogether, painting a poodle in their place. This alteration may have been made several years later.[112]

That Rembrandt struggled with the depiction of full-length figures in the early 1630s is also clear from the picture that lies beneath the Liverpool self portrait (p. 134, fig. 26b). This initial design shows a similar standing figure, the position of whose feet the painter changed before rejecting the composition altogether.[113]

fig. 29a
LUCAS VORSTERMAN I AFTER PETER PAUL RUBENS,
Adoration of the Kings (detail), 1621.
Engraving, 569 × 383 mm.
Amsterdam, Rijksmuseum, Rijksprentenkabinet.

cat. no. 29a

One may wonder at Rembrandt's choice of a poodle to add to this composition. As far as is known, it was not a breed with any specific oriental connotations. The poodle, which is now regarded mainly as a pet, was originally used as a hunting-dog, especially for the shooting of waterfowl.[114] For practical reasons, the furry rear of the animal was shaved clean. This pattern of fur, which recalls the coat of a lion, is clearly visible in Rembrandt's painting. As hunting was the prerogative of royalty and the nobility, the poodle became a sort of status symbol. Thus several French sovereigns owned poodles and Prince Rupert, the son of Frederick V, the Elector Palatine known as the 'Winter King' who had sought refuge in The Hague, had a poodle that answered to the name of Boy. So it is possible that Rembrandt chose this breed to enhance the princely stature of his disguise.

fig. 29b
X-radiograph of cat. no. 29a.

cat. no. 29b

30
Self Portrait
with Loose Hair *c.1631*

Etching, 145 × 117 mm (I), 64 × 60 mm (from II);
six states

Amsterdam, Rijksmuseum, Rijksprentenkabinet,
inv. no. RP-P—1961—976 (II)*

London, British Museum,
inv. no. 1844—5—11—9 (II)

B. / Hollstein 8; Hind 55

IN THE FIRST STATE of this self portrait, the etching-plate was more than twice as large as in the later states. Only a single impression of this first state has remained intact;[115] in two other specimens the head has been cut out.[116] It may be inferred from the original large size that at first Rembrandt had intended to make a half-length portrait.

It was a challenging task for the artist to render the light in the loose hair, which fans out in an almost decorative pattern. The facial expression, with its knitted forehead and eyebrows, is familiar from Rembrandt's self portrait in *The Raising of the Cross* from 1633 (p. 22, fig. 27) and in his etching from around 1642 (cat. no. 58). In the case of the *Self Portrait with Angry Expression* (cat. no. 21) it is clear that the frown expresses anger, because of the wide-open eyes. In the etching described here, as in *The Raising of the Cross*, Rembrandt has depicted himself with an earnest gaze. This self portrait probably dates from the early 1630s, the period in which Rembrandt made the handsome etching *Self Portrait with Hat, Hand on Hip* (cat. no. 32). In the latter piece, however, the face has a more relaxed expression.

31
Model Sheet with
Self Portrait *c.*1631

Etching, 101 × 114 mm (I), 100 × 105 mm (II); two states

Amsterdam, Rijksmuseum, Rijksprentenkabinet, inv. no. RP-P-OB–764 (I; see fig. 31b)

London, British Museum, inv. no. 1848–9–11–187 (I)*

B. / Hollstein 363; Hind 90; Chapman 1990, p. 33 and fig. 39

ARTISTS OCCASIONALLY draw a number of different motifs on a single sheet. In some cases the motifs are intended as sketches or studies; the draughtsman is seeking the most successful depiction, perhaps to use as a preliminary study for a painting or etching. In others the aim is to provide examples to be used by himself and his pupils. The finest model sheet in Rembrandt's oeuvre is the drawing in Birmingham (fig. 31a).[117] Model sheets of this type, in which the drawings were composed with greater care than in the case of sketches, were sometimes made into prints. Rembrandt himself etched several model sheets and there is even an eighteenth-century reference to a model book of Rembrandt's, probably a group of prints bound together in a volume. Whether he put this book together himself is not known.[118]

In some of Rembrandt's etched model sheets, he depicted a self portrait or part of one (see cat. nos. 61 and 64). In this sheet, the portrait is executed in a delicate style. The light around the eyes is rendered subtly, with an arresting chink of light by the left eye. This is one of the many examples in which Rembrandt has registered a particular effect of light in his own face. In several impressions of this print there are remnants of ink, which have been removed in the second state. In the specimen in Amsterdam these remnants are particularly noticeable (fig. 31b). Finally, it is curious that Rembrandt has not depicted a hat, as he has clearly left a space for one in his rendering of the hair and the shadows around the eyes appear to be related to a hat.

Rembrandt revolved the etching-plate 90 degrees three times clockwise in succession to depict other motifs: an old couple leaning on their sticks and above them the head of an old woman with a loose-fitting scarf, a man bent over with a stick, and finally an old man with a cap (to the right of the old couple). Each of these subjects also occurs in individual prints dating from the same period. The fact that the self portrait is part of a model sheet means that individual self portraits, too, could be used as examples: they show us not only the maker himself, but the maker's work as well (see pp. 30–1).

No such obvious self portrait occurs in a drawn model sheet. One small drawn self portrait is known, however, which was made next to the head of a man (fig. 31c). These images were cut out of a larger sheet with a variety of motifs, a fate that befell a good many drawn model sheets as dealers hoped to make a higher profit by selling sketches individually. In contrast to the drawn model sheets, Rembrandt may have intended to sell the etched variants. Besides serving as examples for himself and his pupils, numerous examples could be printed,[119] and buyers would certainly have appreciated the self portrait in the model sheet described here.

fig. 31a
REMBRANDT, *Model Sheet with Heads and Sketches of Figures*, c.1636. Pen and brush in brown and red chalk, 220 × 233 mm. Birmingham, The Barber Institute of Fine Arts.

fig. 31b
REMBRANDT, *Model Sheet with Self Portrait*, c.1631. Etching (first state), 101 × 114 mm. Amsterdam, Rijksmuseum, Rijksprentenkabinet.

fig. 31c
REMBRANDT, *Man with High Cap and Self Portrait*, c.1635. Pen and brown ink, 105 × 96 mm. New York, The Pierpont Morgan Library.

32
Self Portrait with Hat, Hand on Hip 1631–3

Etching, 148 × 130 mm; eleven states

Monogrammed and dated at upper left:
RHL 1631 (in the fifth state) and (in the tenth
state) signed at upper right: *Rembrandt f*

Amsterdam, Rijksmuseum, Rijksprentenkabinet,
inv. no. RP-P-OB-12 (VIII)*

London, British Museum,
inv. no. 1973-U-790 (X)

B. / Hollstein 7; Hind 54; White 1969,
pp. 109–12, 117, 120, 122 and figs. 134–40;
Chapman 1990, pp. 59–62 and figs. 87–92

fig. 32a
REMBRANDT, *Self Portrait*, 1631.
Etching (fourth state), 184 × 130 mm.
Amsterdam, Rijksmuseum, Rijksprentenkabinet.

IN 1631, REMBRANDT had moved from Leiden to Amsterdam and it was in that year that he produced this impressive self portrait. Running to eleven states, its execution occupied him for some considerable time. Perhaps he also took account of the possibility, even then, that collectors might be interested in different states, given that he printed several impressions of each.

In the first four states he portrayed only the head, elaborating small parts of it more each time (fig. 32a). In the fifth state he added his body to the portrait, with a loose-fitting cloak under which he placed his right hand on his hip, while the left rested on the back of a chair. The addition of his monogram and the year 1631 in the upper left corner shows that he considered the print finished at this point.

Later on, Rembrandt elaborated the self portrait further and made some changes, although the differences between successive states become smaller. In the sixth state the suggestion of a little wall, or balustrade, appears on the right and in the seventh Rembrandt decorated the material of the cloak with a design.[120] In the eighth state the little wall vanishes again, while the chair at lower right is indicated more clearly, and the left and upper areas of the background disappear into the shadows. In the tenth state he furnished the ruff with a decorative design and added a new signature in the top right because the previous monogram and year had been effaced by hatching. In the eleventh and last state he restored the white background, with the exception of a small shadowy

area in the lower left corner. The signature has disappeared altogether in this state.

It was not until the beginning of 1633 that Rembrandt started signing with his name rather than a monogram, so the tenth state, to which the signature 'Rembrandt f' was added, can be dated in or after that year.[121] At this time Rembrandt signed in the same way two early impressions of the etching that were still in his possession (depicting only his head), to which he added the body in black chalk. He also added his age: 'AET 27' (figs. 32b and c).[122] So we know that he made the drawings when he was 27 years of age, that is, in 1633–4. He then altered the '7' to a '4', because the little etched portrait dates from 1631, when he was 24 years old (before his birthday on 15 July). After this he also added the date '1631' to the two impressions on which he had made additions in black chalk.

Rembrandt's pose in these two drawn versions from 1631 to 1634 differs considerably from that of the etched figure. The drawn clothing is simpler and displays a resemblance to the costume in a number of painted self portraits of Rembrandt dating from the early 1630s. Only in this period did the artist portray himself in contemporary dress, probably because he had just moved to Amsterdam and wanted to make a certain impression in his new surroundings. The print bears a very close resemblance to the self portrait in Glasgow from 1632 (cat. no. 33). The composition of the sheet in Paris (fig. 32b), in particular, corresponds to that of the painting, which was without a doubt his direct example when making the drawing.[123]

A print made by Paulus Pontius (1603–58) from 1630 (fig. 32d) after Rubens's self portrait in Windsor Castle (p. 47, fig. 11) is usually regarded as the example for the etching described here.[124] That Rembrandt knew this print may in any case be inferred from its similar – drawn – frame (fig. 32b). Rembrandt's pose in a capacious cloak, hand on hip, is very similar, however, to his *Self Portrait in Oriental Attire* from the same year (cat. no. 29a), for which he took his inspiration from a print by Lucas Vorsterman (1595–1675) of 1621 after Rubens's *Adoration of the Kings* (p. 137, fig. 29a).[125] In the print described here, Rembrandt presents himself rather ostentatiously in contemporary, fashionable dress, placing himself among the ranks of the Amsterdam bourgeoisie.

fig. 32b
REMBRANDT, *Self Portrait*, 1631.
Etching (fourth state) and black chalk,
184 × 130 mm. Paris, Bibliothèque Nationale.

fig. 32c (in exhibition)
REMBRANDT, *Self Portrait*, 1631.
Etching (second state) and black chalk,
184 × 130 mm. London, British Museum.

fig. 32d
PAULUS PONTIUS AFTER PETER PAUL RUBENS,
Self Portrait of the Painter, 1630.
Engraving, 366 × 270 mm.
Haarlem, Teylers Museum.

33 (possibly London only)
Self Portrait with Wide-Brimmed Hat 1632

Panel, 64.4 × 47.6 cm (oval)

Signed with monogram and dated at lower right: *RHL van Ryn / 1632*

Glasgow Museums, The Burrell Collection, inv. no. 35/600

Bredius/Gerson 1969, no. 17; *Corpus*, vol. II, no. A 58; Chapman 1990, pp. 30, 47, 59, 61–2, 71 and fig. III

fig. 33a
REMBRANDT, *Portrait of a Man at the Age of 41*, 1633. Panel, 69.5 × 54.7 cm. Pasadena, Norton Simon Art Foundation.

fig. 33b
X-radiograph of cat. no. 33.

IN THIS OVAL painting, as in the etching from the previous year (cat. no. 32), Rembrandt presents himself as a prosperous citizen. He is dressed in the formal attire that was popular among fashionable young men of his time. Headgear such as berets and turbans had given way to the hat with a broad brim, the gentleman's ideal status symbol. The overall impression is austere, but the subject's prosperity is reflected in the carefully rendered details of his apparel, such as his gold hatband, a cloak with velvet facings, a doublet with gold buttons and a falling ruff, of which even the red cord has been depicted (see also p. 62).

Rembrandt thus portrayed himself here in much the same way as the numerous Amsterdam citizens whose portraits he was commissioned to paint (fig. 33a).[126] Although not a single portrait commission is known from his Leiden period, Rembrandt was soon much sought-after as a portraitist in Amsterdam. It is quite conceivable that he used this self portrait as an example to impress potential clients with his artistic skill.

The face is depicted frontally and is clearly recognisable. Never before had Rembrandt rendered his facial features with such care. The first wrinkles are visible around the left eye and he has the beginnings of a double chin. The eyebrows are raised, giving the face a slightly surprised expression. This is the only element that recalls the *tronies* he had painted in the past (compare, for example, cat. no. 7). Aside from the fashionable apparel, the frivolously trimmed moustache and the longish flared hair introduce a note of youthful *élan* into what is otherwise a rather solemn picture.

In common with numerous other self portraits, Rembrandt painted this grand self-advertisement on a used panel (see also cat. no. 26). An X-radiograph of the piece (fig. 33b) shows that the initial design bears a considerable resemblance to one of the self portraits from 1633 (cat. no. 35).

The Haarlem Teylers Museum keeps a drawn copy after this self portrait, as well as a copy after a *Portrait of a Young Woman* from Rembrandt's workshop (figs. 33c and d).[127] The sheets are attributed, on the basis of fragments of signatures, to the Amsterdam painter Dirck van Santvoort (1610/11–80). Both drawings were previously owned by the

Delft collector Valerius Röver (1686–1739), who described them as pendant portraits of Rembrandt and his wife. However, it is unlikely that the 1632 self portrait originally had a companion piece, despite the vogue in this period for pendant portraits of married couples.[128] The frontal composition is ill-suited to being combined with another painting and the woman in the supposed pendant bears not the slightest resemblance to Saskia. Moreover, in 1632 Rembrandt was still considered an eligible bachelor.

fig. 33c
ATTRIBUTED TO DIRCK VAN SANTVOORT,
Portrait of Rembrandt. Drawing, 280 × 194 mm.
Haarlem, Teylers Museum.

fig. 33d
ATTRIBUTED TO DIRCK VAN SANTVOORT,
Portrait of a Young Woman. Drawing, 279 × 194 mm.
Haarlem, Teylers Museum.

34
Self Portrait Wearing a Hat

1632

Panel, 21.8 × 16.3 cm

Signed and dated centre right:
Rembrant . f ᵛ. / 1632

Private Collection

Van de Wetering 1997, p. II, repr., and inside dust jacket; *Corpus*, vol. IV, add. no. 2

ALTHOUGH THE SUBJECT was previously reproduced from a poor copy (whereabouts unknown), the original was only recently recognised by the Rembrandt Research Project, which at the same time correctly identified it as a self portrait.[129] This version had been seen by other scholars, who, however, rejected it as a work by Rembrandt because of its unusually small format and certain weaknesses in the execution. But a convincing case can be made for its authenticity.

Scientific analysis of the panel on which it is painted indicates that it came from the same tree as that used for the well-known *Portrait of Maurits Huygens* (Hamburg, Hamburger Kunsthalle), also dated 1632,[130] which establishes, therefore, that it was produced in Rembrandt's workshop. The complex genesis of the painting, including several radical changes during the course of execution, rules out the possibility that it is a copy after a lost original.

The signature was written while the paint of the background was still wet, proving that it was not, as is sometimes the case, a later addition. Its unusual form, 'Rembrant', omitting the penultimate 'd', can be shown to have been used for only a few months at the end of 1632 and the beginning of 1633. Earlier he had signed with the monogram 'RHL', adding the surname 'van Rijn' in 1632, and from 1633 he began to sign his works regularly 'Rembrandt', a form he used until his death.[131]

Further support that this painting is an authentic self portrait is found in the sitter's attire. Hitherto only the self portrait in Glasgow (cat. no. 33), also dated 1632, showed the artist in fashionable contemporary clothing seen here. Two touched impressions of the etched self portrait (p. 144, figs. 32b and c), as well as the finished print itself (cat. no. 32) document Rembrandt's short-lived interest in portraying himself in such clothing precisely in this period.

The painting has suffered from overcleaning and subsequent retouching in the past, and this would explain such apparent weaknesses as the awkwardly small hand (which, given its brownish-grey tint, should be seen as gloved). Nevertheless, the execution agrees in every respect with what we now know of Rembrandt's working method, as seen here in the handling of the brush, and the use of contours and colour. The painting displays a surprising sense of monumentality, which only increases the longer one looks at this tiny panel.

EvdW

35* *opposite top left*
Self Portrait 1633

Panel, 61 × 48.1 cm (oval)

Signed and dated at the right of the middle:
Rembrandt. f / .1633.

Paris, Musée du Louvre, inv. no. 1744

Bredius/Gerson 1969, no. 18; Foucart 1982, p. 32; *Corpus*, vol. II, no. A 71; Chapman 1990, pp. 62–3, 67, 74, 111, 120 and fig. 97

FROM THE EARLY 1630s onwards, headgear is a recurrent element of Rembrandt's self portraits. In this painting, however, he has depicted himself bare-headed for a change. The frowning face is wreathed in wild strands of hair with a reddish lustre. Rembrandt wears a gold chain and under his clothing a gorget can just be made out, giving the portrait a military air. A similar composition lies concealed beneath the self portrait in Glasgow (see p. 145, fig. 33b).

This painting is not executed as freely as the following self portrait from 1633 (cat. no. 36). The face, in particular, displays a smooth finish. The coarse-grained structure of the paint that generally appears in Rembrandt's work in light areas and reflected light is largely absent here.

36* *opposite top right*
Self Portrait, 1633

Panel, 70.4 × 54 cm (oval)

Signed and dated at the right of the middle:
Rembrandt. / fv 1633

Paris, Musée du Louvre, inv. no. 1745

Bredius/Gerson 1969, no. 19; Foucart 1982, pp. 28–30; *Corpus*, vol. II, no. A 72; Chapman 1990, pp. 62–3, 67, 74, 111, 120 and fig. 96

ASIDE FROM marked similarities of composition, this work displays clear differences from the previous self portrait, dating from the same year (cat. no. 35). Not only does the painter wear a beret in this case, but also the image is livelier. The painter inclines his head somewhat and makes a less introverted impression. The face and hair are painted freely but confidently, with the brown underpainting left partly exposed. The movement of the right arm, with the hand on the chest, breaks up the taut contours of the torso. The dented beret and wavy movement of the gold chain also introduce playful accents into the whole. With his dark clothing, apparently based on sixteenth-century dress, the figure stands out clearly against the light background. The effect of depth is further enhanced by the strong shadow cast on the wall to the right, at the exact point where Rembrandt has placed his signature.

37* *opposite below*
Rembrandt?
Self Portrait *c.*1633

Panel, 56 × 47 cm

Berlin, Staatliche Museen, Gemäldegalerie, Preussischer Kulturbesitz, inv. no. 808

Bredius/Gerson 1969, no. 23; *Corpus*, vol. II, no. C 56; Chapman 1990, p. 43 and fig. 60; Grimm 1991, p. 100; Berlin/Amsterdam/London 1991–2, vol. I, no. 60; New York 1995–6, vol. II, p. 17; Liedtke 1996, p. 43

WHILE THERE is no doubt that this piece portrays Rembrandt, opinions differ as to its attribution. The style of painting is more vigorous and loose than in other self portraits from this period. This discrepancy has prompted some authors to doubt the painting's authenticity, while others see the masters hand in it. An attribution to Rembrandt's pupil Govert Flinck (cat. nos. 93 and 94), as proposed in 1986 by the Rembrandt Research Project, has recently been rejected.

The painting shows by now familiar attributes such as the gorget, gold chain and beret. The composition did not acquire its present form until late in the painting process. An X-radiograph reveals that the figure originally wore no beret and that he was depicted in virtually the same way as in one of the self portraits from 1633 (cat. no. 35).

38
Self Portrait with Beret 1633

Etching, 140 × 115/8 mm (I), 132 × 103 mm (II); two states

Signed and dated at lower left: *Rembrandt f. 1633* (in second state only)

Amsterdam, Rijksmuseum, Rijksprentenkabinet, inv. no. RP-P-OB–32 (II)

London, British Museum, inv. no. 1973-U–839 (II)*

B. / Hollstein 17; Hind 108; Chapman 1990, p. 24, fig. 26

fig. 38a
REMBRANDT, *Portrait of Joris de Caulerij*, 1632. Canvas on panel, 102.5 × 83.8 cm. San Francisco, The Fine Arts Museums.

IN THIS PORTRAIT Rembrandt wears an East Indian scarf that also appears in some of his other works. On his shoulder is a 'point' – a button with laces for attaching armour. A similar fastener is visible on the sleeve of Joris de Caulerij (*c*.1606-after 1661), whose portrait as lieutenant of the militia in The Hague Rembrandt made in 1632 (fig. 38a).[132] The clothing in this etching can therefore be described as military dress, but depicted in rather an informal context.

Rembrandt's face is almost entirely in shadow. Only part of the right cheek and the right ear lobe are illuminated, and the tip of the nose catches a glimmer of light. Lighting of this kind is highly reminiscent of pieces such as Rembrandt's early self portrait in Amsterdam from *c*.1628 (cat. no. 5), although the face in this etching is rendered in deeper shadow.

In the past it was assumed that Rembrandt's aim in placing his face in the shadow in this and other self portraits was to express his imaginative powers or poetic spirit.[133] However, the ingenious application of effects of light and dark points rather to an artistic motive. The strong shadows and contrasts in a number of his self portraits were undoubtedly influenced by the Italian artist Caravaggio (1571–1610), whose paintings were immensely influential in the Netherlands from the 1620s onwards, especially on the group known as the Utrecht 'caravaggists'.

39*
Self Portrait 1634

Panel, 58.3 × 47.4 cm

Signed and dated at lower right: *R..brandt.f / 1634*

Berlin, Staatliche Museen, Gemäldegalerie,
Preussischer Kulturbesitz, inv. no. 810

Bredius/Gerson 1969, no. 21; *Corpus*, vol. II,
no. A 96; Chapman 1990, pp. 24, 30 and fig. 27

THIS COMPOSITION is clearly a variation on the painted self portrait with beret
produced a year earlier (cat. no. 36). The face is depicted from a more frontal
perspective and from closer to, however, enhancing the portraits directness. In addition,
light and dark contrasts are more prominent here. As in the earliest self portraits, part of
the face, including the eyes, is depicted in shadow. The beret set at an angle, the flared
hair and the wavy line of the striped scarf introduce dynamic elements into the painting.

40
Self Portrait with Helmet

1634

Panel, 80.5 × 66 cm (octagonal)

Signed and dated at right, above the shoulder: *Rembrandt: f 1634.* (not autograph)

Cassel, Staatliche Museen Kassel, Gemäldegalerie Alte Meister, inv. no. 237

Bredius/Gerson 1969, no. 22; *Corpus*, vol. II, no. A 97; Chapman 1990, pp. 36, 38, 40–1 and fig. 51

AFTER HIS EXCURSION into the bourgeois self portrait (cat. nos. 33 and 34), Rembrandt returned to the by then familiar formula of the *tronie* and exchanged his fine suit for more fanciful costumes. One important difference with his Leiden period, however, was that he began to place more emphasis on the portrait as such, which undoubtedly stemmed from his activities as a portrait painter. Henceforth, instead of entering fully into the spirit of a role assumed for a *tronie*, as he had done in the past, Rembrandt retained his own identity. This was because he began to pay more attention to his own facial features. It has been suggested that Rembrandt aged rapidly in the early 1630s, a theory based on the wrinkles that appear in the self portraits produced in these years (cat. no. 36).[134] A better explanation would be that he had previously used his face primarily to experiment with light effects and facial expressions. It was only now that he looked in the mirror with the acute, probing gaze of the portraitist.

In the painting from Cassel shown here, Rembrandt leans forward and looks past the viewer into space. As only a small part of the face is in the shadows, idiosyncrasies of his physiognomy such as the asymmetrical frown between the eyebrows and the sagging folds of skin above the eyelids are clearly visible (see also pp. 16-17). The painter has once again depicted himself as a soldier (compare cat. nos. 8 and 14a). He wears a gorget and a gleaming helmet that is furnished with two plumes at the side, one light and one dark. This type of helmet generally has its plume attached at the back, and the twin ridge on the top is also uncommon. Rembrandt has probably depicted a variation on an existing model. Helmets with a similar design but adorned with a wide range of decorations are found in a number of his history pieces.[135]

The lowest portion of the painting makes a somewhat curious impression. As the hands are not visible and the lower part of the body is abruptly cut off by the balustrade, the figure takes on the appearance of a sculpted portrait bust. This was not in fact Rembrandt's invention, but a later addition. In the present state, only the head, the helmet, the gorget and the scarf are by Rembrandt himself. The rest was painted over quite roughly at some later – unknown – date. The signature and date are also not original, although the year 1634 is highly plausible and may have been copied from an authentic inscription that has since been lost. It is difficult to reconstruct the picture's original appearance. In any case, the mahogany panel had its present octagonal format from the outset. The X-radiograph reveals, however, that Rembrandt originally placed the self portrait within an oval plane and painted a frame around it.[136] This is a highly unusual design and no explanation for its use has yet been advanced.

The self portrait in the form of a *tronie* afforded Rembrandt ample opportunity to combine his skill as a portraitist with his ambitions as a history painter. The purchaser of such a piece became the proud owner of both of the painter's specialities in one fell swoop. The fact that it depicted Rembrandt himself will have enhanced the picture's appeal still further. Whereas in Leiden he was known only to a small circle, in Amsterdam he acquired a large public. It is therefore fair to assume that purchasers of his self portraits knew what he looked like, or at the very least were aware of his reputation. Furthermore, by portraying himself so often, Rembrandt himself ensured that his face became well-known. The way he chose to appear in some of his *tronies* was another aspect of this self-advertisement. He regularly posed in historical costumes based on portraits made by fifteenth- and sixteenth-century painters from the northern Netherlands (see cat. no. 36 and pp. 42–4 and 69). By assuming the role of 'old master', Rembrandt presented himself as a worthy follower of his illustrious predecessors.

41
'Self Portrait' as an Oriental Potentate with a Kris 1634

Etching and burin, 124 × 108 (I), 124 × 102 mm (II); two states

Signed and dated at upper left: *Rembrandt f. / 1634*

Amsterdam, Rijksmuseum, Rijksprentenkabinet, inv. no. RP-P-OB–283 (II)*

London, British Museum, inv. no. 1973-U–840 (II)

B. / Hollstein 18; Hind 109; Chapman 1990, p. 43 and fig. 58

fig. 41a
REMBRANDT, *The Capture of Samson*, 1628. Panel, 61.3 × 50.1 cm. Berlin, Staatliche Museen, Gemäldegalerie, Preussischer Kulturbesitz.

IN THIS PRINT Rembrandt has portrayed himself as an oriental potentate. The figure, rendered virtually as a bust, fills almost the entire pictorial plane and is a commanding presence. The ruler wears a cloak with an ermine collar, signifying his status and power, over which hangs a chain. A design is woven into the material of his cloak. The beret, which Rembrandt wears in a number of his self portraits, is pulled down over the forehead, and the feather hugs the line of the beret. As in other pictures in which Rembrandt takes himself as a model and dons exotic apparel, it is unlikely that he actually wore all these clothes. More probably, he added some or even all of them from his imagination or worked after the example of other artists.

In his right hand, the 'oriental potentate' holds a kris against his shoulder. This Indonesian sword has a wavy blade on one side only, which is quite unusual: perhaps it was not depicted after an original model. Moreover, the potentate is holding it incorrectly: the protruding piece at the base of the wavy side of the blade – the so-called 'elephant's trunk' – should rest against the knuckles of the hand, giving protection.[137] In other works by Rembrandt the weapon appears to have been depicted with greater precision. In *The Capture of Samson*, a painting he produced in 1628 (fig. 41a),[138] the artist painted a sheathed kris with great accuracy, and in the large painting *The Blinding of Samson* from 1636 (p. 89, fig. 1g), Samson's eye is pierced with a kris. In the latter painting the attacker holds the knife – which has wavy blades on both sides – by the blade instead of the hilt.[139] The 1656 inventory of Rembrandt's property lists a number of weapons, including Indonesian ones, but there is no mention of a kris.[140]

In the second state of the print, shown here, the etching-plate was reduced in size along the left edge, slicing through the letter 'R' of Rembrandt's signature. At the same time a redundant line enclosing the picture was removed on the right. The print dates from the same year as another print of an Oriental for which Rembrandt took himself as the model (cat. no. 42).

42
'Self Portrait' as an Oriental

1634

Etching, 197 × 162 mm (I), 130 × 108 mm
(oval, from II); three states

Signed and dated at upper left (from II at lower
right): *Rembrandt f / 1634*

Amsterdam, Rijksmuseum, Rijksprentenkabinet,
inv. no. RP-P-OB–42 (I)*

London, British Museum,
inv. no. 1874–11–20–7 (I)

B. / Hollstein 23; Hind 110; Chapman 1990,
pp. 36, 41–3 and figs. 54–5

IN THIS *'Self Portrait' as an Oriental*, Rembrandt's aim was not to make a self portrait as a historical or biblical figure – a popular custom in the seventeenth century (see, for example, cat. no. 81). He posed for this etching of an Oriental without having any particular person in mind (see also cat. no. 29a).[141] It is clear that he subsequently adjusted the image, as the ample proportions of this figure do not resemble those of the young artist. Furthermore he added a wart, to the left of the nose. Warts generally had negative connotations in the seventeenth century.[142] Given these changes, this etching cannot be regarded as a true self portrait, although Rembrandt took his own face as his point of departure.

This splendidly dressed, imposing figure in exotic apparel would not be out of place in one of Rembrandt's biblical scenes. The Oriental sports a handsome moustache, a goatee and long hair, and wears a small fur hat on which a plume is fastened with a brooch. His fur-trimmed cloak is buckled at the front, and below this a chain is visible over a half-length coat with frogging down the front, which, like the gorget around his neck, was part of a contemporary military dress. He also has a sash around his waist. His left hand is on his hip and with his right he leans on some kind of sword.

Before making the print described here, Rembrandt had already produced a large painting of a man in oriental attire, also depicted three-quarter length and standing with his hand on his hip, although the latter wears a turban and leans on a stick.[143] Furthermore, the man represents a general character type, as does, for instance, the full-length portrait of an Oriental in a small print traditionally known as '*The Persian*'.[144] Both the painting and the print are dated 1632.

Only four impressions are known of the first state of the '*Self Portrait*' as an Oriental.[145] It is not known why the image was reduced to an oval portrait in the second state (fig. 42a). A painting from 1633 with an Oriental depicted in profile was also initially rectangular in format and later cut into an oval (fig. 42b),[146] but it is not known whether Rembrandt performed this operation himself.

In the second state of this etching the clothing is depicted less sketchily and is developed into a unified dark image. The plate has so-called ear – projecting pieces used to hold the plate against a template for it to be cut into an oval. In the third and last state of the etching, all traces of this alteration were removed.

fig. 42a
REMBRANDT, '*Self Portrait*' as an Oriental, 1634. Etching (second state), 130 × 108 mm (oval). Amsterdam, Rijksmuseum, Rijksprentenkabinet.

fig. 42b
REMBRANDT, *Oriental*, 1633. Panel, 85.8 × 63.8 cm (oval). Munich, Bayerische Staatsgemälde-sammlungen, Alte Pinakothek.

43*
'Self Portrait' as the Prodigal Son in the Tavern

c.1635

Canvas, 161 × 131 cm

Signed at the left, beside the peacock pie:
Rembrant f (possibly a later replacement of
the original signature)

Dresden, Staatliche Kunstsammlungen,
Gemäldegalerie Alte Meister, inv. no. 1559

Bredius/Gerson 1969, no. 30; *Corpus*, vol. III,
no. A 111; Chapman 1990, pp. 43, 55, 97, 105,
114–20, 127 and fig. 155

THIS PAINTING WAS described as early as 1749 as a portrait of Rembrandt and his wife Saskia. Five years later, however, when it belonged to the collection of the Elector Palatine of Saxony, it had been entitled, more neutrally: 'Seated officer, caressing a female and holding a glass of beer.' Even so, the painting would often be seen later as a double portrait of the Van Rijns. The young lady, who looks over her shoulder at the viewer, certainly resembles the silverpoint portrait that Rembrandt drew of Saskia in 1633 (Berlin, Staatliche Museen, Kupferstichkabinett). The identification of the smiling man as Rembrandt is less convincing, but it should be noted that the face is rather abraded and has been retouched in places.

Even in the twentieth century, numerous authors continued to see the painting as capturing a moment in the young couple's carefree existence. But, partly because of the slate hanging on the back wall – an item used in taverns to keep a tally of who owed what – the scene could be related to the popular theme of the prodigal son in the tavern, based on a New Testament parable (Luke 15: 11–32). This interpretation became more plausible still when analysis of the X-radiograph of the painting revealed that Rembrandt had initially included the figure of a woman playing a musical instrument, a familiar motif in scenes of the prodigal son's sinful life. Although this is a history piece, Rembrandt may well have used himself and his wife as models. Whether he intended this to convey any particular significance, however, as has sometimes been suggested, is highly debatable.

44
Self Portrait with Beret *c.1635*

Etching, 49 × 44 mm; one state

Amsterdam, Rijksmuseum, Rijksprentenkabinet, inv. no. RP-P-1961-970

London, British Museum, inv. no. 1973-U-792*

B. / Hollstein 2; Hind 57

IN THIS ETCHING we see Rembrandt with a peaked beret that he also wears in other pieces. The drawing with red chalk in Washington (cat. no. 45) is largely similar in terms of pose and the play of light, although the light comes from the other side of the face, and in this etching the face is rendered from a more frontal perspective. When making the print, Rembrandt placed the beret on his head at a different angle than in the drawing. This is clear from the fact that both sheets show the peak from the same side. Whereas the drawing shows Rembrandt's mirror image, the print does not: the reverse image on the etching-plate is reversed back again when the etching is printed. The drawing in Washington is usually dated 1637 and the print roughly 1634. Given the similarity between the two pieces, it would appear more plausible that both were made at the same time, around the mid-1630s.

Both works show a long lock of hair hanging down one shoulder. From the drawing we may conclude that Rembrandt added this lock to his own hairstyle, because such a lock of hair, known as *cadenette*, was exclusive to aristocratic circles (see p. 62). Of Rembrandt's many etched self portraits, there are a handful in which he adorns himself with a *cadenette* (cat. nos. 11, 32, 42 and 49).

A similar peaked cap was worn in the sixteenth century by Isaac Claesz van Swanenburgh (1537–1614) in his self portrait of 1568, now in the Stedelijk Museum De Lakenhal, Leiden.[147] Rembrandt hence wore the same cap as the father of his first teacher in Leiden, Jacob Isaacsz van Swanenburgh (1571–1638). In Rembrandt's painted self portrait from 1629 in Boston (cat. no. 10) we also see him wearing a similar cap, although there it is embellished with a feather and a chain.

Curiously, part of the beret in the etching described here has not been developed: there is a white strip above the peak. In the drawing too, the illuminated side above the peak of the cap is elaborated in less detail, but in the etching this strip makes an unfinished impression. That the shoulder area has not been worked out in detail in the etching is less remarkable; this applies also for several other etched self portraits and heads.

45
Self Portrait with Beret

*c.*1635–8

Red chalk, 129 × 119 mm

Inscription on verso: *het Portrait van / Rembrant / van / hem zelve*

Washington, National Gallery of Art, Rosenwald Collection, inv. no. 1943.3.7048

Benesch 1973, vol. II, no. 437; Schatborn 1981, pp. 38, 41; Chapman 1990, p. 48

fig. 45a
Verso of cat. no. 45.

THIS SELF PORTRAIT is drawn in red chalk, which is handled in a variety of ways. The beret is depicted in quite minute detail with a finely pointed chalk, while the shoulders are sketched boldly and part of the chest is drawn in wide sweeps of the same – now blunt – piece of chalk. The beret casts light shadows over the eyes, which fix the viewer with a penetrating gaze. The play of light is accentuated by the contrast between the open areas in the nose and right cheek, and the darker parts of the beret.

This sheet can be dated around 1635–8.[148] In the long strand of hair that falls over one shoulder and the high closed shirt with smocking, Rembrandt's appearance displays similarities with an etched self portrait dated 1638 (cat. no. 49). In both sheets Rembrandt has depicted himself in historical dress and he has the intrusive gaze so characteristic of his self portraits. His headgear, a wide peaked beret, resembles that in a small etched self portrait (cat. no. 44) from *c.*1635. The technique of the drawing discussed here suggests that it was also made in the mid-1630s,[149] possibly around 1637, when Rembrandt used red chalk for his drawings after paintings by several artists, including those by his late master Pieter Lastman (*c.*1583–1633), as well as Leonardo's *Last Supper*.[150] They display the same characteristic combination of a meticulous with an expansive style of drawing.

The provenance of the drawing described here can be traced back to the well-known collector Valerius Röver (1686–1739), who described the sheet, in a handwritten catalogue of his collection, as 'a portrait of Rembrandt with a beret on his head, drawn by himself in red chalk'.[151] It is clear that he did not accord much importance to the back of the drawing, which displayed compositional sketches of the Entombment (fig. 45a). These extremely rough studies were sliced through when the drawing was trimmed. This operation was evidently not performed by Röver though. An old inscription describes the picture as 'a Portrait of / Rembrandt / by / himself'. Catalogue numbers were in general added to the back of Röver's drawings after his death, yet this sheet bears no such number. This means that the sheet (and the inscription?) must have been reduced in size after the sale of his famous collection. In the eighteenth century, sketch-like drawings were held in far less esteem than more highly elaborated sheets, which probably explains the mutilation of this piece.[152]

46
Self Portrait with Saskia 1636

Etching, 104 × 95 mm; three states

Signed and dated at upper left:
Rembrandt. f. / 1636

Amsterdam, Rijksmuseum, Rijksprentenkabinet,
inv. no. RP-P—1961—988 (I)

London, British Museum,
inv. no. 1973-U—1358 (I)*

B. / Hollstein 19; Hind 144; White 1969,
pp. 118—19, fig. 152; Chapman 1990, pp. 82, 134
and fig. 115

fig. 46a
AFTER REMBRANDT, *Rembrandt with his Mother.*
Posthumous print made from two
different etchings, 104 × 95 mm.
Amsterdam, Rijksmuseum, Rijksprentenkabinet.

THIS IS THE ONLY etching in which Rembrandt portrayed himself together with his wife, Saskia van Uylenburgh. The artist is dressed in historical costume and looks directly at us. He wears a shirt with a fairly high white collar under a fur-trimmed cloak; on his head is a sixteenth-century hat with a notched rim and a feather. Saskia also wears old-fashioned clothes and she has a veil on her head, as in two other etchings from the same year.[153] One other work is known in which Rembrandt and Saskia appear together; this is the painting from *c.*1635 for which they probably modelled as the prodigal son and a loose woman in a tavern (cat. no. 43).

This etching with husband and wife is not a domestic scene, but an allusion to the significance of marriage to the artist and his art. Love as the nourishing source of artistic creativity is a common theme in literature of the sixteenth and seventeenth centuries — a theme encapsulated by the Dutch motto 'Liefde baart kunst (Love brings forth art)'.[154] Seventeenth-century Dutch painters depicted this motto in family and double portraits, but this is a unique treatment of the subject in seventeenth-century printmaking.

Rembrandt must have been well aware of the effect of the reversal when printing a double portrait etched on a copperplate: the representation on the plate is the reverse of the impression that eventually appears on paper. The light was intended to fall on both the artist and his wife from the same side. To achieve this, Rembrandt had to portray Saskia too in the mirror, otherwise she would have been illuminated from the wrong side. Furthermore, if Rembrandt had not depicted her in the mirror, her image would have been reversed when the etching was printed, whereas the artist's own image would not have been (because his own mirror image on the etching-plate would have been automatically reversed again when printed). Rembrandt probably wanted to portray both his wife and himself in the same direction.[155] While he was working on this print, Rembrandt moved the outline of his right arm to the left, across the figure of Saskia.

As a right-handed artist, Rembrandt must have been aware that he was holding the chalk in his left hand in the print, as he did when he was sitting for the portrait. This is probably why he has not shown his hand engaged in drawing but at rest, with the chalk in its holder grasped between the index and middle finger.

Several lines are visible on the paper under Rembrandt's hand, depicting two different elementary shapes — the arc of a circle and a rectangular shape. That he has portrayed himself as a draughtsman probably serves to emphasise the importance of draughtsmanship — the 'father' of art — in the creative process.[156] In the series of artists' portraits published by Lampsonius in 1572 (see p. 42), the subjects are generally seated at a table and often rest one arm on it. The attributes that appear in these portraits are always brushes and a palette (p. 71, fig. 17), never a drawing implement and paper, as in this etching by Rembrandt.[157]

In a version of this double portrait that was produced posthumously, Saskia was replaced by Rembrandt's mother (fig. 46a), as she is known from an etching made in 1631.[158] This 'Freudian' exchange was conceived by a later owner of the two copperplates, the aim being to fulfil the demand for a unique state of the print. The plates were printed onto the same sheet of paper one after the other, a different part of the plate being covered with a piece of paper each time.[159] The maker of the print with Rembrandt's mother evidently saw nothing wrong with the fact that the light falls on the two figures from different sides.

47
Self Portrait, Seated *c.1636*

Pen and brush and brown ink, with white
highlights, 123 × 137 mm

Berlin, Staatliche Museen, Kupferstichkabinett,
inv. no. KdZ 1553

Benesch 1973, vol. II, no. 432;
Berlin/Amsterdam/London 1991–2,
vol. II, no. 4

THIS SELF PORTRAIT displays a detailed representation of the face and hair using the
pen, while the clothing is rendered in a more sketchlike manner with the brush.
Light washes have been applied in the background, whereas the foreground has been
delineated briskly with a virtually dry brush. Rembrandt sits at his table and peers
attentively in front of him, lost in contemplation rather than seeking contact with the
viewer. The technical execution is much like that of his first drawn self portraits,
although the painter has clearly aged here.

His hair is shorter than in the self portrait from 1633 in Paris, with which it has
often been compared (cat. no. 35).[160] The most marked resemblance, however, is to
Rembrandt's *Self Portrait with Saskia* from 1636 (cat. no. 46). In both pictures the artist
has short hair and we see him sitting at a table with an artist's attribute. In the drawing
described here it is the oval object hanging on the wall to the right, which has been
identified as a palette, although it is perhaps going too far to expect the viewer to regard
the picture on this account as a 'self portrait as a painter'.[161] Rembrandt depicted
himself at work a number of times (cat. nos. 17, 46, 62, 70, 72, 79, 82 and 83). The
costume in the sheet discussed here is extremely uncommon: the artist's open shirt is
a highly informal mode of dress that is not found in any of Rembrandt's other self
portraits.

48*

Rembrandt and/or workshop

Self Portrait *c.1637*

Panel, 64 × 49 cm (upper edges rounded)

Signed at the right, above the arm: *Rembrandt / f*
(not autograph)

London, The Wallace Collection, inv. no. P 52

Bredius/Gerson 1969, no. 27; *Corpus*, vol. III,
no. C 96

THE FORMULA OF the self portrait with beret from 1633 (cat. no. 36) has been applied again in this piece. The image was painted over an unfinished portrait of a woman, which was originally rectangular in shape. The attribution to Rembrandt is not certain, but the work was probably made in his studio, as the panel comes from the same tree as that of the Berlin self portrait from 1634 (cat. no. 39).

49
Self Portrait in Sixteenth-Century Apparel

1638

Etching, 134 × 103 mm; one state

Signed and dated at upper left: *Rembrandt f / 1638*

Amsterdam, Rijksmuseum, Rijksprentenkabinet, inv. no. RP-P–1961–989*

London, British Museum, inv. no. 1910–2–12–376

B. / Hollstein 20; Hind 156; Chapman 1990, pp. 43, 76 and fig. 59

THIS FIGURE WITH Rembrandt's features is rendered in early sixteenth-century apparel. He wears a velvet plumed beret and a loose-fitting fur-lined cloak with frogging down the front; the shoulder-piece of the cloak is enlivened with a decorative pattern. Under the cloak we see a jerkin with panes at the front, a shirt and a scarf. On the right, the man's long hair falls onto his shoulder. In self portraits and other works for which Rembrandt posed, he generally depicted himself with a moustache and goatee, but seldom with a beard as shown here (see also cat. no. 24).

The hand pressed against his chest, under his cloak, is a motif that may refer to one of the seven deadly sins – sloth: 'A slothful man hideth his hand in his bosom, and will not so much as bring it to his mouth again' (Old Testament, Proverbs 19: 24). This motif appears in seventeenth-century Dutch painting in various types of genre scenes.[162] In a painting made in 1629, Rembrandt depicted a sleeping old man with his hand in his bosom and his other hand under his head to signify melancholy.[163] There is yet a third significance attached to the motif of the hand in the bosom, one expounded in Ripa's handbook *Iconologia*, which explains that the Phlegmatic should be portrayed 'wearing a badger's pelt . . . holding both hands in his bosom'.[164]

This piece has been classified among the self portraits ever since Gersaint's *catalogue raisonné* of Rembrandt's etchings appeared in 1751, but collectors are likely to have recognised Rembrandt's facial features in the print before then. This is probably not a self portrait as such, however, but simply a representation of a richly dressed, exotic figure from a past age, in which Rembrandt has used his own face as the model. It is not known whether he had any particular individual in mind.[165]

50*
'Self Portrait' with Bittern

1639

Panel, 120.7 × 88.3 cm

Signed and dated at upper left, on the
wooden beam: *Rembrandt.ft. 1639*
(possibly not autograph)

Dresden, Staatliche Kunstsammlungen,
Gemäldegalerie Alte Meister, inv. no. 1561

Bredius/Gerson 1969, no. 31; *Corpus*, vol. III,
no. A 133; De Vries 1989, pp. 188–90; Chapman
1990, p. 48 and fig. 72; De Jongh 1991a, p. 19

A MAN WEARING a plumed cap holds up a dead bittern with its legs tied together. He is about to hang the bird on an iron hook, or possibly to take it down from the hook. The full light falls on the open wings, which are depicted with immense attention to physical detail. Because of this emphasis on still-life qualities, the painting occupies a special place in Rembrandt's oeuvre.[166] The human figure plays a purely subordinate role here and is not even mentioned in the description of this (or a similar) image in the 1656 inventory of Rembrandt's property, which refers merely to: 'A bittern depicted from life'.

Some have inclined to identify the man with the plumed cap as the painter himself. The face is largely in shadow, however. Aside from the moustache and wide nose, no specific facial features of Rembrandt are distinguishable. It therefore appears improbable that this painting is intended as a self portrait. At the very most, the painter may have used himself as a model for the sake of convenience. As the man holds a rifle and has a game bag hanging at his hip, he can be classified as a huntsman. Hunting was a favourite pastime of the élite in the seventeenth century, and it has therefore been suggested that Rembrandt was expressing his social ambition here by depicting himself as a member of the privileged classes. Leaving aside the fact that this huntsman perhaps resembles a servant more than a nobleman, the old-fashioned dress and two earrings (see also cat. no. 57) indicate that he does not represent a contemporary individual. He should rather be interpreted as a costumed minor figure who gives the piece a historical character.

For all the conflicting readings that have been suggested for this scene, its significance still remains unclear. Some authors note that the introduction of a bird in seventeenth-century art and literature often had an erotic undertone; in colloquial usage the verb 'vogelen (to bird)' meant sexual intercourse. A dead bird was also a *vanitas* symbol, a meaning that could be underscored here by the gallows-shaped construction in the upper left corner. An ingenious new interpretation was recently added to the plethora of alternative readings. The seventeenth-century Dutch name for the bittern – 'pitoor' – is remarkably similar to *pictor*, the Latin word for painter. It is possible that Rembrandt intended the bird to represent a visual pun on his profession.

51*
Self Portrait c.1639

Panel, 80.5 × 62.8 cm (oval)

Signed and dated at the right, on the balustrade:
Rembrandt f. / 1637 (probably not autographed)

Paris, Musée du Louvre, inv. no. 1746

Bredius/Gerson 1969, no. 29; Foucart 1982, p. 93;
Corpus, vol. III, no. B 10

THIS PAINTING has undergone several transformations in the course of time. The originally rectangular panel was first painted with a biblical scene, probably by one of Rembrandt's studio assistants, though this work never proceeded beyond a preliminary design. Rembrandt subsequently used the panel for a self portrait, which in turn, was later almost completely painted over. Of the present image, only the head and the white collar can be regarded as Rembrandt's work. The rest of the clothing, the long hair and the architecture in the background display a style of painting that has nothing to do with either Rembrandt or his pupils. It is not known why, or when, this rigorous operation was performed. Possibly the self portrait was never finished, or the original paint layer became badly damaged. The signature and the year 1637 are probably also inauthentic. The year given seems too early for this portrait, whose facial features greatly resemble those of the self portrait from 1640 (cat. no. 54).

52 (London only)

Rembrandt?

'Tronie' of a Young Man with Gorget and Beret

(previously regarded as a self portrait)

*c.*1639

Panel, 62.5 × 54 cm

Remainder of signature at lower left: *. . . ndt. f*

Florence, Galleria degli Uffizi, inv. no. 3890

Bredius/Gerson 1969, no. 20; *Corpus*, vol. III, no. B 11; Chapman 1990, p. 43 and fig. 61; Langedijk 1992, pp. 141–3, no. 26

THIS PAINTING, which was not included in the famous collection of self portraits owned by the Florentine Medici family (see pp. 48–50 and cat. no. 85) until the nineteenth century, was long regarded as an authentic self portrait of Rembrandt. It could be an unfinished work by the master that was completed by another artist. The identification of the person portrayed as Rembrandt, however, is highly questionable. The facial features exhibit only the vaguest of similarities to undisputed self portraits. Furthermore, the non-moustachioed face looks too young for Rembrandt's age, assuming that the painting was indeed made in 1639, as the Rembrandt Research Project has posited on stylistic grounds.

53
Self Portrait, Leaning on a Stone Wall 1639

Etching and drypoint, 205 × 164 mm; two states

Signed and dated at upper left: *Rembrandt f. / 1639*

Amsterdam, Rijksmuseum, Rijksprentenkabinet, inv. no. RP-P—1962—10 (II)

London, British Museum, inv. no. 1868—8—22—656 (II)*

B. / Hollstein 21; Hind 168; White 1969, pp. 120—2; Chapman 1990, pp. 69, 71—2, 74—6, 81 and fig. 101

GERSAINT, THE AUTHOR of the first *catalogue raisonné* of Rembrandt's etched oeuvre in 1751, looked on this print as the finest of all his etched self portraits. Rembrandt has portrayed himself from an oblique angle, behind a stone wall on which his arm rests, with his head turned toward us. This pose and the composition are derived from a portrait painted by Titian (active by 1510; died 1576; fig. 53a), which was in Amsterdam in the seventeenth century, in the collection of the diplomat and collector Alfonso Lopez (1572—1649). The painting was mistakenly assumed at the time to depict the Renaissance poet Lodovico Ariosto (1474—1533). On 9 April 1639, at the Amsterdam sale of the collection of Lucas van Uffelen, Lopez also acquired Raphael's *Portrait of Baldassare Castiglione* (fig. 53b), a painting that Rembrandt copied in a drawing that same year (fig. 53c).[167] From that painting he derived a slightly different angle of the head in comparison to Titian's portrait – turned more towards the viewer – as well as the turned-up collar. In his drawn copy, Rembrandt changed the position of Castiglione's beret, setting it at a jauntier angle than in Raphael's painting. The position of the beret in Rembrandt's drawing then served as the point of departure for the hat in the etching from 1639 that is discussed here.[168]

One year later, Rembrandt adopted the same pose for a painted self portrait (cat. no. 54). While in part inspired by the Italian artists mentioned above, it can also be assigned a clear place in the Northern tradition of the self portrait (see p. 44). There are several significant differences, aside from clothing, between the painting and this etching. The figure in the painting has a more monumental character, as his torso is depicted larger in relation to his head and we look up to him, as it were, from a lower vantage-point. Moreover, the figure in the print appears smaller altogether as it has more space around it. The rakish angle of the beret in the etching becomes horizontal in the painting, so that the latter has a more symmetrical composition. Furthermore, the glove worn by Rembrandt in the etching is absent from the painting. In both portraits Rembrandt wears a chain with a small cross – a general allusion to pre-Reformation days, just as his clothing, too, recalls the past.[169] The differences between the etching and painting demonstrate that Rembrandt was constantly creating new pictorial forms, taking earlier examples as his point of departure, sometimes drawing inspiration from his own work.

fig. 53a
TITIAN, *Portrait of a Man*, c.1512.
Canvas, 81.2 × 66.3 cm.
London, National Gallery.

fig. 53b
RAPHAEL, *Portrait of Baldassare Castiglione*, before 1516.
Canvas, 82 × 67 cm. Paris, Musée du Louvre.

In a number of early impressions, Rembrandt elaborated the print with black chalk. Part of a globe is etched to the right of the figure with diagonal hatching across it, as if Rembrandt's shadow is cast on a wall there. In the second state, Rembrandt transferred to the etching-plate the beret as he had expanded it with chalk in two examples of the first state.[170] In some impressions, stones have been drawn in the lower right corner.[171] In others, the barely suggested architecture is elaborated to various degrees,[172] the most detailed example being the print in Melbourne (fig. 53d).[173] In this sheet, a globe drawn in black chalk rests on part of a balustrade situated behind, or possibly on, the stone wall.

The motif of a globe on a balustrade has a special significance in seventeenth-century portraiture. The subjects portrayed intended it to convey that they possessed, or at any rate aspired to, elevated ideals and virtues.[174] It is found most often in portraits made in the open air. Perhaps the small etched lines to the left of the hatching represent a preliminary suggestion of leaves.

In contrast to Titian's painting, and to Rembrandt's painted self portrait from 1640, the wall on which the arm rests looks somewhat dilapidated. This is apparent not merely from the structure of the stones, but also from the grass or moss growing on the wall to the left of Rembrandt's hand, and from the two stones overlapping rather haphazardly behind his back. The dilapidated state of the wall is an allusion to the brevity of earthly life, counterbalancing the status and allure with which Rembrandt has undoubtedly presented himself here.

fig. 53c
Rembrandt after Raphael, *Portrait of Baldassare Castiglione*, 1639. Pen and brown ink with white highlights, 163 × 207 mm.
Vienna, Graphische Sammlung Albertina.

fig. 53d
Rembrandt, *Self Portrait, Leaning on a Stone Wall*, 1639. Etching (first state), 205 × 164 mm.
Melbourne, National Gallery of Victoria.

54
Self Portrait 1640

Canvas, 93 × 80 cm (rounded edges at top)

Signed and dated at lower right: *Rembrandt f 1640*; inscription below signature: *Conterfeycel* (added by another hand, probably in the seventeenth century)

London, National Gallery, inv. no. 672

Bredius/Gerson 1969, no. 34; *Corpus*, vol. III, no. A 139; Chapman 1990, pp. 8, 46, 48, 55, 69, 71–2, 74–8, 79, 81, 87–8, 91, 95, 120, 130–1, 135 and fig. IV

fig. 54a
X-radiograph of cat. no. 54.

THIS DISTINGUISHED self portrait, which Rembrandt painted at the height of his success, is an ingenious expression of his ambitions. Composition and clothing alike highlight his desire to follow in the footsteps of renowned painters from past centuries. Just as in the etching produced in the year before (cat. no. 53), Rembrandt took his inspiration from Raphael's *Portrait of Baldassare Castiglione* (p. 170, fig. 53b) and Titian's so-called portrait of Ariosto (p. 170, fig. 53a). The influence of these Italian examples is less pronounced here, however. The only elements that clearly recall Raphael (1483–1520) are the use of colour and the contours of the figure, while the position of the arm appears to derive from Titian (active by 1510; died 1576). The body is turned more towards the viewer, however, and the entire lower arm, rather than only the elbow, rests on the balustrade. This pose resembles a well-known self portrait from 1498 by the German artist Albrecht Dürer (1471–1528), which had belonged to the collection of Charles I of England (1600–49; see p. 44, fig. 7), together with a self portrait by Rembrandt, since 1636.

The self portrait from 1640 should therefore not be discussed solely in relation to Italian examples, as is usually done, since it also refers to the painting tradition of the North.[175] Moreover, an X-radiograph shows that in Rembrandt's initial design, the fingers of the right hand rested on the balustrade (fig. 54a). This motif is based, as are the picture's rounded upper edges, on well-established usage in northern Netherlandish portrait painting.[176] The clothing, which is rendered in detail, likewise contains numerous allusions to the past. This ensemble was not pulled out of the dressing-up chest but carefully composed from a variety of examples in prints, in particular portraits believed to depict Lucas van Leyden (active 1508; died 1533). The various borrowings were creatively combined into a fictitious whole, which makes an authentic impression as a costume and whose separate components can be dated between 1520 and 1530 (see p. 68). That Rembrandt paid especial attention to clothing can also be inferred from the X-radiograph reproduced here, which shows that the turned-up collar initially had a different shape.

With this self portrait Rembrandt was drawing on the work of famous predecessors from both sides of the Alps. His interest in Albrecht Dürer and Lucas van Leyden may have been partly related to the fact that they, like himself, excelled in both painting and printmaking. The portrait aspect of this piece is more dominant than in the self portraits from the 1630s. The face is painted accurately in short, regular brushstrokes. Each individual hair of the dapper moustache is rendered separately; the familiar lines scratched into the wet paint are confined to a few curls in the neck.[177] Rembrandt's hair looks a good deal shorter than in the etching from the previous year, giving him a more dignified appearance.[178] The clothing has been painted more freely in places, but the overall impression of the painting is smooth and well-balanced. The cloak folded back over the left arm provides an effect of three-dimensionality, as does the light that strikes the wall, making the figure stand out from the background.

174

Although Rembrandt has dressed himself here as a master from bygone days, he has above all remained himself. This is emphasised by the addition *Conterfeycel* (the seventeenth-century Dutch word for portrait) immediately under the signature. This inscription is not in Rembrandt's hand, but probably dates from the seventeenth century. It may have been added by one of the first owners, who wanted to emphasise that he possessed a portrait of the painter, then already famous. A similar addition appears in the inventory of the household effects of the Amsterdam dealer Johannes de Renialme, drawn up in 1657: 'Rembrants contrefeytsel antycks (Rembrandt's likeness *à l'antique*)'.[179] Although this description is too general to be linked to any specific painting, it could easily apply to the self portrait from 1640. For in the seventeenth-century the term 'antycks' was not confined to classical antiquity, but could refer to anything that was not contemporary.[180]

55a* *(left)*

Anonymous artist after Rembrandt?
Portrait of Rembrandt *c.1640*

Canvas, 92.3 × 76.4 cm

Remainder of signature at lower right: *Rembra...*

Woburn Abbey, Bedfordshire, By Kind Permission of the Marquess of Tavistock and the Trustees of the Bedford Estates

Bredius/Gerson 1969, no. 33; *Corpus*, vol. III, no. c 93

55b* *(right)*

Canvas, 94.4 × 74 cm

Ottawa, National Gallery of Canada, inv. no. 4420

Corpus, vol. III, no. c 94

THESE TWO PAINTINGS are probably seventeenth-century copies after a self portrait of Rembrandt that has been lost. Both were made outside the artist's workshop. Partly on the basis of the facial features depicted here, the original self portrait can be placed around 1640, the year in which the well-known painting in London was completed (cat. no. 54). Comparison of the two copies reveals that one of the copyists, in any case, took liberties with the original composition. For instance, where the Woburn Abbey piece has a medallion hanging from the gold chain, the Ottawa copy has a cross. Furthermore, the figure in the latter piece is surrounded by rather more space and appears to be standing before a stone alcove.

56*

Rembrandt?

Self Portrait *c.1641?*

Panel, 62.5 × 50 cm

Signed at the right, level with the shoulder:
Rembrandt f / 163(.)
(possibly not autograph)

Pasadena, Norton Simon Art Foundation

Bredius/Gerson 1969, no. 32; *Corpus*, vol. III,
no. c 97; Grimm 1991, p. 104; Liedtke 1996, p. 43

JUDGING BY THE particular phase in the ageing process as rendered in Rembrandt's face, this piece may be placed between the paintings from 1640 and 1642 (cat. nos. 54 and 57). There is a striking contrast between the meticulously elaborated head and the briskly painted clothing. The hand slipped between the folds of the cloak, which has been conveyed with a few brushstrokes, is a common motif in Rembrandt's self portraits. In an etching from 1638 (cat. no. 49) this gesture is combined, as it is here, with a loose-fitting coat with frogging down the front.

The authenticity of this work, which is of high quality, was recently questioned. However, an attribution to Rembrandt's most gifted pupil Carel Fabritius (cat. no. 92), as suggested in 1989 by the Rembrandt Research Project, has not been endorsed by other experts.

57
Self Portrait 1642

Panel, 69.9 × 58.4 cm

Signed and dated at the right, by the shoulder:
Rembrandt.f.1642

London, The Royal Collection, inv. no. 1156

Bredius/Gerson 1969, no. 37; *Corpus*, vol. IV, no. 1

fig. 57a
X-radiograph of cat. no. 57.

fig. 57b
Infra-red reflectogram of a detail of cat. no. 57.

HAVING BEEN WRITTEN off as a Rembrandt in 1982, even being labelled an 'eighteenth-century imitation', this painting has recently made a remarkable comeback in the master's oeuvre.[181] Although little of the original paint can be seen today, detailed examination has revealed that beneath the copious overpainting lies an authentic self portrait.

The origins of this painting, the reconstruction of which is based on scientific research, are extremely complicated.[182] Broadly speaking, three different stages can be distinguished. The panel was used in Rembrandt's studio, possibly as early as the 1630s, for a self portrait (or a portrait of Rembrandt by a pupil) that was perhaps left incomplete. The paint was partly scraped off and the panel served for another painting with the same subject in 1642. This second version, to which the painter made numerous corrections before it attained its final form, was eventually painted over by another hand.

So this panel consists of two (self) portraits, one on top of the other, of which the uppermost one was substantially reworked at a later date. Remains of the earliest portrait are visible in an X-radiograph (fig. 57a). Above the head it can be seen that the paint was scraped off in diagonal strokes using a sharp object, and that the painter's hand slipped in a few places. The part of the paint that had already dried and was therefore more difficult to remove was left behind on the panel. The resulting silhouette reveals that the headgear and hair were originally different: medium-length flared curls emerged from a simple beret. The face visible in the X-radiograph does not go with the original beret, however, it belongs to the uppermost self portrait. That this conceals an earlier design can be inferred from another examination, this time using infra-red reflectography (fig. 57b). This clearly reveals an eye where now there is an ear, showing that the head was originally placed at a completely different angle. All these data combined enable a reconstruction drawing to be made (fig. 57d). Its composition displays striking similarities to self portraits by Rembrandt from the early 1630s (compare cat. nos. 36 and 39).[183]

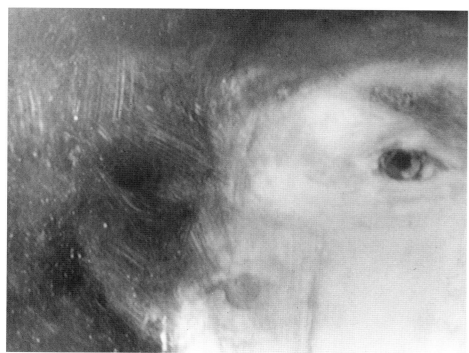

fig. 57d
Reconstruction by the Rembrandt Research
Project of the underlying representation
in cat. no. 57.

Evidently after the original painting was abandoned the panel languished in the workshop for years, until it was used for another self portrait in 1642. The infra-red reflectogram shows that Rembrandt changed his mind several times while making this second version. Next to the left eye, for instance, the contours can just be made out of an eye painted at an earlier stage (fig. 57b), showing that the head was moved slightly to the right. This change may have been related to the shape of the headgear, which was adjusted repeatedly before it settled into its final form (fig. 57c). Some of the *pentimenti* (changes made by the painter himself) in the beret are visible to the naked eye.

The later overpainting – done at an unknown date – is recognisable on the surface from what is clearly a different structure and style of painting. Both the clothing and the right hand, which is placed under the cloak, have been executed rather clumsily. Only in the face have certain parts been left untouched, revealing something of the original quality. Here the style of painting is comparable to Rembrandt's own work. Although the paint is relatively less transparent in the eyes and the shadows, this can be explained by the fact that the painting was made on top of another one.

Although the background too was laid in thickly, the signature, strikingly enough, was left untouched. The handwriting resembles signatures of the master that have been shown to be reliable. Furthermore, the year 1642 is not inconsistent with the facial features of the aging painter, which support a date in the middle of the period 1640–5 (compare cat. nos. 54 and 59).

As far as can be determined, the later overpainting broadly follows the original composition, although initially the beret may have been adorned with a feather. The clothing, which is a combination of sixteenth-century elements, corresponds to that in other self portraits by Rembrandt. The beret and openworked doublet, for instance, which is decorated with two chains, make a particularly old-fashioned impression. The earring, which Rembrandt included in several of his self portraits, was not a common item of jewellery among men in the seventeenth century and emphasises the special character of his costume all the more.

58
Self Portrait with Beret *c.1642*

Etching, 93 × 62 mm; one state

Signed at upper left: *Rembrandt f.*
(almost invisible)

Amsterdam, Rijksmuseum, Rijksprentenkabinet,
inv. no. RP-P-OB—288

London, British Museum, inv. no. 1973-U—894*

B. / Hollstein 26; Hind 157

IN THIS ETCHING Rembrandt wears an old-fashioned jerkin with panes at the front and a beret on his head. The placing of the figure in the pictorial plane is unusual: the left shoulder is lower and further forward than the right, which is only partially represented. To the left, Rembrandt's shadow falls on a weather-beaten wall. The contrasts in the image are quite strong and it is therefore logical to assume that the artist, the left side of whose face is in the shadow, is illuminated by the sun. This may arouse the mistaken impression that he is screwing up his eyes because of the bright light: rather, the expression is one of earnestness and solicitous attention, with the forehead and eyebrows puckered into wrinkles. In the *Self Portrait with Loose Hair* from about 1631, Rembrandt portrayed himself with an identical expression (cat. no. 30), and we see it again in *The Raising of the Cross* from 1633 (p. 22, fig. 27). In this painting, where he is one of the bystanders who help to erect the cross, the artist also wears a beret and old-fashioned attire. Rembrandt probably set out to depict the same earnestness in his prints.

The self portrait described here may be dated around 1642 on the basis of the regular, open hatching that is characteristic of several etchings from this period.[184] Rembrandt is no longer a young man here; his facial features are very similar to those in the self portrait in Karlsruhe made in (or around) 1645 (cat. no. 60).

59

Rembrandt?

Self Portrait with Beret and Two Gold Chains

*c.*1642–3

Panel, 72.2 × 58.3 cm

Madrid, Museo Thyssen-Bornemisza, inv. no. 1976.90

Bredius/Gerson 1969, no. 36; *Corpus*, vol. IV, no. 2

As in the case of the self portrait in the Royal Collection (cat. no. 57), the poor condition in which this panel has been preserved makes it extremely difficult to arrive at a sound assessment of it. Important parts of the original paint layer have been lost or rubbed off, probably through unduly vigorous attempts at cleaning. Its present appearance is to a large extent determined by retouches, and the background has been painted over completely by another hand. It was perhaps at this stage that a feather was covered up which originally adorned the beret and is now visible only with the use of infra-red reflectography (fig. 59a).[185] It also appears that the panel was trimmed on all four sides, possibly distorting the proportions of the composition.

The authenticity of this piece was not disputed in the literature until Rembrandt specialist Horst Gerson wrote in 1968, 'there are many strange features which make me doubt the attribution to artist and period'.[186] The piece then vanished silently from Rembrandt's oeuvre and it was not until 1990 that a meticulous analysis appeared of the problem of attribution. The conclusion reached was that the painting had been produced by a workshop assistant or one of the master's followers.[187] Technical research had not produced any evidence for doubting the panel's seventeenth-century origins, which Gerson had called in question, but on the basis of painting technique and artistic quality an attribution to Rembrandt was rejected. That the painting must in any case have been produced in his workshop was confirmed in 1994, when the age of the panel was further investigated:[188] the research showed that the wood used for this panel came from the same tree as the panels of four undisputed Rembrandts.

After careful consideration of all the arguments, and taking the poor condition of the panel into account, the Rembrandt Research Project concluded that this painting may be attributable to Rembrandt after all. Aside from technical and stylistic aspects, the rendering of details of the subject's physiognomy played an important part in the evidence. The picture displays all the details most characteristic of Rembrandt's appearance, such as the wrinkled frown, the drooping folds of skin over the eyes and the furrows above the bridge of the nose, which occur in his self portraits from 1640

fig. 59a
Infra-red reflectogram of a detail of cat. no. 59.

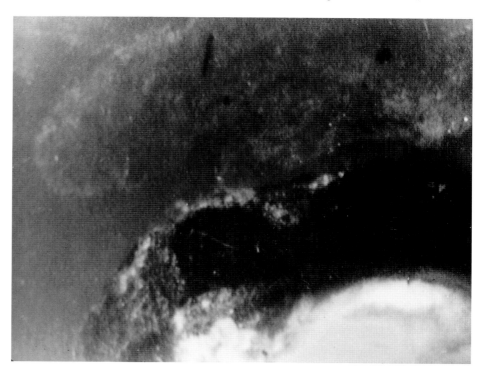

181

onwards (see also pp. 16–17). In itself, however, this does not exclude the possibility that the piece is a copy after a lost original. However, the attention paid to idiosyncratic features of the face that may appear at first sight to be insignificant, and which a copyist could easily have overlooked, makes an attribution to the master himself more plausible. The painting documents a stage in Rembrandt's aging process that is otherwise unknown to us, and that can be dated in the rough period 1640–5. In comparison to the painting from 1642 in the Royal Collection (cat. no. 57), the face appears less full and the skin under the chin seems to have sagged a little more.

Rembrandt is dressed completely in black, the only accents being provided by the collar of his white shirt, the fur trimmings of his doublet and the two gold chains. As both the head and body are depicted from a more or less frontal perspective, this self portrait lacks an element of tension. Furthermore, the lack of nuance in clothing and background, possibly a consequence of the extensive overpainting, contributes to the austere character of this piece.

60*
Self Portrait, c.1645?

Panel, 68.5 × 56.5 cm (oval)

Remainder of signature at lower right: *Rem . . .*

Karlsruhe, Staatliche Kunsthalle, inv. no. 238

Bredius/Gerson 1969, no. 38; Chapman 1990, pp. 63, 79 and fig. 110; *Corpus*, vol. IV, no. 5

THE POSE THAT Rembrandt has adopted here corresponds to some extent to the type of composition he favoured in the 1630s (see, for example, cat. nos. 35–6, 39 and 48). The painting was probably originally rectangular, and reduced later – possibly at the beginning of the eighteenth century – to an oval. The fact that the signature has been cut off on the right indicates, at any rate, that the panel was originally larger.

The head is modelled meticulously in warm and cool flesh tints, avoiding sharp transitions. The careful rendering of details in the physiognomy is reflected most clearly by the soft skin of the full, blood-red lips, a feature to which Rembrandt did not usually pay a great deal of attention. Because of the painstaking elaboration, it is apparent that the flesh has slackened and that the cheeks sag more than before. The deep frown and taut muscles by the left eye reveal the subject's concentration. Interestingly, Rembrandt has neither moustache nor goatee here, both of which are fixed features of his self portraits from the early 1630s onwards. In the etching from 1648 (cat. no. 62), however, they reappear.

More pronounced even than in some self portraits from previous years (cat. nos. 54 and 56) is the sharp contrast between the delicate manner in which the face has been painted and the sketchy delineation of the torso. The clothing is indeed depicted so roughly that it is hard to make out what Rembrandt is wearing. The bulge in the right side of the red cloak should probably be interpreted as indicating an arm held against the

chest. The viewer can see with the naked eye changes that the painter has made in a number of places, for instance by both shoulders. To the left of the head, the top paint layer is abraded, exposing a second ear belonging to an earlier composition that lies beneath the present one. X-ray examination has revealed that the earlier painting was a portrait of a man, which was probably not painted by Rembrandt or one of his assistants. Perhaps the panel was purchased second-hand, from the estate of a deceased artist for instance. After 1645, the year in which this painting is dated, Rembrandt's steady output of painted self portraits virtually stagnated; it was not until 1652 that he would pick up the thread once again (cat. no. 65).

61

Model Sheet with
Self Portrait *c.1645*

Etching, 78 × 69 mm; one state

Amsterdam, Rijksmuseum, Rijksprentenkabinet,
inv. no. RP-P-OB—778*

London, British Museum, inv. no. 1836—4—12—2

B. / Hollstein 372; Hind 155

THIS IS THE second out of a total of three model sheets in which Rembrandt included his portrait (compare cat. nos. 31 and 64). Unlike the other self portraits, in this etching the beret was executed before the face, of which just a fraction is shown:[189] only the left eye has been elaborated. In its present form, the etching-plate would have been too small for the whole head; perhaps it was originally larger. In the shadows above the beret we see that Rembrandt has depicted an eye, and the little lines to the right of the beret may be identified as a strand of hair. The most important motif in the etching, however, is the tree, beside which a little figure is visible, standing by a hill. As in the case of other model sheets, this part of the image is etched in a different direction from the portrait.

The style of the tree and the loose style of etching recall *The 'Omval'* and *The Boathouse*, both of which date from 1645.[190] The face most resembles that in the self portrait in Karlsruhe from (or around?) 1645 (cat. no. 60), but in the painting Rembrandt wears a smaller beret. On the basis of the similarities with the above works, the model sheet described here can also be dated in the mid-1640s.

62

Self Portrait at the Window, Drawing on an Etching-Plate 1648

Etching, drypoint needle and burin,
160 × 130 mm; five states

Signed and dated at upper left: *Rembrandt. f 1648*
(from second state)

Amsterdam, Rijksmuseum, Rijksprentenkabinet,
inv. no. RP-P-OB–39 (I)*

London, British Museum,
inv. no. 1855–4–14–260 (I)

B. / Hollstein 22; Hind 229; White 1969,
pp. 132–4; Chapman 1990, pp. 79, 81–4, 86–8,
135, 157, note 13 and figs. 112–14

fig. 62a
REMBRANDT, *Self portrait at the Window, drawing
on an Etching-Plate*, 1648. Etching (fourth state),
160 × 130 mm. Amsterdam, Rijksmuseum,
Rijksprentenkabinet.

IN CONTRAST TO the ambitious, grandiose self portrait from 1639 (cat. no. 53),
Rembrandt depicted himself almost ten years later as an artist. He is working at the
window and is dressed not in rich apparel and a beret, but in a shirt, a painter's coat and a
narrow-rimmed hat – the same hat he wears in his full-length drawn self portrait (cat.
no. 63). The long curls and goatee of the 1639 portrait have gone, while a less elegant
moustache has remained. Whereas in the 1639 print Rembrandt is placed against an open
background, here we see him in an enclosed space, the dark walls of which contrast
sharply with the light from the window. This window consists solely of a frame and a
ledge, devoid of styles, jambs or latch, giving it the appearance of a somewhat crude
opening in the wall, especially in the first state of the print. In this proof, Rembrandt
used the drypoint needle for the warm, velvety lines on the figure, which wear has
rendered imperceptible, or almost so, in later impressions. Here, the resting hand is not
yet shaded and the face still has to be developed in detail.

Rembrandt sits working at a small table. He is using the etching-needle to draw his
reflection and his elbow rests on the window-ledge. The etching-plate, invisible to the
viewer, lies on a folded cloth placed on top of a book, which in turn rests on a second,
larger book.[191] In the first state of the print, the section above and to the right of the
smaller book (including part of the cloth and the artist's right hand) has not yet been
elaborated. In 1658 Rembrandt produced another etched self portrait (cat. no. 72),

in which he is depicted at work on an etching-plate even more clearly than in the piece described here, dating from ten years earlier.

In the second state Rembrandt added a piece of cloth at the top of the window, on which he wrote his name. This recalls the cloth that he had hanging above the window in his workshop, and which he used to modify the light, as shown in a drawing by Rembrandt that is preserved in Oxford.[192] In the fourth state, the frame and cloth were shaded with hatching. Rembrandt then added a view of an un-Dutch hilly landscape with houses (fig. 62a),[193] which displays a stylistic resemblance to some of the landscapes rendered from memory that appear in the background of etched or drawn biblical scenes.[194]

63
Full-Length Self Portrait

*c.*1650

Pen and brown ink on brownish paper,
203 × 134 mm

On a strip pasted to the paper: *getekent door Rembrant van Rhijn naer sijn selver / sooals hij in sijn schilderkamer gekleet was*; on the cardboard mount: *Rembrant avec l'habit dans lequel / il avoit accoutumé de peindre*

Amsterdam, Museum Het Rembrandthuis, inv. no. 246

Benesch 1973, vol. V, no. 1171; Chapman 1990, p. 87 and fig. 124; Ornstein-van Slooten/ Holtrop/Schatborn 1991, no. 5; Melbourne/Canberra 1997–8, no. 85

THIS IS THE only drawing in which Rembrandt made a full-length portrait of himself. He is dressed in a long, large coat, that is bound with a sash around the waist. The exact contours of this sash are unclear because Rembrandt wiped away excess ink at this spot, causing slight damage even to the paper. The drawing has been executed very vigorously, with accents added in various places.

Rembrandt wears a narrow-rimmed cylindrical hat like the one in his etched self portrait from 1648 (cat. no. 62). Given the similar characterisation of the wide face with the frowning eyes and pursed lips, and details such as the woolly tufts of hair near the ears, this drawing does not appear to have been made much later than the etching. His pose, hands on hips and thumbs hooked behind the sash, is remarkably similar to that in the self portrait of 1652 (cat. no. 65).

Several *repentirs*, alterations made while drawing, are discernible in this vigorous sketch. The right hand appears initially to have been placed slightly higher up. In the first design, the left foot was placed further back; with a few strokes of the pen this was changed into a static pose, which makes a more monumental impression. Vigorous hatching behind the figure is suggestive of light emanating from the front right corner. In spite of the crude delineation of the eyes, nose and mouth, Rembrandt is immediately recognisable. In the painting of 1652, in contrast, every detail of the face is represented. The drawing may have served as a design for this half-length portrait. In view of the presumed relationships to the etching from 1648 and the painting from 1652, the drawing can be dated *c.*1650.[195]

The inscription in a late seventeenth-century handwriting was pasted onto this piece by someone who claimed to know what Rembrandt looked like in his workshop. It reads: 'Drawn by Rembrandt van Rijn after his own image / as he was attired in his studio' (see pp. 64–5). Still, although Rembrandt is indeed shown here in working clothes, he is not depicted as a painter with a palette and brush, nor is he shown at work, as in the etching of 1648. Both drawing and inscription have been cut out and pasted onto a thick cardboard mount. The owner of the sheet then furnished with a drawn border first the drawing and then the ensemble. Later on, a French translation was added, which reads:

'Rembrant avec l'habit dans lequel / il avoit accoutumé de peindre.' The handwriting in which these words were written was later identified as that of the art connoisseur and collector of drawings Pierre-Jean Mariette (1694–1774).[196] In 1741, Mariette wrote the auction catalogue of the collection of Pierre Crozat (1665–1740) – the earliest known owner of this sheet – and it may have been on this occasion that he added this French translation. It appears from the catalogue that Crozat had acquired a large number of Rembrandt drawings from the French diplomat and art critic Roger de Piles (1635–1709), who purchased drawings in the Netherlands in 1693, possibly including the one described here.[197]

64
Model Sheet with Self Portrait *c.1651*

Etching, 111 × 92 mm; one state

Signed and dated at lower right: *Rf. 1651* (not autograph)

Amsterdam, Rijksmuseum, Rijksprentenkabinet, inv. no. RP-P-OB—776

London, British Museum, inv. no. 1973-U—994*

B. / Hollstein 370; Hind 230; White 1969, p. 168

THIS MODEL SHEET bears certain similarities to an etching produced twenty years earlier, which also displays several different motifs in combination with a self portrait (cat. no. 31). Here we see a beggar wearing a high cap, with a begging bowl in his outstretched arms, and – at a ninety-degree angle – a mother and child. The contours of the latter figure overlap the shadows beneath the portrait, and the beggar is placed directly beside Rembrandt's head. Formally speaking, these figures constitute a more cohesive group of motifs than in the earlier model sheet, although in this case too they are not depicted in the same direction. A third model sheet depicting different motifs with Rembrandt's portrait (or part of it) was made around 1645 (see cat. no. 61).

The signature and the year 1651 under the mother and child are probably not autograph. It was only in his early period that Rembrandt used the initial 'R' and the letter 'f' ('fecit', Latin for made). Nonetheless, the model sheet may be dated around 1651: the open hatching and the dark sections, which have been developed in places, display a marked similarity to an etching of a family of beggars dating from around 1652.[198]

65
Self Portrait 1652

Canvas, 112.1 × 81 cm

Signed and dated at lower left: *.......dt.f.1652*

Vienna, Kunsthistorisches Museum, inv. no. 411

Bredius/Gerson 1969, no. 42; Chapman 1990, pp. 48, 87, 91, 134 and fig. 123; *Corpus*, vol. IV, no. 8

I N 1652 REMBRANDT painted a self portrait again, the first for many years (see cat. no. 60). He appears to have derived fresh inspiration in the interim, as the painting from Vienna is one of his most successful and original creations. The way in which he has represented himself here is very different from previous works. Hands on hips, with a somewhat defiant air, he faces the viewer in a frontal pose. His penetrating gaze, too, radiates self-assurance. As the portrait extends to below the waist, much of the picture is taken up with clothing, which is painted in an extremely free style.

The painter is plainly dressed. Over a black doublet with a stand-up collar he wears a brown robe, tied with a sash. This attire, though contemporary, scarcely makes a fashionable impression. It was probably working attire, designed chiefly to be practical and comfortable (see p. 65). In a drawing of *c*.1650 (cat. no. 63), Rembrandt not only adopts the same pose, but is also similarly dressed. According to the drawing's inscription, which is not autograph but probably dates from the seventeenth century, Rembrandt wore these clothes 'in his studio'.

One striking difference in comparison to the drawing is the type of hat. In the painting, Rembrandt does not wear a top hat but a black gathered beret, which makes a sixteenth-century impression and is probably derived from engraved artists' portraits. The beret, which had by then become Rembrandt's trademark (see p. 68), is the only reference to the past in this piece.

66*

Rembrandt?

Self Portrait 1654

Canvas, 72 × 58.5 cm

Signed and dated: *Rembrandt / f.1654*
(probably not autograph)

Cassel, Staatliche Kunstsammlungen,
Schloss Wilhelmshöhe, inv. no. 244

Bredius/Gerson 1969, no. 43;
Corpus, vol. IV, no. 9

THE DELFT COLLECTOR Valerius Röver (1686–1739) described this painting, which belonged to his collection from 1721 onwards, as 'the Portrait of Rembrandt ... painted by himself in his best period'. Nowadays, though, the attribution to Rembrandt is deemed highly questionable, but the poor condition of the canvas makes it difficult to resolve the question conclusively. The abraded paint layer, which has been painted over and is covered by a yellowed layer of varnish, was badly damaged in a sulphuric acid attack in 1977. It is therefore impossible to gain an impression of the original style of painting. Technical examination has made it clear, however, that the image was painted over an unfinished portrait of a woman, which was probably made in Rembrandt's workshop.

67*

Rembrandt?
Self Portrait 1655

Panel, 66 × 53 cm

Signed and dated at upper left: *Rembrandt f / 1655*

Vienna, Kunsthistorisches Museum,
inv. no. 9040

Bredius/Gerson 1969, no. 44;
Corpus, vol. IV, no. 11

A S IN THE CASE of the previous portrait (cat. no. 66) this painting is in such poor
condition that its authenticity can no longer be properly assessed. While the face
displays a superficial resemblance to Rembrandt, details of the subject's physiognomy
are scarcely perceptible. Since the man's gaze does not appear to be fixed on the viewer,
which is very unusual for a self portrait, this painting is unlikely to have been executed
by Rembrandt.

68 *

Rembrandt?

Self Portrait *c.1655*

Canvas, 69 × 59 cm

Signed at the right, above the shoulder: *Remb.....*

Florence, Galleria degli Uffizi, inv. no. 1890

Bredius/Gerson 1969, no. 45;
Corpus, vol. IV, no. 12

THIS PAINTING, which displays compositional similarities to the 1655 piece from Vienna (cat. no. 67), has been regarded since 1953 as an old copy. However, the Rembrandt Research Project recently concluded it probably is an authentic work after all, albeit in a poor condition. A striking detail is the odd kink in the jaw, which is depicted nowhere else as prominently as it is here. As in numerous other self portraits, this one was painted over an earlier image, in this case a still life.

69*
Self Portrait *c.1655*

Panel, 48.9 × 40.2 cm

Signed at upper left: *Rembrandt. f* (not autograph)

Vienna, Kunsthistorisches Museum, inv. no. 414

Bredius/Gerson 1969, no. 49; Chapman 1990, p. 87; *Corpus*, vol. IV, no. 13

M ANY LATE SELF portraits by Rembrandt have been poorly preserved. In this painting too, parts of the face have been overcleaned and subsequently overpainted. In this case, the condition may have been adversely affected by the fact that Rembrandt used a panel made of walnut, a wood that is particularly prone to shrink. As a result, cracks appeared in the panel in the course of time, which worked their way into the layer of paint and were retouched by a later hand. At some point another panel was attached at the back for additional support. Furthermore, it is possible that large parts of the painting were in such poor condition by then that it was decided to reduce the picture drastically in size. The lower edge still exhibits traces of the saw, and the image appears to have been cut along the other sides too. As a result, hardly any space has been left around the head with the wide-rimmed hat. Where the original paint is still present, the face can be seen to have been painted in a varied technique, using a combination of smooth brush-strokes and impasto. The facial features exhibit a striking resemblance to those of the large self portrait from 1652 (cat. no. 65), in which the head is likewise depicted frontally and with the same play of light. Judging by the more flaccid skin and sagging double chin, this small self portrait was probably made a few years later, around 1655. As in the large piece of 1652, Rembrandt has depicted himself here in everyday attire. Under a brown robe we see a red woollen undergarment that was worn to keep out the cold and was generally concealed under other clothes (see p. 66). That Rembrandt is depicted in his undershirt emphasises the informal nature of this self portrait.

70a*

ANONYMOUS ARTIST AFTER REMBRANDT

Portrait of Rembrandt with Pen, Inkpot and Sketchbook

*c.*1657

Canvas, *c.*74.5 × 61 cm (oval)

Signed and dated at upper left: *. . .brandt 165(3?)*
(not autograph)

San Francisco, The Fine Arts Museums of
San Francisco, Roscoe and Margaret Oakes
Collection, inv. no. 75.2.7

Bredius/Gerson 1969, no. 47; Chapman 1990,
p. 88 and fig. 127; *Corpus*, vol. IV, no. 10
(version 2)

70b*

Canvas, 75 × 62.3 cm

England, Private Collection

Bredius/Gerson 1969, no. 47 A;
Corpus, vol. IV, no. 10 (version 3)

70c*

Canvas, 85.5 × 65 cm
Signed and dated at lower right: *Rembrandt f 1657*
(not autograph)

Dresden, Staatliche Kunstsammlungen,
Gemäldegalerie Alte Meister, inv. no. 1569

Bredius/Gerson 1969, no. 46;
Corpus, vol. IV, no. 10 (version 4)

cat. no. 70a

THE UNUSUAL composition of this self portrait, which has been lost, is known from six painted copies, three of which are depicted here,[199] and a mezzotint (fig. 70a) by Jacob Gole (1660–1724). In terms of quality and condition, the paintings are rather mediocre, and the reproductive print probably gives the most reliable impression of the original. This is the only painted self portrait in which the artist has depicted himself as a draughtsman (compare cat. no. 46). We see Rembrandt drawing in a sketchbook with a cut feather, grasping an open inkpot in the other hand.

cat. no. 70b

cat. no. 70c

fig. 70a
JACOB GOLE, *Portrait of Rembrandt with Pen, Inkpot and Sketchbook*. Mezzotint, 322 × 236 mm. Amsterdam, Rijksmuseum, Rijksprentenkabinet.

71*
Self Portrait 1658

Canvas, 131 × 102 cm

Signed and dated at lower right, on the armrest:
Rembran.. / f. 1658

New York, The Frick Collection, inv. no. 06.1.97

Bredius/Gerson 1969, no. 50; Chapman 1990,
pp. 31, 48, 75, 88, 90, 92, 94–5, 121 and fig. V;
Corpus, vol. IV, no. 14

THE SIZE AND monumentality of the composition combine with the virtuoso painting technique to make this piece, beyond doubt, one of the most impressive of Rembrandt's self portraits. The master has depicted himself life-sized, seated in a frontal pose in an armchair. He may have worked with the aid of a large mirror (see pp. 11–12). The paint surface exhibits an extremely complex and varied structure, in which the paint was applied in several successive layers. The gold brocade scarf, in particular, is executed in remarkably free and audacious brushstrokes. The yellow jerkin and red sash, which has a pomegranate-shaped metal object dangling from it, confer a delightful colourfulness on the whole. The costume is composed of sixteenth-century components, to which several oriental motifs have been added (see p. 70). The figure's dignified appearance and rich attire have prompted some authors to hypothesise that Rembrandt portrayed himself as a prince. It seems more plausible, however, that here, as in numerous other self portraits, he assumed the identity of a celebrated painter from the past. In this case, the shiny gold material of his jerkin may have a special significance. In his *Schilder-Boeck*, published in 1604, Karel van Mander (1548–1606) describes famous sixteenth-century painters such as Jan Gossaert (active 1503, died 1532; p. 43, fig. 5) and Lucas van Leyden (active 1508, died 1533; p. 69, fig. 13) wearing gold-coloured garments to advertise their eminence.[200]

72
Self Portrait, Drawing on an Etching-Plate 1658

Etching on Japanese paper, 117 × 63 mm; one state

Signed and dated at lower centre:
Rembrandt f. 1658 Aet...

Paris, Musée du Petit Palais, Dutuit Collection,
inv. no. 7681

Hollstein S. 379; Hind 300A; White 1969, p. 149,
fig. 210; Boon 1969, pp. 4–9; Paris 1986, no. 100;
Chapman 1990, pp. 88, 95 and fig. 128

fig. 72a
REMBRANDT, *Self Portrait, Drawing on an
Etching-Plate*, 1658. Etching, 117 × 63 mm.
Vienna, Graphische Sammlung Albertina.

IT IS PARTICULARLY in some of his late self portraits that Rembrandt depicted himself as an artist. This last etched self portrait dates from 1658, the year in which he turned 52. Only two impressions are known of this etching: besides this pale specimen there is a better impression preserved in Vienna, also on Japanese paper (fig. 72a).[201] The print is rather narrow and Rembrandt has portrayed himself from very close by. While most of the shoulders and arms are cut off by the edge of the picture, the hands have been depicted clearly: the fingers and nails are quite distinct. The light surface in the left background, on which Rembrandt's head casts a shadow, may be the back of a chair. As the face and the cap are bathed in light, they contrast sharply with the extremely dark background.

The artist sits at a table on which lie several folded sheets of paper. In his right hand he wields an etching needle and in his left he holds an etching-plate that is placed on a soft engraving cushion to prevent it from slipping. Another such cushion may perhaps be depicted in the drawn self portrait in Rotterdam, which has been interpreted in a variety of ways (see cat. no. 77). Rembrandt wears the same white painter's cap in the self portraits in Paris from 1660 (cat. no. 79) and Kenwood House from about 1665–9 (cat. no. 83), in which he poses as a painter, with palette and brushes.

So rare are the impressions of this *Self Portrait, Drawing on an Etching-Plate* that the etching was not known to Gersaint, the compiler of the first catalogue of prints by Rembrandt in 1751.[202] Later on, several authors questioned its authenticity.[203] There is nothing about either the style of the self portrait or the signature, however, to fuel such doubts.[204] The regular lines with their varying tone, combined with the way in which the spaces are left partly open and the shadows rendered in irregular lines, are all characteristic of some of Rembrandt's late etchings.[205]

73
Self Portrait with Beret and Turned-Up Collar 1659

Canvas, 84.4 × 66 cm

Signed and dated at the left, by the chin:
Rembrandt f. 165(9)

Washington, National Gallery of Art, Andrew
W. Mellon Collection, inv. no. 1937.1.72

Bredius/Gerson 1969, no. 51;
Corpus, vol. IV, no. 18

WHEN MAKING A self portrait, the most practical arrangement for a right-handed painter such as Rembrandt would be to place the mirror to the left of the easel, so that the painting arm would not block his view (compare p. 11, fig. 4). In the mirror image thus obtained, the body would then incline somewhat to the right, how much depending on the angle with the mirror. The head would be placed at a slight angle to the torso, with the tip of the nose pointing to the right from the viewers vantage-point, and the left cheek would figure most prominently in the picture. This is the pose seen in most of Rembrandt's self portraits. Sometimes he adopted a frontal perspective, but the artist painted himself turning to the left only twice: in this self portrait from 1659 and the *Self Portrait as Zeuxis* from around 1662 (cat. no. 82).

This reversal gives a different view of Rembrandt's face. There is a small blemish on the right cheek, for instance, which is normally in the shadows, and on the right ear lobe there is a pimple. The light comes not from the left, as usual, but from the upper right, illuminating the face almost frontally. In this lighting, the right-hand side of his face is noticeably hollow-cheeked. The painter has portrayed himself here seated, his hands resting serenely in his lap. The red shape behind him, with its straight edge on the right, probably indicates the back of the chair, while the red patch in the lower left corner is a tablecloth.

It has been suggested that the unusual pose adopted in this self portrait was based on Raphael's famous *Portrait of Baldassare Castiglione*, after which Rembrandt had drawn a copy in 1639 when it was in Amsterdam (see pp. 170 and 172, figs. 53b and 53c).[206] There are certainly striking similarities to Raphael's composition, for instance in the position of the folded hands and the contours of the cloak draped over the left arm. However, it is open to question whether Rembrandt had any definite intention in mind with this paraphrase.[207] In comparison to his self portrait from 1640 (cat. no. 54), which combines the same example by Raphael with borrowings from Titian, Dürer and Lucas van Leyden, this painting is simpler in character and the clothing has no explicit allusions to glorious moments in the history of painting. A light coloured cap, which shows up under

fig. 73a
X-radiograph of cat. no. 73.

X-radiography (fig. 73a), was painted out by the master himself and replaced by a black beret. As a cap of this type occurs only in Rembrandt's self portraits with painters' attributes, it is possible that in this piece too, he initially intended to depict himself at work. We can only speculate as to why he should have changed his mind, but this alteration removed the only way of alluding to the painting profession.[208]

One possible explanation for the unusual pose in this painting is that Rembrandt wanted to introduce some variation into his succession of self portraits produced towards the end of the 1650s. In the style of painting, too, there is a discernible tendency to strike out in a new direction. The dynamic brushwork in the face, which makes a stark contrast with the even strokes used to paint the clothing and background, is extremely unusual even for a late Rembrandt (fig. 73b). The individual strokes have been left clearly visible and the capricious movements of the brush appear separate from the shapes they denote. Spots of reflected light on the nose, forehead and cheeks lie on top of the canvas, while quite close by, the greenish-grey colour of the ground (or possibly an intermediate layer applied locally) has been left exposed. The entire painting is characterised by contrasts of this kind. Vaguely adumbrated portions are furnished with sharp, drawing-like lines, as in the short hairs on the fur of the cloak. In the woolly hair protruding from the beret, the curls have been scratched into the wet paint with angular movements. The effect is to bring certain hairs to the fore and to make the immediate surroundings recede into the background. The contrasts between distant and close, indistinct and sharp, warm and cool colours, as well as flat and impasto brushstrokes do much to enhance the liveliness of this self portrait, in which the clothing and background have been kept extremely subdued.

The unusually free and sketch-like execution has sown doubts as to the painting's attribution. A plausible explanation might be, however, that Rembrandt stopped painting at a stage at which he usually carried on elaborating details and smoothing over abrupt transitions.[209] The faces in the self portraits in the Frick Collection (cat. no. 71) and the Metropolitan Museum of Art in New York (cat. no. 80) were also laid in with impasto brushstrokes, but these were subsequently covered with smoother painted layers and fine strokes. In the self portrait in Edinburgh (cat. no. 74) the final elaboration was completed down to the smallest detail. In the painting discussed here, on the other hand, the rough design for the face is still on the surface. Other parts of the picture, such as the beret and the light on the shoulders, have been worked out more thoroughly, and the whole makes a finished impression. Apparently the result achieved in this piece satisfied the painter at an early stage. According to the painters' biographer Arnold Houbraken (1660–1719), Rembrandt's motto was 'that a work is finished when the master has achieved his intention in it' (see p. 34).[210]

see p. 34

fig. 73b
Detail of cat. no. 73.

74

(London only)

Self Portrait with Beret and Turned-Up Collar 1659?

Canvas, 52.7 × 42.7 cm

Signed and dated at lower right:
Rembrandt / f.165(9?)

His Grace The Duke of Sutherland (on loan
to the National Gallery of Scotland, Edinburgh)

Bredius/Gerson 1969, no. 48;
Corpus, vol. IV, no. 15

THERE IS NO OTHER self portrait of Rembrandt that gives the viewer such a sense of confrontation with the painter. The suggestion of physical presence is evoked partly by the placement of the subject close to the edge of the picture and the relatively large rendering of the head.[211] As the torso is moved away from the centre and the head is turned at a fairly abrupt angle, with the cheek pressed against the raised collar of the doublet, the picture seems to capture a fleeting moment in time. In comparison to other self portraits, there is an avoidance of strong shadows; the uniform lighting exposes every unevenness in the face. The nose, the ridge of which traces a concave line down to its broad tip, is especially pronounced.

From our modern vantage-point, the rendering of the face in this self portrait resembles the eye of the camera, and the term 'photographic realism' has often been used in discussing it.[212] The anachronistic impression one has of looking at a photograph is enhanced by the painterly execution, which is unusually meticulous for Rembrandt. This is particulary clear in comparison to the self portrait from Washington (cat. no. 73), in which the illuminated parts of the face are painted in wide sweeps of the brush. In this piece Rembrandt adopted a far more careful approach; fuzzy spots of paint, thin lines and transparent layers are juxtaposed or overlap, but nowhere is the paint applied thickly. The forms are modelled softly in a wide variety of hues, and the different parts of the face are forged into a whole without any abruptness of line. Only the curly hair is painted with somewhat more vigorous brushstrokes, with some of the lines being scratched into the paint. This has been done in far less haste, however, than in the painting in Washington, and the highlights in the hair have been applied with care. The velvet beret has indeed been painted with a strikingly smooth touch, with the illuminated contours being indicated with a delicate line.

Whatever the great differences in brushwork, however, the self portraits in Edinburgh and Washington probably stem from the same period. Not only do they broadly correspond in terms of clothing, but also the physiognomy in the two pieces indicates the same phase of the aging process. Unfortunately, the date on the painting described here is not conclusive, as the last digit is nearly illegible. It seems quite possible, however, that it was originally a '9'.

Other self portraits from the late 1650s are worked out less elaborately, although the brushwork is in general restrained. Rembrandt apparently varied between two different levels of finishing in the late 1650s, of which the paintings in Edinburgh and Washington represent the opposite extremes.

75
Self Portrait with Beret, Unfinished _c.1659_

Panel, 30.7 × 24.3 cm

Aix-en-Provence, Musée Granet, inv. no. 860–1–171

Bredius/Gerson 1969, no. 58; _Corpus_, vol. IV, no. 16

Up to the middle of the twentieth century, this painting was accepted as an original by Rembrandt, but in 1969 it was dismissed as a later imitation by Gerson, whose opinion, with one exception, has been followed by other scholars.[213] However, recent examination of the panel by the Rembrandt Research Project suggests that not only is it unquestionably a seventeenth-century painting, but also on technical and stylistic grounds it should be accepted as an authentic work by Rembrandt, painted around 1659, but never finished.

Compared with other late self portraits, which are life-size, it is, unusually, much smaller. For works on a similar scale one has to turn back to self portraits done in 1632. Rosenberg, who saw in it 'all the boldness and immediacy of a Goya', believed that this difference from other contemporary self portraits could be explained by it being a preliminary study for a life-size painting.[214] But this is very unlikely since Rembrandt invariably painted directly on the final work, without the aid of a sketch. It should, therefore, be considered a work in its own right, intended for sale.

The artist, whose raised right shoulder suggests that it exactly records the image seen in the mirror, wears a black gown with a turned-up collar, and a brown beret sits at an angle on his head. Although the position of the head differs, Rembrandt painted himself in the same clothing in the self portraits in Washington (cat. no. 73) and Edinburgh (cat. no. 74).

Despite the thick, discoloured varnish, and the deterioration of the paint layer through age, the very sketchy execution of this small panel is still apparent. This is notable in the background, which was worked up to its present state in two separate stages. The striking and most effective combination of precise definition and very free brushstrokes describing the head and clothing can also be found in contemporary drawings, particularly in the self portrait in Vienna (cat. no. 78), which also shows the artist in similar dress.

CW

76

Attributed to Rembrandt

Self Portrait with Beret *c.1659*

Canvas, 68 × 56.5 cm

Stuttgart, Staatsgalerie, inv. no. 2614

Bauch 1966, no. 337; *Corpus*, vol. IV, no. 17

THE EMERGENCE OF this painting from the obscurity of a private collection and its acquisition for a very substantial sum of money by the Staatsgalerie in Stuttgart in 1961 gave rise to a highly charged debate about whether it was by Rembrandt or not, and even about in which century it was painted.[215] It became the first painting attributed to Rembrandt in which the answer to its authenticity was sought through scientific examination, a process which is now regularly used. At the time scholars were divided in their opinions, but only one catalogue of Rembrandt's paintings accepted it as an original.[216] Since then it has not entered the canon of works seriously considered as by Rembrandt. In deciding its authenticity it has to be borne in mind that the painting is in poor condition, with numerous paint losses, and it has suffered from later heavy-handed cleaning.

Building on the technical examinations made in the laboratory in the 1960s, the Rembrandt Research Project has convincingly established that it is a seventeenth-century painting and not from a later period. From our rapidly growing knowledge of Rembrandt's methods through scientific examination, it can be shown that the unusual quartz ground used on this painting can be found in a considerable number of other paintings by Rembrandt or his school. Moreover, the canvas is typical of that used by the artist, and it may possibly have come from the same roll of canvas used in Rembrandt's painting of *Jacob wrestling with the Angel* of *c*.1659 (Berlin, Staatliche Museen, Gemäldegalerie).[217]

The Rembrandt Research Project has also made a serious case for reconsidering the possibility that the painting might be by Rembrandt himself, rather than by a pupil or imitator. In view of the numerous changes made during the course of execution, it is most unlikely to be a copy after the master. It has been suggested that it is by Arent de Gelder (cat. no. 95), who was a pupil of Rembrandt in the early 1660s.[218] But, apart from the lack of any compelling comparison in De Gelder's work, the alterations made to the head, the collar and other parts of the costume, as well as the reduction in the number of highlights, can be matched in other authentic paintings by Rembrandt executed in the late 1650s. Moreover, the actual technique of painting can be similarly paralleled. The different type of beret, which radiography reveals originally covered the sitter's head, is the same as that in the self portrait in Edinburgh (cat. no. 74) and the 1659 self portrait in Washington (cat. no. 73). It may be unfinished, which would explain the lack of a signature.

This represents the first occasion on which the painting has been exhibited side by side with a group of authentic Rembrandt self portraits, and it will provide a stimulating opportunity to decide its exact status.

CW

77
Self Portrait *c*.1660

Pen and brown ink, 69 × 62 mm

Rotterdam, Museum Boijmans Van Beuningen, inv. no. R. 108

Benesch 1973, vol. V, no. 1176; Giltaij 1988, no. 34

REMBRANDT HAS portrayed himself from a frontal perspective in this drawing, wearing a hat that seems to be rendered in some detail, but whose shape, on further inspection, is rather obscure. Perhaps it is intended to be a painter's beret, like the one in the New York painting dated 1660 (cat. no. 80).[219] The rest of the little portrait, too, has been conveyed with a few simple strokes (compare cat. no. 45), as Rembrandt's reed pen did not permit subtlety of detail. Two brown blobs denote the eyes, whose penetrating gaze beneath the puckered frown of the eyebrows is characteristic of Rembrandt's self portraits.

The figure is enclosed within a lightly delineated frame, as if Rembrandt wished to convey the mirror at which he sat working. The artist is seated at a table and his hand, rendered in the form of a flattened oval, is slightly raised. The small line under this hand was formerly taken to denote a reed pen, the implication being that the artist was depicting himself at work.[220] This is not very likely, however, partly because the position of the hand would not be a very comfortable one for drawing and partly because it is too high above the point of the supposed pen. The diagonal hatching at the lower centre, which appears to have been merged into a cohesive whole with smears of the finger, also calls this interpretation in question. This hatching serves to suggest the back of a piece of paper that Rembrandt is holding up: a print or drawing. Rembrandt has probably depicted himself here not as an artist but as an art connoisseur. The picture displays certain similarities to the etched portrait of the apothecary Abraham Francen from *c*.1657 (fig. 77a).[221] This collector also sits at a table and is holding up a sheet of paper for close inspection.

fig. 77a
REMBRANDT, *Portrait of Abraham Francen*, c.1657.
Etching (second state), 158 × 208 mm.
Amsterdam, Rijksmuseum, Rijksprentenkabinet.

78
Self Portrait c.1660

Pen and brownish-black ink, brush and grey and white ink on brownish paper, 82 × 71 mm

Vienna, Graphische Sammlung Albertina, inv. no. 25.449

Vienna 1969–70, no. 60; Benesch 1973, vol. V, no. 1177; New York 1997, no. 60

I N THIS DRAWING, Rembrandt stares with wide-open eyes and a stern expression. On his head he wears a white cap, as in the painted self portraits in Paris and at Kenwood House (cat. nos. 79 and 83) showing him at work. The sheet probably served as a preliminary study for the self portrait in Paris dated 1660, so it may be assumed to have originated around that time. The representation of the face and collar resembles the unfinished self portrait in Aix-en-Provence that is attributed to Rembrandt and dated around 1659 (cat. no. 75).

The resemblance to the self portraits at Kenwood House and Paris has inspired some scholars to interpret a line on the right of the drawing as part of the edge of a painting on an easel, as in the paintings referred to above. But Rembrandt has depicted himself here not as a painter but as an art connoisseur, as is clear from a piece of paper at the lower left corner.[222] This is also how he portrayed himself in the drawing in Rotterdam (cat. no. 77). However, as the sheet discussed here has been cut along the lower edge, it is unfortunately impossible to determine exactly what action is depicted.

This small sketch has been made using a rather complicated technique. The support consists of a brownish sheet on which the contours of the figure were drawn with a reed pen; the details were then elaborated with white and grey washes. At one of the final stages of the finishing process, Rembrandt added white highlights to the cap with opaque paint. That the washes in the background were made by another hand, as has sometimes been assumed, would appear to be a misconception.[223]

The deliberately bright lighting of the painter's cap against the dark background was the clinching argument for Otto Benesch, the eminent scholar of Rembrandt's drawn oeuvre who purchased this sheet in 1927 for the Albertina in Vienna, to attribute the piece to Rembrandt.[224] The rapid and expressive treatment of the facial features displays the masterful hand of Rembrandt. This, combined with the unmistakable resemblance to the paintings referred to above, leaves no doubt as to the drawing's authenticity. The critical expression on the face of the artist – with its curly eyebrow at the left – makes a striking 'signature'.

79*
Self Portrait at the Easel 1660

Canvas, 110.9 × 90.6 cm

Signed and dated at lower right: *Rem . . . / f.1660*

Paris, Musée du Louvre, inv. no. 1747

Bredius/Gerson 1969, no. 53; Foucart 1982, pp. 72–5; Chapman 1990, pp. 90, 95–7, 99, 101, 121, 122, 135 and fig. 139; *Corpus*, vol. IV, no. 19

IN THIS WORK from 1660, Rembrandt poses for the first time with his painter's attributes, behind the easel. Previously he had omitted from his self portraits any direct allusion to the painting profession, with the exception of *The Painter in his Studio* from *c.*1629 (cat. no. 17) in which his identity, however, was of secondary importance. After 1660, he would depict himself on several occasions with palette, brushes and maulstick (cat. nos. 82 and 83), although he sometimes painted these items out again later (see, for example, cat. no. 84).

Here Rembrandt is seated in a chair, a common position in which to paint in the seventeenth century (see cat. no. 17). A wooden panel is set up on the easel, which is rather odd, as the self portrait described here is painted on canvas. Although the painter's clothing contains sixteenth-century elements, the white cap was a contemporary item of headgear, which men wore around the house. It appears from the inventory of his estate that Rembrandt possessed a number of linen 'men's caps' (see p. 72). He probably wore one at home, including when he was painting.

X-ray analysis of this painting reveals that Rembrandt initially depicted himself in a large, dark beret, like the one he wears, for instance, in another self portrait from 1660 (cat. no. 80). As the top layer of paint is abraded in places, we can see with the naked eye that Rembrandt altered other parts of the composition too. Remains of an earlier design glimmer through, from which it may be inferred that the body initially had a more frontal pose and the hand with the brushes was positioned further to the right.

80*
Self Portrait 1660

Canvas, 81 × 67.6 cm

Signed and dated at lower right:
Rembrandt / f. 1660

New York, The Metropolitan Museum of Art,
Bequest of Benjamin Altman, inv. no. 14.40.618

Bredius/Gerson 1969, no. 54; New York 1982,
pp. 67–71; Tümpel 1986, p. 368, no. A 73;
Chapman 1990, pp. 87–8 and fig. 125; New York
1995–6, vol. I, p. 20, figs. 14–15 and p. 48, figs.
50–1; vol. II, no. 15; *Corpus*, vol. IV, no. 20

THE COMPLICATED genesis of this self portrait and the way it was painted refute the doubts that have recently been expressed concerning its authenticity.[225] Technical examination has revealed that this piece underwent the process, so characteristic of late paintings by Rembrandt, of constant changes in the composition, especially in the shape and size of the hat. The face was laid in using vigorous, confident brushstrokes that were subsequently toned down, in part, with thin, smoother layers of paint – a technique found in several of the master's self portraits (see, for example, cat. nos. 71 and 74). The facial expression, largely defined by the wrinkled frown and raised eyebrows, displays a striking similarity to the *Self Portrait as the Apostle Paul* (cat. no. 81) that was made the following year.

Just as in the large self portrait from Vienna, produced in 1652 (cat. no. 65), Rembrandt has depicted himself here in working clothes. In contrast to the detailed delineation of the face, the brown coat is rendered quite sketchily. The numerous coloured strokes and stripes, which appear to suggest light reflected in shiny material, are a striking feature of this part of the painting.

81

Self Portrait
as the Apostle Paul 1661

Canvas, 93.2 × 79.1 cm

Signed and dated at the left, next to the shoulder:
Rembrandt.f. / 1661

Amsterdam, Rijksmuseum, inv. no. A 4050

Bredius/Gerson 1969, no. 59; Chapman 1990,
pp. 9, 35, 63, 105, 120–7, 129 and fig. VII; *Corpus*,
vol. IV, no. 21; on the provenance of the painting
see p. 51

fig. 81a
REMBRANDT, *The Apostle Paul in Captivity*, 1627.
Panel, 72.8 × 60.2 cm. Stuttgart, Staatsgalerie.

fig. 81b
REMBRANDT (AND STUDIO?), *The Apostle Paul
in Captivity*, c.1657. Canvas, 131.5 × 104.4 cm.
Washington, National Gallery of Art,
Widener Collection.

fig. 81c
REMBRANDT, *An Elderly Man as Saint Paul*, 165(9?).
Canvas, 102 × 85.5 cm. London, National Gallery.

IN THIS PAINTING, Rembrandt for the first time assumed the role of a well-known historical character. The hilt of a sword projects from his doublet, and he is holding a half unrolled manuscript. Both objects are attributes of the apostle Paul, one of the earliest and most influential preachers of the gospel. The sword refers not only to Paul's martyrdom – he was beheaded – but also to the 'sword of the Spirit' from his Epistle to the Ephesians (New Testament, 6: 17). It is possible that Rembrandt intended this epistle to be depicted in the scroll-shaped manuscript. The Hebrew-looking letters at the upper left of the front sheet have been read as 'EFESIS' ('Ephesus').[226] On his head Rembrandt wears not the painter's cap familiar from other late self portraits but a sort of turban, undoubtedly an allusion to the Middle East of the Bible.

During the most recent restoration in 1990–1, the bars of a window were discovered in the background on the right, so that this scene can be interpreted as depicting Paul in captivity. The apostle was imprisoned no fewer than four times. The bars could also be read metaphorically: in the letter to the Ephesians, which he is supposed to have written in prison, Paul refers to himself several times as 'the prisoner of Jesus Christ' or 'the prisoner of the Lord' (3: 1 and 4: 1).[227] In this context, the strong light that beams down from the upper left and illuminates both face and manuscript could also have a symbolic meaning. For in the letter to the Ephesians, Paul uses light as a metaphor for faith: 'walk as children of light, for the fruit of the Spirit is in all goodness and righteousness and truth and Awake thou that sleepest, and arise from the dead, and Christ shall give thee light' (5: 8–14).

Rembrandt was particularly interested in the apostle Paul, as evidenced by his numerous representations of the saint throughout his career. In one of his earliest works – from 1627 – the imprisoned apostle has stopped writing for the moment and has withdrawn into himself (fig. 81a).[228] That he is lost in contemplation is clear from the raised eyebrows and wrinkled brow. A similar expression can be seen in the *Self Portrait as the Apostle Paul*, and although the face also betrays a degree of surprise, it will primarily have been intended to appear pensive. Indeed, a seventeenth-century manual for artists

notes that a wrinkled brow generally indicates 'the contemplation of many great things'.[229]

In the visual arts, Paul is almost always depicted as an old man with a long beard, with a receding hairline. Rembrandt's 1627 portrait is entirely in line with this tradition. Not long afterwards he painted the saint again with the same facial features and in later pieces from his workshop too Paul has a full beard.[230] For a painting made in or around 1657 (fig. 81b) an elderly model was used who often posed for Rembrandt – in 1661 for instance, the year in which this self portrait was made.[231] This makes it unlikely that Rembrandt depicted himself as Paul for lack of a suitable model, as has previously been assumed.[232] In the biography of fellow artist Adriaen van der Werff (1659–1722), written around 1720 by his son-in-law, it is said that Rembrandt lived in an age in which 'beards were the commonest thing in the world' and that in Amsterdam he could have as a model 'any face worth painting'.[233]

Hence, Rembrandt, whose own facial features are clearly recognisable here, made a deliberate choice to depict himself as Paul. It has been suggested that in this self portrait he was expressing a special affinity to the apostle. According to this theory, his identification with Paul related not only to his religious faith but also to his art: 'Rembrandt, having throughout his life repeatedly depicted the events and the lessons of the scriptures, perceived his artistic mission as explicator of the Bible as akin to Paul's teaching mission.'[234] Psychological interpretations of this kind are hard to prove. We know that in seventeenth-century Protestant circles Paul was considered as the most important preacher of the Christian faith, and this could be one of the reasons why Rembrandt felt a special kinship to him.

That Rembrandt portrayed himself as Paul is less curious than it now appears. Many people living in the seventeenth century had themselves portrayed as a biblical or mythological character. Rembrandt and his pupils too painted *portraits historiés* of this kind. In the late 1650s and early 1660s, numerous half-figures of apostles and evangelists were created in Rembrandt's studio, some of which display clear portrait-like features.[235] Thus in or around 1659, an unknown old man with a short grey beard had himself immortalised as Paul in a painting by Rembrandt, complete with sword and book (fig. 81c). It has sometimes been assumed that all these apostle figures belonged to a single series. This is unlikely, however, as they are too dissimilar in terms of size, style of painting and quality.[236] A more likely explanation is that there was a vogue for this type of picture around 1660, which could have prompted Rembrandt to portray himself in this way too.

It has already been noted that Rembrandt did not always finish his late self portraits in the same way (see also cat. nos. 73 and 83). Here he chose a vigorous style of painting, in which the paint was largely applied wet-in-wet. Especially in the turban, we see clearly how Rembrandt applied thick daubs of paint in different hues over one another to give a convincing impression of the way in which the wrapped material is stretched across the forehead (p. 33, fig. 49). With the numerous accents and highlights applied in the face and clothing, the whole nonetheless makes a finished impression. The painter has scratched lines into the paint along the four edges of the canvas, furnishing the completed representation with a kind of frame. To date, no other painting by the master has been found with a line framing the picture in this way.[237] Possibly the canvas was originally somewhat larger, and Rembrandt was indicating its eventual format. In so doing he left parts of the lower arms and the manuscript out of the picture, enhancing the effect of the painting as a slice of reality.

215

82
Self Portrait as Zeuxis c.1662

Canvas, 82.5 × 65 cm

Cologne, Wallraf-Richartz-Museum,
inv. no. 2526

Bredius/Gerson 1969, no. 61; Chapman 1990,
pp. 95, 101–4, 128 and fig. 145;
Corpus, vol. IV, no. 22

NOT LONG AFTER depicting himself as the apostle Paul (cat. no. 81), Rembrandt posed once again as a historical figure. This time he cast himself in the role of a renowned fellow artist from classical antiquity. The Greek painter Zeuxis, who flourished in Athens in the late fifth century BC, was praised for his great skill as a painter. He could not only depict reality with peerless illusionism, but actually surpassed it. When commissioned to make a painting of Helen of Troy, the most beautiful woman in the world, Zeuxis had the five best-looking girls from the neighbourhood pose for him and then combined the finest parts of each girl's body into a paragon of beauty. This anecdote was often related in the late seventeenth century to support the academic view that the painter should select only the beautiful things from nature and reject all that is ugly.

A less well-known anecdote puts the Greek painter in a very different light. In the appendix to his *Schilder-Boeck*, Karel van Mander (1548–1606) recounts that the aged Zeuxis died literally by suffocating with laughter while making a portrait of 'a wrinkled, droll old woman'.[238] This tale seems to have appealed greatly to the imagination of Rembrandt's circle. His pupil Samuel van Hoogstraten (cat. no. 96) mentions it twice in his *Inleyding tot de hooge schoole der schilderkonst* (Introduction to the Art of Painting), published in 1678 (p. 26, fig. 36).[239] Another pupil of Rembrandt's, Arent de Gelder (cat. no. 95) painted the subject in 1685, in combination with a self portrait (fig. 82a).[240] The painter is seated at his easel and glances over his shoulder with a wide grin. Posing at the far left is the 'droll old woman' with an apple or orange in her hand – possibly an ironic allusion to the golden apple presented to Venus as fairest of the godesses.

De Gelder's painting points the way, as it were, to the true subject of Rembrandt's self portrait, which was for many years an iconographical mystery.[241] A comparison of the two works reveals striking similarities. In both cases, the protagonist turns and grins at the viewer. Rembrandt has expressed his merriment by painting the eyes slightly screwed up, the eyebrows raised and the mouth half-open.[242] That he himself sat for the portrait is apparent from the shape of his head and from characteristic facial features

fig. 82a
ARENT DE GELDER, *Self Portrait as Zeuxis*, 1685.
Canvas, 142 × 169 cm. Frankfurt am Main,
Städelsches Kunstinstitut.

such as his prominent, broad-tipped nose. The white cap and the maulstick identify him as a painter; the diagonal stripes at the bottom of the picture probably represent paintbrushes.[243] The reference to the painting profession was initially clearer still, as Rembrandt had intended to depict himself at work. The X-radiograph shows that the left hand (the right from the point of view of the figure in the painting) was initially raised and held a brush (fig. 82b).[244]

In themselves, the smirk and the painter's attributes are not conclusive evidence of the subject. The key to interpreting Rembrandt's painting is the curious figure on the left, who is only partly visible.[245] With some difficulty we perceive at the top an unattractive face with a large nose and jutting chin. Around the figure's neck hang several linked chains, and the lower part of the body is rendered very indistinctly. Some have taken the figure to represent a philosopher or an ancient bust, prompting the most varied interpretations.[246] Comparison with the scene painted by De Gelder reveals, however, that it must be the ugly old woman who triggered Zeuxis' fatal fit of laughter. This is confirmed by the earliest known reference to Rembrandt's painting, in an auction catalogue dating from 1758. It describes the scene, which must have been more clearly visible than it is today, as 'Rembrandt painting an old Woman'.[247] Rembrandt has not in

fig. 82b
X-radiograph of cat. no. 82.

fig. 82c

REMBRANDT, *Homer*, 1663. Canvas, 107 × 82 cm. The Hague, Mauritshuis.

fact depicted the old woman herself here, but the portrait that Zeuxis is making of her. To the right of the female figure is a dark area that stands out against the somewhat lighter background. This probably denotes the edge of a canvas or panel that is set up in front of the painter on an – invisible – easel. On further inspection we also see that Rembrandt has placed his maulstick against the work he is painting.

No Dutch painters other than Rembrandt and De Gelder ever chose this subject. De Gelder may have seen his teacher's painting while working in the latter's Amsterdam workshop between about 1662 and 1664, and taken it as a point of departure, years later, for his own piece. Nonetheless, there are significant discrepancies in size and degree of detail between the two paintings. It has been suggested that Rembrandt's painting was originally as large as De Gelder's and virtually identical in composition.[248] But it may be inferred from the cusping (see cat. no. 85) that is visible on the left that the canvas cannot have been more than about ten centimetres larger on that side.[249] Along the other three sides, too, only narrow strips are missing. De Gelder must therefore have expanded Rembrandt's example on his own initiative, something he also did with other compositions that he derived from his teacher.[250]

The question remains, why did Rembrandt and, in his footsteps, Arent de Gelder, combine the story of Zeuxis with a self portrait? Some have sought to explain it by citing the art theoretical debates that waged in the latter half of the seventeenth century.[251] Followers of the increasingly popular Classicism saw Zeuxis as their champion, because he had achieved ideal beauty in his portrait of Helen of Troy. These same Classicists rebuked Rembrandt for his stubborn refusal to idealise reality. In reaction to this, Rembrandt would have portrayed himself as Zeuxis painting an ugly subject. However, there is as yet no evidence that Rembrandt's work attracted this type of criticism during his lifetime.

Another explanation that merits consideration concerns a different aspect of Zeuxis' fame – his gift for depicting emotions.[252] This is emphasised in the aforementioned book by Rembrandt's pupil Van Hoogstraten, who twice refers to the anecdote of Zeuxis laughing himself to death. Rembrandt too was greatly preoccupied with rendering emotional states, which Van Mander calls one of the most important elements of the art of painting (see cat. nos. 22 and 23). This was expressed not only in his history pieces but also in his self portraits, especially those produced as etchings. It is not inconceivable that in adopting the role of the celebrated Zeuxis, Rembrandt wanted to emphasise this particular aspect of his talent. By choosing the story in which the Greek painter laughs himself to death, he also included a passing allusion to the relative nature of all earthly things. That Rembrandt was alluding here to his own approaching death seems far-fetched. More to the point, we may note that the aging artist had by no means lost his sense of humour.

Partly inspired by the notion that Rembrandt was referring to his own mortality in this piece, some authors have situated this self portrait at the end of his life.[253] On stylistic grounds, however, the painting should be dated somewhat earlier, around 1662. The paint has been applied just as freely and with as much impasto as in *Homer* (fig. 82c), a painting that Rembrandt worked on in the years 1661–3. In both cases, the shiny gold shawl is painted with long brushstrokes and thick highlights applied with the palette-knife. The heads, too, which have been modelled in the wet paint with vigorous movements, are rendered in a very similar manner. If this self portrait was indeed made in the same period as *Homer*, this coincides with Arent de Gelder's presence in Rembrandt's workshop.

83
Self Portrait with
Two Circles *c.*1665–9

Canvas, 114.3 × 94 cm

London, English Heritage, Kenwood House,
The Iveagh Bequest, inv. no. 57

Bredius/Gerson 1969, no. 52; Chapman 1990,
pp. 95, 97–101, 102, 121–2, 135 and fig. VI;
Corpus, vol. IV, no. 23

fig. 83a
X-radiograph of cat. no. 83.

THERE ARE FEW self portraits that have appealed to the imagination so much over the centuries as this painting from Kenwood House. This is not only because of its great pictorial qualities and monumentality but also because of the two enigmatic circles, or rather parts of circles, behind the painter. Countless explanations have been advanced for this curious background feature.[254] The short slanting stripes in the upper right corner have been interpreted as the wrinkles of a hung canvas. But in that case, the circumference of the right-hand circle would be pulled slightly out of line, which it is not. Rather, the suggestion is created that the curved lines are drawn directly on the back wall. An alternative theory is that the lines denote the hemispheres in a map of the world, a common wall decoration in Dutch interiors. But the circles are too far apart for such a map, nor do they contain any topographical marks, not even in the initial design. Other hypotheses range from kabbalistic signs and the *rota aristotelis* (the Aristotelian concept of the world in its true form, in which the first mover gives matter form so it can be united with the soul) to symbols of *ars* and *exercitatio* (theory and practice). To offset these in some cases rather fanciful interpretations, it has been suggested that the circles play a purely aesthetic role, serving to emphasise the underlying geometrical structure of the composition.

One of the more plausible arguments links the circles to a well-known *topos* from the theory of art, namely the ability to draw a circle freehand as evidence of consummate artistic skill.[255] Because of its closed form, the circle was associated with perfection and eternity, and was therefore ideal as a symbol of artistic excellence. In his *Schilder-Boeck*, for instance, Karel van Mander (1548–1606) relates the anecdote of 'Giotto's O'. The Italian artist Giotto (1266/7–1337), when asked to supply proof of his artistic skill for the pope, complied by drawing a perfect circle with a single fluent movement.[256] With this story in mind, one might interpret the circles behind Rembrandt as a reference to his master craftsmanship (compare cat. no. 46). However, close scrutiny reveals that the curves were not drawn in a single movement at all, but in a succession of short brushstrokes. The theory also fails to account for the fact that there are two of them. Still, of all the proposed interpretations, this one remains thus far the most attractive.

That Rembrandt intended this self portrait as a comment on his artistic skill is all the more plausible given his demonstrative pose with his painter's attributes. In his right hand he holds a rectangular palette, a maulstick and several brushes, and the reddish-brown patch under his hand could denote a painting rag. Along the upper right edge of the representation the stretcher of a canvas is just visible; the accompanying easel falls outside the pictorial plane. X-radiography reveals that Rembrandt had initially intended to depict himself at work (fig. 83a). In his first design, the body was angled more to the right and the painter was applying a brush to the canvas with his raised hand. In the left hand he held several more brushes, together with the maulstick he used to support his painting hand.

With a few swift but effective brushstrokes, Rembrandt then altered this active pose to a more frontal angle, moving all the painter's attributes to the right and depicting his other hand resting on his hip. This change is characteristic of Rembrandt's ambivalent attitude towards working with a mirror. On the one hand he was apparently driven by a desire to record things exactly as he saw them reflected, but on the other hand he did not want the viewer to recognise the picture immediately as a mirror image. This may well explain why he etched so many of his self portraits, as in this technique the mirror image is reversed again when prints are pulled from the etching-plate.[257]

The end result radiates considerably more serenity and monumentality than the

initial design. The sketchlike execution of the hands and painter's attributes arouses the impression that Rembrandt made these changes within a few seconds (fig. 83b), but did not develop them in detail. Other parts of the painting too appear to be unfinished.[258] The white cap, for instance, consists largely of a few white streaks and the fur trimmings of the *tabbaard* (a gown originating in the sixteenth century, which was worn by painters in Rembrandt's time) have been quickly dashed off. The contours of the torso are suggested with wide brushstrokes on the right and left, with traces of the brush still visible. The many scratches in the wet paint, for instance in the decorated edge (the so-called smocking) of the white shirt, appear to have been intended as provisional indications. Similar scratches are found in the moustache and above the left eye socket. All in all, the head and background are elaborated in the greatest detail. As Rembrandt stands further away from the viewer here than in his other self portraits, the by now familiar wrinkles and folds of skin are less noticeable. The way in which the richly varied flesh tints merge into one another gives the face an extremely lifelike quality. The question of whether this self portrait is in fact unfinished, as has been assumed, is difficult to answer and not particularly relevant, given the overwhelming impression the painting makes in its present state.

fig. 83b
Detail of cat. no. 83.

84
Self Portrait at the Age of 63

1669

Canvas, 86 × 70.5 cm

Signed and dated at lower left, next to the back:
... t: f / 1669

London, National Gallery, inv. no. 221

Bredius/Gerson 1969, no. 55; Chapman 1990,
pp. 128, 130–2 and fig. VIII; *Corpus*, vol. IV, no. 24

Rembrandt continued painting self portraits until his death. The work shown here is from the last year of his life. The year 1669 it displays was in fact only discovered a few decades ago during restoration.[259] Until then, the self portrait had been assigned a much earlier date, in the early 1660s, and it was believed that in the last phase of his life Rembrandt had felt both his artistic and mental faculties declining (see cat. no. 86). But this painting demonstrates the opposite. The artist has depicted himself with conspicuous vitality. He looks at the viewer with an acute gaze, while the hint of a smile plays around his lips. The history of the painting's development, which can be traced in the X-radiograph (fig. 84a), likewise indicates that Rembrandt tackled this piece full of inspiration and verve. He made numerous changes in the course of his work to achieve the best possible result.[260]

In the first design the hands were not folded; in his right hand the artist held a long, thin object, probably a paintbrush. Thus here as in his other late self portraits, Rembrandt started off depicting himself at work and later changed his mind. He made a comparable change to the hat, which was initially more similar to the white cap in his self portraits in Paris, Cologne and Kenwood House (cat. nos. 79 and 82–3).[261] Since Rembrandt is endowed with a painter's attributes in all these pieces, the conclusion seems justified that he wore a cap of this kind while working. When he painted out the brush in the work described here, he found it necessary to replace this painter's cap with a flat hat of reddish-brown material worn over an undercap. Some alterations were also made to the clothing. In the initial design, the collar of a shirt appears to be depicted, but the dark fur collar of the doublet was later painted over it. The white paint of the earlier collar is still dimly visible through the present coat of paint, however.

The clothing that Rembrandt wears in the definitive version of the painting is not contemporary. He took the apparel from engraved artists' portraits, just as he had done almost thirty years before in the stately self portrait from 1640 (cat. no. 54). This time he did not choose a sixteenth-century painter, but went back even further in time. The high-necked doublet with the little fur collar can be found in the portraits of Dieric Bouts

fig. 84a
X-radiograph of cat. no. 84.

223

(1400?–1475) and Rogier van der Weyden (1399–1464), which were published in 1572 by Domenicus Lampsonius and again in 1610 by Hendrick Hondius (see p. 71, fig. 17). Thus Rembrandt depicted himself here not as a practising painter – as was his initial intention and as he had done in the self portraits in Paris and Kenwood House – but in the guise of a master from the past.

Aside from the fact that Rembrandt changed his mind about how he wanted to present himself while making this self portrait, he may also have had aesthetic reasons for some of the changes described above. The omission of the paintbrush and the folding of the hands introduces a more serene note into the composition, and does not distract attention from the face. A similar effect is achieved by making the cap smaller and giving it the same warm colour as the doublet. Furthermore, the light hues are toned down in several places, as in the white of the original collar for instance, which again leads the viewer's eye to the face, where the forehead and tip of the nose receive most light. The light falling on the blank rear wall, too, which forms a halo, as it were, around the head, draws attention to the painter's wrinkled face. In comparison with the self portrait from 1640, in which the painter was still depicting himself in smart attire and with a provocative air, this portrait radiates more directness and simplicity.[262]

The fact that the 63-year-old Rembrandt has made constant adjustments to this self portrait by no means conjures up the image of an artist who has lost his flair. To the aging master, painting was still a creative process, which was not finished until the final brushstroke had been applied.

85

(The Hague only)

Self Portrait *c.1669*

Canvas, 71 × 54 cm

Florence, Galleria degli Uffizi, inv. no. 1871

Bredius/Gerson 1969, no. 60; Chapman 1990, p. 130 and fig. 168; *Corpus*, vol. IV, no. 25

THIS PAINTING originates from the famous gallery of self portraits of Cardinal Leopoldo de' Medici (1617–75) in Florence (p. 49, fig. 12). The piece is already listed in an inventory of the Medici collection enumerating the acquisitions made in the years 1663–71. It was probably purchased directly from the artist by Leopoldo's nephew, Cosimo III de' Medici (1642–1723), who travelled to the Netherlands in 1667 and again in 1669.[263] During his first journey he visited several painters' workshops on 29 December, including that of 'Reinbrent, pittore famoso (the famous painter Rembrandt)'. It is improbable that Cosimo purchased the self portrait on this occasion. His travel journal expressly states that none of the painters he visited had completed works on the premises, so that the Florentine had to visit private collections to see paintings by the masters concerned.

On 29 June 1669, three months before Rembrandt's death, Cosimo undertook a second journey to Amsterdam and again visited several workshops, on this occasion purchasing some of the paintings he admired. The less detailed travel journal refers merely to the 'più eccellenti maestri (the finest masters)'. There seems little doubt that this included Rembrandt, who had after all been called a 'pittore famoso' in the journal of two years earlier. Although there is no conclusive evidence for it, Cosimo seems likely to have come into the possession of the self portrait discussed here at this time.

A dating of the painting in or shortly before 1669 would also appear probable on the basis of Rembrandt's physiognomy. The puffed-up face, showing clear signs of age, greatly resembles the self portraits from London and The Hague (cat. nos. 84 and 86), which are known to have been painted in the last year of the artist's life. Unfortunately, it is not easy to assess the style of painting because of the poor condition in which the canvas has been preserved.[264] For the same reason, details of the clothing are hard to pick out, such as the collar (of a white shirt?) and the upper section of the jerkin. It is unclear whether the painter is wearing a chain or a ribbon on his chest, nor can we establish exactly what sort of object is hanging from it.[265]

fig. 85a
X-radiograph of cat. no. 85.

On his head the painter wears a wide gathered beret, a type of headgear that was common in the sixteenth century and can be seen, for instance, in Raphael's famous portrait of Baldassare Castiglione (p. 170, fig. 53b). In this portrait, which served as a source of inspiration for an etched and a painted self portrait, executed in 1639 and 1640 respectively (cat. nos. 53 and 54), we also encounter a hairnet of the type that Rembrandt wears here under his beret. Hairnets were popular in the sixteenth century among men with long hair.[266] This net, like the other items of his apparel, may be interpreted as an allusion to a former time, certainly given the fact that by 1669 Rembrandt had already lost much of his hair. In this painting it appears that he has once again adopted the role of a celebrated artist from the past.

The painting was originally of a different size. It has been suggested that the canvas was enlarged in the seventeenth century to make it the same size as the other self portraits in the Medici collection.[267] The narrow additions attached along three sides date from a later time, however, and there is good reason to assume that the canvas was actually reduced in size quite drastically prior to this operation. For none of the sides displays cusping — the ripples that appear in the weave when unprepared canvas is stretched; when the ground is applied, these distortions are fixed in the paint layer. The absence of cusping on four sides generally suggests that the painted canvas has been reduced in size. This is also indicated by the abrupt way in which the figure is cut off by the edge of the picture on the left, and the absence of a signature.[268]

From the X-radiograph too it may be inferred that this self portrait was originally larger (fig. 85a). In the lower right corner, brushstrokes are visible that appear to belong to an initial design for the hands, most of which must have been lost when the canvas was cut. It is now no longer possible to ascertain whether the hands could be seen in the completed painting, or whether Rembrandt had painted them out again. It can be deduced from the X-radiograph, however, that the composition of the costume and the shape of the beret have been altered substantially. The aging artist kept making improvements while working on this piece, and did not flinch from the constant changes this entailed.

86 Self Portrait 1669

Canvas, 63.5 × 57.8 cm

Signed and dated at the left, above the shoulder:
Rembrandt / f.1669

The Hague, Royal Cabinet of Paintings
Mauritshuis, inv. no. 840

Bredius/Gerson 1969, no. 62; Chapman 1990,
pp. 128, 130, 131–2 and fig. 169; *Corpus*, vol. IV,
no. 26

FOR MANY YEARS this painting was the only self portrait known to have been executed by Rembrandt in the year of his death. This provoked countless reflections on the artist's approaching death that could supposedly be read in his features: 'Under the purple headscarf with its narrow gold stripes the face has a pensive gaze, silent and alone . . . The end was not far away.'[269] Prevailing views of Rembrandt's last year changed dramatically, however, when the year 1669 was discovered on the self portrait in London (cat. no. 84), in which no-one had hitherto discerned an empty look or signs of exhaustion. The painting from Florence (cat. no. 85), which almost certainly dates from the same period, also displays a spry old man who meets the beholder's gaze with an alert eye.

In comparison with the self portraits in London and Florence, the double chin has sagged a little more here, the cheeks are more sunken and the grey hair longer. These details suggest that the painter must be somewhat older, and that this is indeed the last known self portrait by Rembrandt.[270] Aside from the understandable signs of age, the face does not really exhibit those indications of mental decline that earlier authors claimed to detect. This image was probably fostered in part by the romantic notion of the unsung genius, which had taken hold of the popular imagination since Vincent van Gogh (1853–90), and also by the style of painting. The facial features display a certain vagueness, caused by the fact that the details of the face are not fully developed here.

Recent research in the conservation studio of the Mauritshuis has given us more information concerning the way in which the painting came into being.[271] On the greyish-brown ground a preliminary design was laid in with dark brown paint, to which thin white paint and organic red were added. At the next stage, the painter used flesh tints for the further development of the face, applying thick white highlights on the brow and prominent parts such as the nose, cheekbone and chin. Because of the loose manner of painting, which is clearly visible, for instance, in the pouches under the left eye, the brown underlayer and ground was left exposed in several places, such as by the eyes, around the mouth and at the neck.

At later stages of the painting process too, these places remained 'open', indicating a limited degree of finishing. Little was done to make the details in the face more precise. At the final stage, the painter did introduce numerous reddish-brown touches, for instance near the left corner of the mouth and the ear lobe, but these have been added so casually that they seem more like preliminary indications. This also applies to the red stroke with which the right contour of the face was laid in. Under the nose, only a dark shadowy edge denotes the presence of a moustache, while the tuft of hair on the chin is suggested by a single streak. Because of these indistinct elements, the face lacks a clear expression, which may have been what prompted romantics to discern a certain world-weariness in it.

Although other parts of the painting too have been left at an early stage of completion, the self portrait is nonetheless impressive as a whole. The grey hair has scarcely been developed beyond the first design, beyond a few sporadic lines and reddish-brown streaks. By the left temple, a few hairs have been scratched into the wet paint, a technique that Rembrandt mastered in his youth and continued to apply throughout his career. The clothing scarcely has any specific features here: under the black coat, from the top of which the V-neck of a white shirt emerges, a red garment can just be made out, which Rembrandt has painted out. Thus in the preliminary design, the clothing resembled that in the self portrait in Kenwood House (cat. no. 83).

The headgear, which is hard to identify and looks more like a lopsided turban than anything else, has been painted with long strokes. The X-radiograph shows that Rembrandt had initially planned to give himself a white cap (fig. 86a), of the kind he probably wore while working (see cat. no. 84). In several other self portraits too he later painted out this cap (cat. nos. 73 and 84). One has the impression that Rembrandt started off, for the sake of convenience, by painting what he saw in the mirror and turned to further details of his apparel only afterwards. When he decided to portray himself with a painter's tools the cap could remain; otherwise it was replaced.

One could easily surmise that this relatively less elaborated self portrait was left unfinished at Rembrandt's death, were it not that details are also sometimes sparse in other self portraits (see, for example, cat. no. 73). Moreover, a very clear signature has been added on the left, the authenticity of which has never been disputed. Rembrandt must have considered the work completed, and had evidently — to quote once again the words of the biographer Houbraken — 'achieved his intention in it'. [272]

fig. 86a
X-radiograph of cat. no. 86.

Pupils of Rembrandt

Ariane van Suchtelen

87

FERDINAND BOL
(Dordrecht 1616–1680 Amsterdam)

Self Portrait at the Age of 30

1646

Canvas, 100 × 84 cm

Signed and dated to the left of centre:
f bol fecit / 1646 (?)[273]

Dordrecht, Dordrechts Museum,
inv. no. 887–372

Blankert 1982, pp. 58, 118, no. 60; Sumowski
1983–95, vol. I, no. 135; Chapman 1990, p. 53
and fig. 83; Melbourne/Canberra 1997–8, no. 45

FERDINAND BOL was already an accomplished painter when he arrived at Rembrandt's workshop in 1635–6, so he would have been able to contribute to the studio's output straight away.[274] That he successfully mastered Rembrandt's style is apparent from this self portrait of 1646.[275] The identification of the painting is corroborated by its resemblance to the *Self Portrait with Palette* from 1653 (fig. 87a), which has a pendant portrait of his wife Elysabeth Dell.[276] A preliminary study for the latter self portrait is preserved in Paris (fig. 87b).[277]

Bol has portrayed himself here literally larger than life, making a rhetorical gesture with his gloved right hand. Over a shirt with a collar tied in convoluted folds he wears a garment with a straight neckline, in a style freely adapted from sixteenth-century fashions. The beret and the chain around his neck strengthen the impression that the painter has dressed himself – emulating Rembrandt – 'in antique style', whereas the hairstyle, moustache and small goatee, like the red velvet cloak, are contemporary elements.[278]

Bol took his inspiration for this slightly averted pose, with his bent right arm parallel to the pictorial plane, from Rembrandt's self portrait of 1640 (cat. no. 54). Bol appears to have followed the development of this masterpiece from close by. Thus two portraits of Bol, one of which is dated 1647 (fig. 87c), derive from an initial design for Rembrandt's well-known self portrait, when the left hand that was later painted out by Rembrandt still appeared on the balustrade (see p. 173, fig. 54a).[279] A drawing attributed to Bol reproduces Rembrandt's painting in its final form, without the left hand (fig. 87d).[280] This copy was probably drawn in the master's workshop in 1640 or shortly thereafter, and demonstrates that the edges of Rembrandt's self portrait were rounded at the top either when it was made or shortly afterwards.[281]

fig. 87a
FERDINAND BOL, *Self Portrait with Palette*, 1653.
Canvas, 105 × 82.5 cm (rounded at top).
London, Private Collection (photograph RKD,
The Hague).

fig. 87b
FERDINAND BOL, *Self Portrait*, c.1653. Pen and brown
ink, 122 × 95 mm. Paris, Musée du Louvre.

Previous page
Self Portrait (cat. no. 92, detail).

fig. 87c
FERDINAND BOL, 'Self Portrait', 1647.
Canvas, 101 × 88 cm. Toledo, Ohio,
Toledo Museum of Art.

fig. 87d
FERDINAND BOL, Portrait of Rembrandt, 1640
or later. Red and black chalk, grey wash,
178 × 128 mm (rounded at top).
Washington, National Gallery of Art,
Rosenwald Collection.

88

FERDINAND BOL

Self Portrait   *c.*1650–5

Black chalk, grey wash, 160 × 132 mm
(brown wash in the upper corners executed later
by another hand)

Vienna, Graphische Sammlung Albertina,
inv. no. 9395

Sumowski 1979–92, vol. I, no. 106

A T AN AUCTION held in 1773, this drawing was attributed to Rembrandt and described as a 'Portrait of Ferdinand Bol'. In 1792 the sheet was put up for sale again, this time with the correct attribution to Bol. By then it was no longer regarded as a portrait, but as 'A man wearing Old Dutch costume'. Later still, probably after its publication in a print by Adam von Bartsch (1757–1821), the picture became known as a self portrait of the painter from Dordrecht.[282]

The smiling expression of the man with the plumed beret, who leans forward on a cushion in a window opening, makes it clear that this picture is strictly speaking not a portrait but a *tronie*, an image of a particular type or character. The emphasis in this genre was on the fanciful clothing, for instance, or on the depiction of a certain state of mind. Because of its historical apparel, contemporaries will have recognised this figure as a *tronie* 'in antique style'.

As it was quite common for artists to use their own face as a model when drawing or painting a *tronie*, something that Rembrandt himself did, especially in his early work, it is not surprising that this wash drawing exhibits Bol's facial features. Thus the Paris self portrait, sketched in pen (p. 234, fig. 87b) likewise displays wide pouches under the eyes, and both the latter sheet and the self portrait in Dordrecht (cat. no. 87) exhibit a similar nose, with the centre of the nasal bone slightly raised. As the features in the drawing discussed here are roughly the same as those in the sketch from around 1653, the sheet may be tentatively dated 1650–5.

The imaginary historical costume has been freely adapted from Rembrandt's pictures of costumes, as may be seen in his etched self portrait from 1638 (cat. no. 49). The pose with the right arm on a stone support recalls Rembrandt's painted self portrait from 1640 (cat. no. 54). The motif of leaning forwards in a window, however, derives from Gerrit Dou, Bol's most illustrious predecessor in Rembrandt's workshop (compare p. 238, fig. 89b).

89

Gerrit Dou
(Leiden 1613–1675 Leiden)

Self Portrait *c.1645–6*

Panel (rounded at the top), 12.4 × 8.3 cm

Signed at upper left, in the lower edge of the
curtain: *GDOU* (*GD* intertwined)

The Hague, Royal Cabinet of Paintings
Mauritshuis (on loan from a private collection)

Melbourne/Canberra 1997–8, no. 40

H AVING FIRST TRAINED as a glass engraver, on 14 February 1628 the 14-year-old Gerrit
Dou apprenticed himself, according to the Leiden city biographer Jan Jansz Orlers
(1570–1646), to the masterful and renowned Mr Rembrandt, himself a mere 21 years of
age.[283] Dou stayed a pupil of Rembrandt until the latter left for Amsterdam at the end of
1631, and developed the detailed style of Rembrandt's Leiden period, with its deceptively
realistic rendering of materials, into his own trademark. As early as 1641, Orlers wrote
that Dou's paintings 'were much prized by connoisseurs of art and sold dear'. Dou, the
father of the Leiden *fijnschilders* ('fine painters', artists dedicated to verisimilitude in
depicting materials), achieved great fame in his lifetime and could ask extremely high
prices for his paintings.

Dou was the only one of Rembrandt's pupils who made more than the occasional
self portrait. We now know an estimated twelve painted self portraits by him,[284]
of which the example shown here – his smallest self portrait – was rediscovered only
recently. As in the case of Rembrandt, it may well have been Dou's fame that made
a self portrait by him an object coveted by art collectors (see p. 28). Dou's self
portraits differ from Rembrandt's in that they always contain staffage that is replete
with meaning.

In the self portrait discussed here, whose modest dimensions and meticulous
execution give it the character of a precious gem, Dou appears to present himself as
a history painter. In the right background a completed history piece stands on the easel,
Rest on the Flight into Egypt, which probably represents an existing composition from his

workshop.[285] The globe and lute on the table, the parasol behind the easel and the shield and stool with part of a suit of armour on the right in front of the painter's easel are attributes from a history painter's workshop: Dou's compositions are full of objects of this kind (see p. 120, fig. 17a).

Dou depicted himself in almost exactly the same fashionable apparel in a self portrait in which he holds up a family portrait with his parents and brother (fig. 89a).[286] Comparison with the facial features in the allegorical self portrait in Dresden, dated 1647 (p. 29, fig. 42),[287] in which the painter is somewhat fuller in the face, shows that the painting described here was made earlier, probably shortly after 1645.[288] A self portrait from around 1652, in which Dou portrayed himself leaning out of a window with a palette in his hand,[289] contains a similar background scene on the right with a painting — in this case unfortunately unidentifiable — resting on an easel (fig. 89b).

fig. 89a
GERRIT DOU, *Self Portrait with Family Portrait*.
Panel, 27 × 23 cm. Brunswick, Herzog Anton
Ulrich-Museum.

fig. 89b
(AFTER?) GERRIT DOU, *Self Portrait by a Window*,
c.1652. Panel, 23 × 17 cm. Salzburg,
Residenzgalerie.

90

WILLEM DROST
(Amsterdam 1633–1663? Amsterdam)

Self Portrait at the Age of 19, Drawing or Etching

1652

Etching, 64 × 52 mm; one state

Signed and dated at upper right: *W Drost / 1652*

Amsterdam, Rijksmuseum, Rijksprentenkabinet, inv. no. RP-P-OB–2

Hollstein, vol. VI, p. 4, no. 1

fig. 90a
WILLEM DROST, *Self Portrait*, c.1660. Canvas, 72 × 64 cm. Florence, Galleria degli Uffizi.

THIS ETCHED self portrait from 1652 is the earliest dated work by Willem Drost. The artist has depicted himself in contemporary dress, drawing or etching on a support that he is holding in place against his chest.[290] His gaze is fixed on the viewer as he works, giving the illusion that he is recording directly what he sees – undoubtedly his own reflection in a mirror. Since this reflection as recorded on the etching-plate was reversed once again when printed, the pencil was automatically switched from his left hand, as seen in the mirror, back into his right hand.

The type of self portrait in which the artist depicts himself drawing or etching was undertaken earlier by Rembrandt (cat. nos. 46, 62 and 72) and also inspired some of the master's other pupils (see cat. no. 95).[291] The style of the etching discussed here, modelled with hatching in different directions – variously close together and more widely spaced – resembles Rembrandt's etchings from around 1650.[292] When Drost etched this self portrait at the age of 19, he may still have been apprenticed to Rembrandt.

Willem Drost was born in Amsterdam in 1633 as the son of Jan Barentsz (1587–1639) from Antwerp, who is described successively as a bookbinder, a bookseller and a schoolmaster.[293] Drost was probably apprenticed to Rembrandt around 1650, and around the mid-1650s he left for Italy, where he worked first in Rome and then in Venice. A painted self portrait by Drost, purchased in 1685 by Cosimo III de' Medici (1642–1723), Grand Duke of Tuscany, for his gallery of artists' portraits and self portraits (see p. 49, fig. 12), can be connected to his stay in Venice around 1660 (fig. 90a).[294] It is clear from the painting that Drost had left his Rembrandtesque style far behind him by then.

91

(The Hague only)

GERBRAND VAN DEN EECKHOUT

(Amsterdam 1621–1674 Amsterdam)

Self Portrait at the Age of 26

1647

Tip of the brush and grey and black ink, grey wash over a sketch in black chalk, the background elaborated with black chalk, 264 × 200 mm

Signed and dated at upper right:
GV D Eeckhout / A° 1647[295]

Paris, Institut Néerlandais, Frits Lugt Collection, inv. no. 854a

Sumowski 1979–92, vol. III, no. 613; Paris/Haarlem 1997–8, no. 51

HIS LEFT HAND resting on the right, the subject gazes at the viewer from under his beret. He is clad in a velvet, fur-lined cloak with a decorative edge, under which he wears a garment with a straight neckline over a shirt with smocking. This apparel, combined with the beret, will have been recognised by contemporaries as 'antique'. The costume is an imaginative reworking of sixteenth-century dress, which Rembrandt frequently depicted with great accuracy. Details such as the turned-up collar and the fur lining of the cloak appear to have been derived, for instance, from Rembrandt's self portrait from 1640 (cat. no. 54), a painting that evidently exerted a profound influence on his pupils. The placing of the figure and the pose with the right arm parallel to the pictorial plane resting on some sort of table are clearly based on this composition.[296] As an emulation of Rembrandt's masterpiece, Van den Eeckhout's drawing may be interpreted as a tribute to his former teacher, who was also, according to the painters' biographer Arnold Houbraken (1660–1719), his 'great friend'.[297]

There appears little reason to doubt the traditional identification of this drawing, which is elaborated with the brush, as a self portrait,[298] although there are no other contemporary portraits (or self portraits) of the artist to support it.[299] After all, it stands to reason that the artist would have chosen a self portrait in which to emulate Rembrandt's famous example. For Van den Eeckhout, who was probably apprenticed to Rembrandt around 1635–40, this drawn self portrait was to be his only venture into the genre.

92

Carel Fabritius

(Midden-Beemster 1622–1654 Delft)

Self Portrait *c.1645*

Panel, 65 × 49 cm

Signed at upper right: *fabritius / f*

Rotterdam, Museum Boijmans Van Beuningen, inv. no. 1205

Brown 1981, p. 123, no. 4; Sumowski 1983–95, vol. II, no. 603; Giltaij/Jansen 1988, no. 7; Chapman 1990, p. 87 and fig. 126

With its wide brushstrokes and warm palette, this painting by Carel Fabritius recalls the work of Rembrandt, to whom he was apprenticed from 1641 to 1643. There is a portrait of the same man in a painting from 1654 in the National Gallery in London, which has long been regarded as a self portrait (fig. 92a).[300] In the panel shown here, Fabritius wears an imaginary garment with a horizontal neckline that recalls sixteenth-century fashion.[301] In the half-open shirt underneath it there is a *pentimento* that can be seen with the naked eye: where now there appears to be a suggestion of hair – an unprecedented detail in seventeenth-century portraiture – the shirt was initially more closed.

The figure has been placed unusually low in the pictorial plane against the background of a greenish-brown wall with crumbling plaster. The bright light from the upper left creates stark shadows in the face, which is modelled with patches of paint in a variety of tints applied with a dry impasto technique. Where the patches of colour do not merge into one another, the painted ground shows through. Above and to the left of the forehead, a few twisted lines scratched into the wet paint suggest springy curls. The painter's name, too, has been scratched into the wet paint in elegant handwriting using a sharp object – possibly the tip of the paintbrush.

Fabritius had already learnt the basic principles of painting from his father, an amateur painter as well as a schoolmaster, when he left Midden-Beemster, newly married at the age of 19, and moved to Amsterdam. There he was to complete his training in Rembrandt's workshop. Samuel van Hoogstraten (cat. no. 96), who was five years his junior, referred to him later as a fellow-pupil of Rembrandt.[302] As an advanced pupil, he must have been able to contribute to the workshop's output quite soon. The inventory of the estate of Fabritius's first wife, who died as early as April 1643, may provide an indication of what Fabritius painted while he was with Rembrandt.[303] For it is not unreasonable to speculate that one or more of the paintings it lists were by her husband. Of the fourteen paintings specified by subject, six are described as *tronies*, including a '*tronie* as a warrior', a '*tronie* in antique style' and a '*tronie* with shadows'. In the latter piece the painter had evidently practised conveying the effect of shadows in the face, a skill that was also useful in painting portraits.

None of the paintings mentioned, which Fabritius may have made during his apprenticeship to Rembrandt, can be traced today. Recently, however, several portraits that must have been produced in Rembrandt's workshop have been attributed to Carel Fabritius.[304] The similarities with the characteristic painting technique in this *Self Portrait* will certainly have played a role in these attributions.

The picture we have of the oeuvre of Rembrandt's talented pupil, who was killed in 1654 when a gunpowder depot exploded in Delft, is all in all a patchy one. Only some twelve to fourteen paintings by him have been preserved. A signed *Raising of Lazarus* from the Muzeum Narodowe in Warsaw, may be the earliest preserved painting by Fabritius.[305] It is still very Rembrandtesque in style and composition. The *Portrait of Abraham de Potter* of 1648/9 from the Rijksmuseum in Amsterdam displays a smoother finish in comparison to the painting in Warsaw and the self portrait described here, which is far removed from Rembrandt's example. It is therefore logical to assume that this self portrait was painted earlier than the piece of 1648/9, possibly around 1645.[306] The somewhat fuller facial features in the London self portrait from 1654, the year of Fabritius's death, could be explained by the difference in age.

fig. 92a
CAREL FABRITIUS, *A Young Man in a Fur Cap and a Cuirass (Self Portrait)*, 1654.
Canvas, 70.5 × 61.5 cm.
London, National Gallery.

93

GOVERT FLINCK

(Cleves 1615–1660 Amsterdam)

Self Portrait Aged 24, 1639

Panel, 65.8 × 54.4 cm

Signed and dated at lower right: *G. flinck / 1639*

London, National Gallery, inv. no. 4068

Von Moltke 1965, no. 226; Sumowski 1983–95,
vol. II, no. 666; MacLaren/Brown 1991, vol. I,
p. 141, no. 4068

MINOR DAMAGE to the signature on this self portrait by Govert Flinck recalls the
attempts that were once made to present the piece as a Rembrandt. The false
Rembrandt signature over the partly erased name of Flinck was removed again during
restoration work in 1925.[307] That this painting, Rembrandtesque as it is in style,
colouring, composition and apparel, should have easily passed for a Rembrandt is not at
all surprising. As early a writer as the painters' biographer Arnold Houbraken
(1660–1719) observed that paintings by Flinck changed hands as authentic works by his
master.[308]

After training with Lambert Jacobsz (*c.*1598–1636) in Leeuwarden, Flinck moved to
Amsterdam in or around 1633, where, according to Houbraken, he first had the
opportunity to demonstrate his artistic skills. In Amsterdam he boarded with the art
dealer Hendrick van Uylenburgh (1587–1661) and, again according to Houbraken, he
apprenticed himself for a year to Rembrandt – who also had rooms with Van
Uylenburgh at the time. Houbraken comments that it was profitable for Flinck, who
must have already been an accomplished painter by this time, to master the 'handling of
paint and manner of painting' favoured by Rembrandt, who was so fashionable in this
period: 'since every aspect of Rembrandt's touch was praised at that time, everything had
to be cast in that mould if it was to please the world.'[309] That Flinck was uniquely able to
master Rembrandt's style of painting – which he unlearnt again afterwards only with the

greatest of difficulty, as Houbraken relates – is also clear from this self portrait of 1639. In both pose and costume, this self portrait shows similarities with the painting in Pasadena (cat. no. 56).[310]

Flinck has depicted himself against a light green background, wearing a black *tabbaard* (a gown originating in the sixteenth century, which was worn by painters in Rembrandt's time) with braiding and a beret decorated with a gold chain. He has chosen to emulate his teacher here in donning costume 'in antique style'. Unlike the historical costumes favoured by Rembrandt, however, Flinck's apparel is a product of his own imagination, which seems to be quite common among Rembrandt's pupils.

The face is modelled with short, bristly brushstrokes, and red accents give colour to the cheeks and nose. In the hair, for which a space was left in the background, the colour of the ground shows through, serving as a basis for the curls that have been applied with light and dark strokes. The *tabbaard* is sketched with vigorous black strokes, with the gleaming lights in the braiding providing striking accents.

Some tried to see Rembrandt's features in this portrait, until it was identified as a self portrait of his pupil in 1965. The likeness with a portrait of Flinck engraved by Abraham Blootelingh (1640–90) and with his self portrait in his *Civic Guard: Festivities Celebrating the Conclusion of the Treaty of Münster*, painted in 1648 for the Amsterdam arbalesters' guild (fig. 93a), was decisive in its identification.[311]

fig. 93a
GOVERT FLINCK, *Civic Guard: Festivities Celebrating the Conclusion of the Treaty of Münster* (detail of self portrait), 1648. Canvas, 265 × 513 cm. Amsterdam, Amsterdams Historisch Museum.

94

GOVERT FLINCK

'Self Portrait' 1643

Black chalk, Indian ink, grey wash, 255 × 180 mm

Signed and dated at lower left: *G flinck f 1643*

Weimar, Kunstsammlungen zu Weimar, Schlossmuseum, inv. no. KK 4947

Von Moltke 1965, no. D 139; Sumowski 1979–92, vol. IV, no. 867

fig. 94a
Govert Flinck, '*Self Portrait*'. Black chalk, grey wash, 109 × 98 mm. Leiden, Print Room of Leiden University.

IN AN UNDEFINED space, with a sketchily delineated curtain serving as the background, a half-figure is depicted from a fairly low vantage-point, creating a slight suggestion of smugness. His attire identifies the man as a soldier: he wears a military collar and a belt for attaching a sword or standard, while the object in his hand could perhaps be interpreted as a staff of office. The object behind his elbow may be the hilt of his sword. The beret does not belong to this military dress, but with its old-fashioned air it places the scene, as it were, outside its own time.

In this drawing from 1643, Govert Flinck appears to have used his own face as a model for a depiction of the military type. A character head of this kind was designated at the time as a *tronie* and did not, therefore, have to be recognisable as a portrait. Despite the presence of his self portrait in his 1648 portrait of the Amsterdam arbalesters' guild (p. 244, fig. 93a), Flinck himself was not a member of the civic guard.[312] His soldierly attire in the drawing shown here is therefore unrelated to his personal background.

Although some doubt might be expressed as to whether this is indeed Flinck's self portrait, the shape of the mouth with its arched lips seems to correspond to the painted self portrait of 1639 (cat. no. 93). Furthermore, the physiognomy resembles a second drawing by Flinck that has also been identified as a self portrait (fig. 94a).[313] This identification may have been based in part on the palette held by the subject, who is portrayed from the same angle as the model in the drawing discussed here.

Flinck derived the composition of his drawing from Rembrandt's etched self portrait of 1639 (cat. no. 53). The figure's pose, with the left shoulder turned towards the viewer, the arm resting on a low stone wall, the cloak draped over the wall and the beret set at a rakish angle to the head all correspond quite closely to Rembrandt's invention.

95

ARENT DE GELDER

(Dordrecht 1645–1727 Dordrecht)

Self Portrait, Drawing *c.1661–3*

Pen and brown ink, paintbrush and white paint,
118 × 103 mm

Amsterdam, Rijksmuseum, Rijksprentenkabinet,
inv. no. RP-T–1975–56

Amsterdam 1984–5, no. 4; Dordrecht/Cologne
1998–9, no. 60

THIS DRAWING HAS been added by Peter Schatborn to the drawn oeuvre of Arent de Gelder, which consists of about twenty attributed drawings. The core of the oeuvre is the *Group of Orientals*, a sheet attributed with confidence to the artist on the basis of a painting by him in the Mauritshuis, The Hague.[314] The technique of the latter drawing, one characteristic feature of which is its plethora of small wavy lines, is also recognisable in the self portrait described here.[315]

De Gelder has portrayed himself leaning forwards, drawing at a table. A few small lines suffice to suggest historical clothing: a plumed beret, a *tabbaard* (a house-gown) and a garment worn over the shirt with a horizontal neckline. He would not have seen the antique attire he wears here in the mirror, but must have fabricated it from his own imagination. His right hand, which has white highlights, has not been depicted very convincingly. Perhaps De Gelder had difficulty correcting his mirror image, in that he wanted to show himself drawing with his right, not his left hand. That De Gelder was in fact right-handed can be inferred from his painted *Self Portrait as Zeuxis* of 1685 (p. 216, fig. 82a), where he is a right-handed painter, holding his palette with brushes and maulstick in his left hand.[316] This portrait also displays a striking difference in size between the eyes, recalling the comment of the painters' biographer Jacob Campo Weyerman (1677–1747) that De Gelder was 'improbably cross-eyed'.[317] There is no trace of this affliction in the drawn self portrait described here.

After a period of apprenticeship with his fellow townsman Samuel van Hoogstraten (cat. no. 96), De Gelder left in 1659–61 for Amsterdam, where Houbraken says he spent two years training with Rembrandt, before eventually settling in Dordrecht once again. He was the last in a series of Rembrandt pupils from Dordrecht, who included Ferdinand Bol (cat. nos. 87 and 88), Nicolaes Maes (1634–93) and his own teacher Van Hoogstraten.[318] Inspired by Rembrandt's late work, De Gelder was to develop a markedly individual style, one to which he would adhere for the rest of his life, since he was financially independent and hence unhampered by the vogue for Classicism. The sheet discussed here, like most of De Gelder's drawings, was probably made while the artist was still training with Rembrandt.[319]

96

SAMUEL VAN HOOGSTRATEN
(Dordrecht 1627–1678 Dordrecht)

Self Portrait at the Age of 17, with Still Life 1644

Panel, 58 × 74 cm

On the base of the column, to the right:
S. van Hoochstraten 1644

Rotterdam, Museum Boijmans Van Beuningen,
inv. no. 1386

Sumowski 1983–95, vol. II, no. 849; Giltaij/
Jansen 1988, no. 10; Chapman 1990, p. 29 and
fig. 32; Brusati 1995, pp. 44–5, 346, no. 1

SAMUEL VAN HOOGSTRATEN was only 17 years of age when he painted this original self portrait in 1644. The resemblance to his drawn self portrait of 1649, confirmed as such by a poem by his friend Carel van Nispen, is the basis for the identification of this painting as a self portrait (fig. 96a).[320] Two other early self portraits, one in The Hague (fig. 96b) and the other in the collection of the Prince of Liechtenstein, dated 1644 and 1645 respectively, are more traditional in conception.[321]

After the death of his father, the Dordrecht genre and landscape painter Dirck van Hoogstraten (*c.*1595–1640), in December 1640, Rembrandt became Samuel's second teacher, as he relates in his book *Inleyding tot de hooge schoole der schilderkonst* (Introduction to the Art of Painting) published in 1678 (p. 26, fig. 36).[322] The fact that Van Hoogstraten signed and dated in full the painting described here does not necessarily mean that he had left Rembrandt's workshop by 1644.[323] In 1646 he spent several sessions with Rembrandt drawing from models, when they each sketched the same male nude from a different angle.[324] Van Hoogstraten's first painted history piece, the *Adoration of the Shepherds* from 1647 in the Dordrecht Museum, contains striking borrowings from some of his teacher's recent compositions.[325] All things considered, it is a plausible hypothesis that Van Hoogstraten stayed with Rembrandt until about 1647 – by the beginning of 1648, in

any case, he was back in Dordrecht.[326] We can therefore assume that the self portrait discussed here was painted during his apprenticeship to Rembrandt. This makes the originality of the composition all the more remarkable. Unlike the other early self portraits by Rembrandt's pupils (cat. nos. 87–95), it displays no similarities whatsoever to Rembrandt's oeuvre. The subdued colouring and the artist's virtuoso handling of the brush, however, do testify to the master's influence.

Van Hoogstraten has portrayed himself studying a book, rapt in concentration. His mouth is half-open, as if he is muttering the words to himself. The fact that he wears nothing over his shirt is extremely unusual in seventeenth-century portraiture, as well as the fact that he does not look at the beholder. On the table to the right, Van Hoogstraten has depicted a miscellaneous collection of objects: an hourglass, a skull, a candlestick with a lopsided, extinguished candle, a few books and some rolled-up sheets of paper, covered in writing. In the right background, a base with a column can just be made out in the darkness. The objects on the table can be interpreted as *vanitas* symbols and have been linked to an emblem from Gabriël Rollenhagens *Nucleus Emblematum* (Cologne 1611).[327] The column in the upper right corner, too, fits into this interpretation. It is not uncommon for still-life paintings to combine *vanitas* symbols with images of study in this way.[328] Thus the hourglass can stand for the time needed for study, time that must not be lost. One might say that in this youthful self portrait, the painter and writer Samuel van Hoogstraten was already indicating that his professional ambitions were not confined to painting.

fig. 96a
SAMUEL VAN HOOGSTRATEN, *Self Portrait*, 1649.
Pen and brown ink, brown wash, red chalk,
143 × 172 mm. Munich, Staatliche
Graphische Sammlung.

fig. 96b
SAMUEL VAN HOOGSTRATEN, *Self Portrait*, 1644.
Panel, 63 × 48 cm. The Hague, Museum Bredius.

Notes to the catalogue entries

Edwin Buijsen wishes to acknowledge the following individuals: Philip Akkerman, The Hague; Graham Baraclough, English Heritage, London; Marie-Christine Boucher, Musée du Petit Palais, Paris; Xanthe Brooke, Walker Art Gallery, Liverpool; Caterina Caneva, Galleria degli Uffizi, Florence; Rudi Ekkart, Netherlands Institute for Art History, The Hague; Susan Galassi, The Frick Collection, New York; Wouter Kloek, Rijksmuseum, Amsterdam; Walter Liedtke, The Metropolitan Museum of Art, New York; Viola Pemberton-Pigott, The Royal Collection, London; Cathy Power, English Heritage, London; Christiaan Vogelaar, Stedelijk Museum De Lakenhal, Leiden; Arie Wallert, Rijksmuseum, Amsterdam; Arthur Wheelock, National Gallery of Art, Washington, as well as Rachel Billinge, National Gallery, London and Caroline van der Elst, Petria Noble, Carol Pottasch and Jørgen Wadum, conservators of the Mauritshuis.

1   For the numerous attempts to identify the subject depicted here, see e.g. Broos 1975–6, pp. 203–4; M.L. Wurfbain in Leiden 1976–7, pp. 66–8; *Corpus*, vol. I, p. 112; Bruyn 1987; Van Straten 1991.

2   On the technique of the young Rembrandt, see Van de Wetering 1982 and Van de Wetering 1997, pp. 11–44.

3   *Corpus*, vol. I, p. 107 and fig. 2 on p. 105.

4   *Corpus*, vol. I, no. A 1; Paris/Lyon 1991, pp. 118–20.

5   *Corpus*, vol. I, no. A 9.

6   Chapman 1990, p. 15; Grimm 1991, p. 15.

7   Ekkart 1989, figs. 1 and 3. For other examples, see Raupp 1984, pp. 243–66.

8   According to an ingenious hypothesis, these two works, which are virtually the same size, are the 'two fine large pieces by Rembrandt' from the estate of the Leiden scholar Petrus Scriverius (1576–1660). Even leaving aside the fact that Rembrandt used standard sizes in this period, so that the two panels are not necessarily companion pieces, this description is so vague that the identification is scarcely justifiable (on this hypothesis, see M.L. Wurfbain in Leiden 1976–7, pp. 66–8; Dudok van Heel 1978, p. 169; Schwartz 1984, pp. 36–8, and for a response to it, see Van Straten 1991, pp. 97 and 106, note 23). On the use of standard sizes in Rembrandt's early work, see Van de Wetering 1997, p. 13.

9   With thanks to Marieke de Winkel for pointing out this latter detail.

10   Bergström 1966, pp. 164–6; *Corpus*, vol. II, no. A 69; Tümpel 1986, p. 136; Berlin/Amsterdam/London 1991–2, vol. 1, p. 158; Chapman 1990, pp. 108–14. For another possible self portrait in a history piece, see cat. no. 43.

11   Martin 1923–4. See also Haverkamp Begemann 1982, p. 81.

12   B. 54.

13   *Rest on the Flight into Egypt* (B. 559) and *The Circumcision* (S. 398).

14   Amsterdam, Rijksmuseum, Rijksprentenkabinet and Paris, Bibliothèque Nationale. The latter specimen is indeed printed so badly that Rembrandt filled it in with a pen.

15   In a later state, Rembrandt elaborated Joseph's beard; from the fourth state onwards, the execution is no longer autograph.

16   Middleton 1878, p. 30, no. 19. In the second state, of which only one impression is known, the shadow under the chin was deepened (the unique specimen is in Paris, Musée du Louvre, De Rothschild Collection). De Vries (1883, p. 295) established that the self portrait had been made on the plate of *The Flight into Egypt*. There is another example of the self portrait in which Mary's head can still be seen in the De Rothschild Collection in Paris (this impression was formerly in the Rijksprentenkabinet, but was sold as a duplicate on 2 May 1882).

17   B. 304; in the third state the print was reduced in size, and this *repoussoir* disappeared. In *Beggars Behind a Hillock* (B. 165) there is a similar, even more obtrusive *repoussoir*.

18   Chapman 1990, pp. 23–33; for a reaction, see De Jongh 1991a, p. 18.

19   On the concept of the *tronie*, see De Vries 1989; J. van der Veen in Melbourne/Canberra 1997–8 and the bibliography included there. See also the essays by Ernst van de Wetering and Marieke de Winkel in this catalogue.

20   Amsterdam 1996, pp. 51–64.

21   Bauch 1962; *Corpus*, vol. I, pp. 172–3.

22   Benesch 1973, vol. I, no. 35; Royalton-Kisch 1992, no. 2.

23   See *Corpus*, vol. I, no. A 22. The 1637 inventory of the property of the Frisian painter and art dealer Lambert Jacobsz includes a copy after Rembrandt, the description of which corresponds to the composition described here: 'A soldier with black hair, an iron collar and a scarf around the neck, after Remb.' (Strauss/Van der Meulen 1979, p. 144, no. 1637/4).

24   See Janson 1980, fig. p. 94; Janson 1981, pp. 8–13, and *Corpus*, vol. I, p. 238.

25   While Grimm (1991, p. 28) regarded the version from Indianapolis as the prototype, he did not believe it was by Rembrandt. He suggested an attribution to Gerrit Dou (cat. no. 89).

26   *Corpus*, vol. I, no. A 22. After being accepted as an original work by the Rembrandt Research Project (RRP), though one of its members (Ernst van de Wetering) had already expressed his doubts, the RRP now no longer believes that this work is by the master. Janson (1980, pp. 92–6 and 1981, pp. 11–13) suggested an attribution to Jan Lievens, while in Ozaki 1989 it is linked to Dou (for other views on the attribution of this piece, see note 24 to the latter article).

27   Part of the frame may have been placed in the wrong position, ending up in the lower right corner.

28   Heesakkers 1987, p. 86: 'Rembrandt, on the other hand, likes to devote his full concentration to a small painting, and achieves in this miniature form a result that will be sought in vain in the large pieces of other artists.'

29   Amsterdam 1991, no. 29.

30   B. 280.

31   Chapman 1990, pp. 50–4; Liverpool 1994–5, p. 48.

32   See e.g. *Corpus*, vol. I, nos. A 41–2; vol. II, no. A 94.

33   *Corpus*, vol. I, pp. 223–4; Broos 1987, pp. 297–8.

34   Grimm 1991, pp. 28 and 124, note 37, where this is seen as an argument for doubting both the identity of the piece as a self portrait and its attribution to Rembrandt.

35   White (1984, p. 16) believed that this piece was not a self portrait intended to bolster the artist's reputation, but that Rembrandt merely used himself as a model here.

36   Schatborn 1985, p. 2.

37   Benesch 1947, p. 8.

38   See e.g. Wright 1982, p. 20; Tümpel 1986, p. 65, and Berlin/Amsterdam/London 1991–2, vol. I, no. 4.

39   *Corpus*, vol. I, p. 8.

40   Grimm 1991, pp. 20–8. The attribution of the Nuremberg painting to Rembrandt was adopted by Tacke (1995, pp. 187–91. no. 91), who stopped short of expressing a definite view, however, on the authorship of the Hague piece. In Van de Wetering 1997, p. 160, fig. 203, the Hague painting is included without further comment as 'Attr. to Rembrandt' (in the reprint that appeared at the end of 1998, an illustration of the Nuremberg painting replaces that of the Hague piece).

41   See *Corpus*, vol. I, p. 230; Tacke 1995, pp. 187–8 and Hofstede de Groot 1895, pp. 53–4.

42   This comparative analysis took place on 7–8 October 1998 in the restoration workshop of the Germanisches Nationalmuseum (GN), Nuremberg, in the presence of Martina Homolka (picture conservator at the GN) and a delegation representing the Mauritshuis, comprising Frits Duparc, Jørgen Wadum, Christopher White, Edwin Buijsen and Adri Verburg. On this occasion the two paintings were subjected to thorough scrutiny, including examination using IRR (infra-red reflectography) and CCD (Focal Plane Silicium Array) cameras (see also note 43). The author of the present catalogue entry made grateful use of Jørgen Wadum's account of this meeting (*A Comparative Study of Rembrandt's Self-Portraits (1629) in Nuremberg and The Hague*, 16 November 1998) and of the findings of Ernst van de Wetering, who studied the two works independently (transcript of notes related by telephone, 6 October 1998). A forthcoming Mauritshuis publication will dwell at greater length on the technical aspects of the two works and the relationship between them.

43   This underdrawing was first discovered by Jørgen Wadum and Caroline van der Elst when they examined the piece in the restoration workshop of the Mauritshuis in the spring of 1998 (see Van der Elst's account). An earlier technical examination had not revealed any underdrawing (see De Vries/Tóth-Ubbens/Froentjes 1978, pp. 41–7, no. I). During the comparison with the Nuremberg painting (see note 42) an IRR camera (Hamamatsu C 2400-03 with N2606 vidicon), belonging to the Netherlands Institute for Art History (RKD) in The Hague, was used as well as the CCD camera of Adri Verburg, Middelburg. The images were digitized with a Framegrabber and the montage was done using Adobe Photoshop 5.0.

44   In the early self portrait from Amsterdam (cat. no. 5), infra-red reflectography did not reveal any underdrawing. With a number of works from Rembrandt's circle, this painting was examined by Jørgen Wadum, Edwin Buijsen and Adri Verburg in the Rijksmuseum, Amsterdam, on 26 October 1998, using the RKD's IRR camera (see also notes 53 and 56).

45 Verbal observation by Peter Schatborn, spring 1998.

46 This was suggested in 1992 by Volker Manuth; see Tacke 1995, pp. 188–9 and 191, note 7.

47 One of the pieces of evidence advanced by Grimm (1991, p. 24) in support of his identification of the Nuremberg painting as the original was the X-radiograph, which reveals some minor *pentimenti*. Contrary to an assertion made by the RRP (*Corpus*, vol. I, p. 228), no changes of this kind, made during the painting process, show up in the X-radiograph of the Hague painting. In itself, however, this observation says nothing about the correctness of the attribution of the Nuremberg piece, as IRR examination has since revealed changes to the Hague painting too, although only at the underdrawing stage.

48 The light on the face of the Hague painting closely resembles a drawn self portrait by Rembrandt from the same period (cat. no. 13). It is conceivable that the maker of the Hague painting used this drawing as a second example, but the relationship between the two pieces needs further investigation.

49 This signature was discovered as far back as 1887, but the RRP could no longer find it (*Corpus*, vol. I, p. 230), nor could Tacke (1995, p. 188). In the examination conducted on 7–8 October 1998 (see note 42), the signature turned out to be visible.

50 The observations reported here derive from Ernst van de Wetering's account, as referred to in note 42.

51 It seems unlikely that the Hague painting was made many years after the original, as dendrochronological analysis, performed by Dr P. Klein in 1995, revealed that the panel could have been used in as early as 1619. In the case of the Nuremberg panel, which Klein also examined in 1995, the earliest possible year of use is estimated as 1623. The wood of this panel comes from the same tree as that of a painting from Rembrandt's immediate circle, which was long held to be an authentic self portrait (*Corpus*, vol. I, no. C 34; p. 127, fig. 22a).

52 On De Jouderville's work, see e.g. Ernst van de Wetering in Amsterdam/Groningen 1983, pp. 59–69; Van de Wetering 1986, pp. 78–90; Sumowski 1983–95, vol. II, pp. 1434–52; Berlin/Amsterdam/London 1991–2, vol. I, pp. 308–13; The Hague 1992, pp. 193–7. The RRP expanded De Jouderville's oeuvre with several works from Rembrandt's studio previously attributed to the master himself (*Corpus*, vol. II, no. C 54 and p. 838, corrigenda and addenda, no. A 23). Although these pieces are closer in quality to the Hague painting, these attributions are as yet too tentative to serve as the basis for an argument (see also Liedtke 1996, pp. 39 and 41–2).

53 This painting was examined in the Rijksmuseum, Amsterdam, on 26 October 1998 (see note 44); no traces were found of any underdrawing. For the view that this painting could be a portrait of Rembrandt by Lievens, see Brunswick 1979, no. 19. However, Grimm (1991, p. 32) considers that the facial features depicted make it impossible that the piece represents Rembrandt. On the artistic rivalry between Lievens and Rembrandt, see Leiden 1991–2.

54 Compare e.g. the half figures of a young girl and an old woman that Lievens painted in c.1625–9 (Melbourne/Canberra 1997–8, nos. 34–5).

55 Sumowski 1983–95, vol. I, no. 245; Amsterdam 1989, no. 1.

56 This painting was examined on 26 October 1998 in the Rijksmuseum, Amsterdam (see note 44).

57 Couprie 1994, fig. 11. See also Van de Wetering 1991–2.

58 Van Gelder 1953, p. 291.

59 Couprie 1994, pp. 69 and 81.

60 Slive 1964, p. 486; Van de Wetering 1976–7, p. 26; *Corpus*, vol. I, p. 211; Berlin/Amsterdam/London 1991–2, vol. I, p. 130; Couprie 1994, p. 70.

61 Van de Wetering 1997, p. 88 and fig. 148 on p. 118.

62 For a detailed justification of this hypothesis, see Van de Wetering 1976–7; Van de Wetering 1991–2, pp. 41–4 and Van de Wetering 1997, pp. 75–89. For a reaction to it, see Schwartz 1984, p. 55. For other, less convincing readings of the picture, see Bauer 1977; Bal 1991, pp. 247–85; Harrison 1992 and Couprie 1994, pp. 88–9.

63 Melbourne/Canberra 1997–8, no. 39.

64 See e.g. Sumowski 1983, vol. I, nos. 261–2 and 270.

65 Translated from Latin; Heesakkers 1987, pp. 89–90 and Leiden 1991–2, p. 131.

66 See Froentjes 1969; De Vries/Tóth-Ubbens/Froentjes 1978, pp. 49–51; *Corpus*, vol. I, p. 424; Berlin/Amsterdam/London 1991–2, vol. I, p. 140.

67 Phoenix/Kansas City/The Hague 1998–9, no. 46.

68 *Corpus*, vol. I, nos. B 5–6; both paintings are now universally accepted as by Rembrandt.

69 Van Mander 1604b, fol. 48 recto, line 20; Miedema 1973, vol. I, pp. 258–9; vol. II, p. 599. See also Broos 1987, p. 176.

70 Suggested by Schatborn 1986, p. 61.

71 Compare also Amsterdam 1996, nos. 13–14.

72 Rembrandt wears a similar fur hat in cat. no. 9.

73 De Winkel 1995, passim.

74 In the painting in Stockholm (cat. no. 18), Rembrandt wears the same clothes, but without a fur hat.

75 Van Hoogstraten 1678, p. 110.

76 Houbraken 1718–21, vol. I, pp. 257–8 (on Rembrandt's many and varied sketches).

77 B. 73; White 1969.

78 Houbraken 1718–21, vol. I, facing p. 258; Van Mander refers explicitly to wide-open eyes in his *Grondt der edel vry schilder-const* in connection with the depiction of cruelty and wrath, citing by way of illustration Michelangelo's rendering of the ferryman Charon in his *Last Judgment*: 'thus should the iris of the eyes be placed within white borders both above and below, by opening the eyes wide' (Van Mander 1604b, fol. 27 verso, line 60; Miedema 1973, vol. I, p. 177).

79 Chapman (1990, p. 19) compares the head to the man on the ladder in *The Deposition* (B. 81). But while the latter does indeed have Rembrandt's facial features, his expression is bitter and mournful rather than angry.

80 Berlin/Amsterdam/London 1991–2, vol. II, no. 2.

81 Two impressions of this print (in Berlin and London) are printed on cartridge paper (see White 1969, pp. 14–15, note 15); the fifth and sixth state are not by Rembrandt.

82 Van Mander 1604b, fol. 25 recto, line 28; Miedema 1973, vol. I, pp. 166–7.

83 Van Mander 1604b, fol. 25 verso, line 36; Miedema 1973, vol. I, pp. 168–9.

84 *Corpus*, vol. I , no. B 6. The painting's authenticity was wrongly called in question; see also Schatborn 1986, p. 61.

85 Bredius/Gerson 1969, no. 5 and *Corpus*, vol. I, no. C 34.

86 Van Mander 1604b, fol. 25 recto, line 29; Miedema 1973, vol. I, pp. 166–7; Koerner (1986, pp. 18–19) linked this and the following passages (Van Mander 1604b, fol. 25 recto and 26 verso, lines 30 and 44; Miedema 1973, vol. I, pp. 172–3) to Moses' expression in the painting in Berlin (Bredius/Gerson 1969, no. 527).

87 *Corpus*, vol. I, no. A 35.

88 Van Mander 1604b, fol. 26 verso, line 44; Miedema 1973, vol. I, pp. 172–3.

89 New Hollstein 143.

90 On the identification of the figures, see Jacobowitz/Stepanek 1983, p. 82, no. 23.

91 Lieure 1924–7, vol. V, pp. 41–5, nos. 479–503, vol. VI, figs. 479–503.

92 Lieure 1924–7, vol. V, p. 43, no. 490, vol. VI, fig. 490.

93 Stratton 1986, pp. 78–9.

94 B. / Hollstein 176 and 131.

95 For a psychological interpretation, see Held 1984, pp. 33–4.

96 B. / Hollstein 177.

97 Münz 298, p. 174, fig. 9 (e); see Amsterdam 1996, p. 17, note 30.

98 Millar 1958–60, p. 57, no. 87; Strauss/Van der Meulen 1979, p. 179, no. 1639/11; see also Hoff 1935, pp. 33–43; White 1962, pp. 177–80; White 1982, pp. xxxvi-xxxviii; Liverpool 1994–5, p. 48.

99 Hoff 1935, pp. 39–42.

100 For a reasoned argument in favour of this year, see White 1962, p. 180; *Corpus*, vol. I, p. 321.

101 Orlers 1641, p. 377; see also Hoff 1935, p. 35 and White 1962, p. 179.

102 *Corpus*, vol. I, no. A 32; vol. II, pp. 839–40; W. Liedtke in New York 1995–6, vol. II, p. 10.

103 For palimpsests in Rembrandt's workshop, see Van de Wetering 1982, pp. 31–3.

104 *Corpus*, vol. I, p. 32.

105 *An Old Woman* (fig. 26a), one of the two other paintings that Robert Kerr presented as gifts to Charles I, is also painted over another representation (*Corpus*, vol. I, p. 317, fig. 2).

106 Amsterdam 1996, no. 27.

107 B. 262 (c.1632) and B. 263 (1631, fig. 28a). In addition, the figures in e.g. *The Blind Fiddler* from 1631 (B. 138) and *Peasant with his Hands behind his Back* from the same year (B. 135) also wear fur hats. The painting referred to is in Innsbruck, Tiroler Landesmuseum Ferdinandeum (*Corpus*, vol. I, no. A 29).

108 E.g. an old woman reading, who may represent the prophetess Anna; see *Corpus*, vol. I, no. A 37. The figures in Rembrandt's history pieces with biblical scenes also wear oriental dress.

109 Translated from Latin; Heesakkers 1987, p. 88, and Leiden 1991–2, p. 130. For Lievens's painting, now in Potsdam, see Schneider/Ekkart 1973, no. 152 and fig. 15.

110 Strauss/van der Meulen 1979, p. 144, no. 1637/4.

111 For the attribution to De Jouderville, see *Corpus*, vol. III, p. 17.

112 See *Corpus*, vol. I, p. 379.

113 Similar standing figures occur in an etching from 1632 and two drawings from around 1630–1; see B. 152 and Benesch 1973, vol. I, nos. 44–5.

114 The information given here has been derived from the website of the Poodle History Project (www3.sympatico.ca/emily.cain/).

115 Paris, Musée du Louvre (Boon 71).

116 Amsterdam, Rijksmuseum, Rijksprentenkabinet and Paris, Musée du Louvre, De Rothschild Collection.

117 Benesch 1973, vol. II, no. 340; Berlin/Amsterdam/London 1991–2, vol. II, no. 8, and Melbourne/Canberra 1997–8, no. 79.

118 Dezallier d'Argenville 1745–52, vol. II: 'son livre à dessiner est de dix à douze feuilles' (see Emmens 1968, pp. 157–8).

119 Compare H. Bevers in Berlin/Amsterdam/London 1991–2, vol. II, etching no. 5.

120 The cloak is not embroidered, as indicated in the old title (with thanks to Marieke de Winkel for pointing this out).

121 Van de Wetering 1997, inside dust-jacket; Royalton-Kisch 1992, p. 46, note 5.

122 London, British Museum, second state (White 1969, fig. 135; Royalton-Kisch 1992, pp. 43–6, no. 8a); Paris, Bibliothèque Nationale, fourth state (White 1969, fig. 136; Royalton Kisch 1992, p. 45, fig. c). A third small print elaborated with chalk follows the clothing of the etching in later states: London, British Museum, third state (Royalton-Kisch 1992, p. 43, fig. 8a).

123 *Corpus*, vol. II, no. A 58.

124 Chapman 1990, fig. 94.

125 White 1969; *Corpus*, vol. I, no. A 40. For Vorsterman's print after Rubens (Hollstein 9), see Amsterdam 1985–6, no. 22.

126 Rembrandt regularly adopted an oval format for portraits; see e.g. *Corpus*, vol. II, nos. A 59–60, A 62, A 82, A 83, A 86–7 and A 104.

127 *Corpus*, vol. II, pp. 236–7, 678–9; Plomp 1997, pp. 388–9.

128 Another painting was also regarded at one time as the counterpart of the Glasgow painting; see *Corpus*, vol. II, pp. 234–5 and no. C 59.

129 Bredius/Gerson 1969, no. 157 (as *Portrait of a Young Man*, not by Rembrandt). This entry has been written on the basis of the draft entry for the fourth volume of the *Corpus*.

130 *Corpus*, vol. II, no. A 57.

131 For a more detailed discussion of the different forms of signature used by Rembrandt, see Van de Wetering 1997, inside dust jacket and *Corpus*, vol. IV, add. no. 2.

132 *Corpus*, vol. II, no. A 53.

133 Chapman 1990, p. 31.

134 Tümpel 1986, p. 199.

135 See e.g. *Corpus*, vol. II, no. A 70; vol. III, no. A 116.

136 *Corpus*, vol. II, fig. on p. 527.

137 Van Duuren 1996, p. 66.

138 *Corpus*, vol. I, no. A 24; The Hague 1997–8, no. 21.

139 *Corpus*, vol. III, no. A 116.

140 Strauss/Van der Meulen 1979, no. 1656/12, no. 313, p. 383: '60 pieces including Indonesian rifles, axes, spears, assegais and bows'.

141 According to Chapman (1990, pp. 41–2 and fig. 56), the figure was based on the *Portrait of Theodoricus of Aquitaine* that was published in M. Vosmerus, *Principes Hollandiae et Zelandiae*, Antwerp 1578.

142 The *Woordenboek der Nederlandse Taal* (Dictionary of the Dutch Language) includes under the lemma corresponding to 'wart' quotations from Gheschier (1643) and Sprankhuisen (1648) describing warts as excrescences of the 'impure' body and blood from a wart as a disseminator of evil.

143 New York, The Metropolitan Museum of Art; *Corpus*, vol. II, no. A 48.

144 B. 152.

145 Two in Amsterdam and London, and two in Paris (Musée du Louvre, De Rothschild Collection and Bibliothèque Nationale). The provenance of these four examples can be traced back to the eighteenth century.

146 *Corpus*, vol. II, no. A 73.

147 Amsterdam 1986, no. 337.

148 The dating given in Benesch 1973, vol. II, no. 437 ('About 1637'), is based on the comparison with the painted self portrait in Paris (cat. no. 51) that the Rembrandt Research Project does not, however, accept as fully autograph and dates *c.*1639 (see *Corpus*, vol. III, no. B 10).

149 Benesch 1973, vol. II, nos. 280 a and e (*c.*1635).

150 Benesch 1973, vol. II, nos. 443–4 (after Leonardo) and nos. 448–9 (after Lastman).

151 Amsterdam, Universiteitsbibliotheek, UB II-A–18, portfolio 8, fol. 93.

152 Schatborn 1981, p. 39.

153 B. 365 and 367. In the painted portrait in the Rijksmuseum, Amsterdam, Saskia is similarly portrayed in sixteenth-century dress and wearing a veil (*Corpus*, vol. II, no. A 75).

154 E. de Jongh in Haarlem 1986, p. 58; Smith (1982, p. 139) believed that the double portrait was inspired by friendship portraits.

155 Schwartz (1977) believed that Saskia had been depicted in mirror image, on the basis of comparison with B. 365. Schneider (1995, p. 225) believed that Rembrandt portrayed Saskia in mirror image and himself from memory; finally, Chapman (1990, p. 82) pointed out that Rembrandt had depicted Saskia rather small in comparison to his own self portrait.

156 It is Van Mander who refers to draughtsmanship as the father of art (Chapman 1990, p. 82).

157 An exception is the portrait of Vermeyen, who is depicted drawing an oriental landscape in a sketchbook (Lampsonius/Cock 1572, p. 15).

158 B. 349.

159 The process is described thus by Gersaint in his 1751 catalogue.

160 P. Schatborn in Berlin/Amsterdam/London 1991–2, vol. II, p. 34, note 8.

161 P. Schatborn in Berlin/Amsterdam/London/1991–2, vol. II, no. 4. Three other drawn 'self portraits' from the 1630s have been attributed to Rembrandt: Paris, Musée du Louvre (Benesch 1973, vol. II, p. 126, no. A 18a and fig. 626: 'a work of the School'; Wright 1982, p. 45, no. 3 and fig. 24); Marseille, Musée des Beaux-Arts (Benesch 1973, vol. II, no. 430 and fig. 517: 'About 1633'; Wright 1982, p. 45, no. 5 and fig. 43). The attribution of the first sheet is controversial, while the likeness of the second is not apparent. The latter objection also applies to the drawing in New York, The Metropolitan Museum of Art, Robert Lehman Collection (Benesch 1973, vol. II, p. 102, no. 434 and fig. 525; Wright 1982, p. 45, no. 7 and fig. 54).

162 Koslow 1975.

163 Turin, Galleria Sabauda; *Corpus*, vol. I, no. A 17.

164 Ripa 1644, p. 76. The woodcut that accompanies this passage depicts an old man wearing an exotic cap. A similar illustration appears in the 1603 Italian edition (Koslow 1975, fig. 30).

165 Döring compares Rembrandt's print (in Brunswick 1997, pp. 11–12) to the portrait of Gossaert in Lampsonius's print series with painters' portraits, published in 1572 (p. 43, fig. 5). There are indeed certain formal similarities, but Gossaert does not place his hand inside his cloak; furthermore, part of his other arm is visible at the bottom of the print.

166 The only comparable work is *Two Dead Peacocks and a Girl* from the Rijksmuseum, Amsterdam, which may be dated around the same time (*Corpus*, vol. III, no. A 134; Berlin/Amsterdam/London 1991–2, vol. I, no. 30).

167 Benesch 1973, vol. II, no. 451.

168 De Jongh (1969) believed that Titian's painting served as Rembrandt's sole example here. He also thought that the rakish angle of the beret in the etched self portrait determined the position of the hat in the drawing after Raphael that is shown here (see also *Corpus*, vol. III, under no. A 139).

169 With thanks to Marieke de Winkel for this observation; the figure in an etching from 1641 also wears a small cross of this type (B. 261).

170 Amsterdam, Rijksmuseum, Rijksprentenkabinet and London, British Museum.

171 Madrid, Biblioteca Nacional (Huidobro/Santiago 1998, no. 14); Amsterdam, Rijksmuseum, Rijksprentenkabinet (Boon 1963, no. 149); Munich, Staatliche Graphische Sammlung (Grimm 1991, p. 109, fig. 196).

172 London, British Museum; White 1969, fig. 158.

173 Melbourne/Canberra 1997–8, no. 103.

174 De Jongh 1995, p. 230.

175 De Jongh (1969) considered Titian's so-called portrait of the poet Ariosto as Rembrandt's most important example, and he saw this self portrait as a contribution to the *paragone* debate (the polemic concerning the question of whether painting or poetry was the superior art form). On the relationship to Dürer, see Dickey 1994, pp. 123–8.

176 Rembrandt probably painted his self portrait on a rectangular canvas, but left the upper corners unpainted in order to be able to mount the picture in a frame with an arched inner contour. Later on, both the upper corners and part of the upper edge of the canvas were cut (see *Corpus*, vol. III, p. 375; London 1988–9, p. 82, and Berlin/Amsterdam/London 1991–2, vol. I, p. 218).

177 London 1988–9, p. 84.

178 In Melbourne/Canberra 1997–8, p. 128, this short hairstyle is linked to the criticism of the fashionable long hair that was expressed within the Protestant Church from 1640 onwards. Rembrandt, however, already depicted himself with short hair in 1636 (compare cat. nos. 46–7). On Rembrandt's hairstyle, see also Dickey 1994, p. 164, note 62.

179 Strauss/Van der Meulen 1979, p. 397, no. 1657/2, no. 292.

180 J. van der Veen in Melbourne/Canberra 1997–8, p. 71.

181 For the different views on the degree of authenticity of this painting, see Winkler 1957, p. 143 (who believes that the original was painted over completely); White 1982, p. 111–12 (eighteenth-century imitation); Van de Wetering/Broekhoff 1996 (heavily painted over with some parts of the original left intact).

182 For the results of the scientific research, see Groen 1988; Van de Wetering/Broekhoff 1996 and *Corpus*, vol. IV, no. 1. The author wishes to acknowledge Viola Pemberton-Pigott of the Royal Collection for her kind assistance.

183 According to dendrochronological examination performed by Dr P. Klein, it is quite possible that the panel was first used in or around 1630 (see *Corpus*, vol. IV, no. 1).

184 E.g. B. 118 and 356.

185 The feathered beret appears in a copy that was probably made outside Rembrandt's workshop. It may be inferred from this that the feather also graced the finished painting and was not painted over by Rembrandt himself (*Corpus*, vol. IV, no. 2).

186 Gerson 1968, p. 498, no. 240.

187 Gaskell 1990, pp. 134–9, no. 25, as 'workshop or follower of Rembrandt Harmensz. van Rijn'.

188 The dendrochronological examination was performed in May 1994 by Dr P. Klein.

189 In drawings too, Rembrandt sometimes depicted the headgear before starting on the face. The verso of *The Standing Man with a Stick*, for instance, displays the sketch of a cap (Amsterdam, Rijksmuseum, Rijksprentenkabinet; Benesch 1973, vol. I, no. 32, verso; Schatborn 1985, no. 4 verso).

190 B. 209 and 231.

191 Van Gelder 1943.

192 Oxford, Ashmolean Museum; Benesch 1973, vol. V, no. 1161.

193 Not all authors agree that the landscape is by Rembrandt; see e.g. Boon and White in Hollstein, and White 1969, p. 134, note 4. The watermark in the paper on which the fourth state is printed is from Rembrandt's time (Ash/Fletcher 1998, p. 185, G. c). Additions in the fifth state, however, are not contemporary (Ash/Fletcher 1998, p. 226).

194 Compare, e.g. the drawing with the *Baptism of the Eunuch* (Ottawa, National Gallery of Canada; Benesch 1973, vol. V, no. 909).

195 Benesch (1973, vol. V, no. 1171) dated the sheet c.1655–6.

196 Mahon 1967, p. 63; see also Frerichs 1970, pp. 42–3.

197 The sheet was furnished with a separate, glowing description in the Crozat catalogue along with a 'counterpart' (which was in fact wrongly ascribed to Rembrandt): 'Son portrait & celui de sa Mere, faits par lui-même' (Schatborn 1981, p. 41; for the supposed pendant, see Benesch 1973, vol. VI, p. 391, under no. A 105 with fig.).

198 B. 131; also comparable are dated prints from 1652 (B. 65) and 1654 (B. 64 and 87).

199 For a detailed discussion of the various copies of the lost self portrait, see *Corpus*, vol. IV, no. 20 (with illustrations of the three copies that are not depicted here).

200 Van Mander 1604a, fol. 214 verso; see *Corpus*, vol. IV, under no. 14.

201 Paris 1986, p. 202, fig. 117. The Paris sheet derives from the well-known eighteenth-century collection of John Barnard (Lugt 1419).

202 The print was added to Gersaint's catalogue shortly after his death in 1751 by the publishers Helle and Glomy (G. 11). According to an inscription on a copy made after the etching by François Basan, the original was preserved in the collection of the famous collector Pierre Mariette (1634–1716), whose collector's mark is found on the back of the specimen in Vienna (Boon 1969, p. 7).

203 For instance by Von Bartsch, Von Seidlitz, Rovinski, Coppier, Boon and Björklund (Hollstein, vol. XVIII, p. 169, no. S. 379).

204 The date and signature are quite similar to those on the etching *Christ and the Woman of Samaria*, also executed in 1658 (B. 70; detail of the signature of this etching in Paris 1986, p. 204, fig. 119).

205 Especially B. 199, 200 and 205.

206 Wheelock 1995, p. 262.

207 It seems a little far-fetched to suggest that Rembrandt was basing himself on Raphael's *Portrait of Baldassare Castiglione* in order to parade his ambitions as a *pictor doctus* (learned painter), as argued in Wheelock 1995, p. 264.

208 A similar situation arises in the self portrait from 1669 in London (cat. no. 84), in which, apart from the painter's cap, a brush was also painted over.

209 This explanation was suggested by the Rembrandt Research Project, partly in response to Christian Tümpel, who classified the painting as a product of the workshop in his monograph on Rembrandt (Tümpel 1986, p. 428, no. A 72).

210 Houbraken 1718–21, vol. I, p. 259.

211 This effect was lost in an enlargement of the canvas in the nineteenth century, which was reversed again before 1935 (*Corpus*, vol. IV, no. 15). C. Wright (1982, p. 31) mistakenly assumed that the sections of the painting removed at that time had belonged to the original (on this point, see also Bailey 1992).

212 See e.g. Clark 1978, p. 26.

213 Bredius/Gerson 1969, p. 552, no. 58. This entry has been written on the basis of the draft entry for the fourth volume of the *Corpus*. Apart from the latter, Wright (1982, no. 54), has been the only recent author to defend it.

214 Rosenberg 1964, p. 51.

215 This entry has been written on the basis of the draft entry for the fourth volume of the *Corpus*.

216 Bauch 1966, no. 337.

217 Bredius/Gerson 1969, no. 528.

218 For example, by J. Bruyn in Berlin/Amsterdam/London 1991–2, vol. I, p. 85.

219 W. Liedtke in New York 1995–6, vol. II, no. 15. The self portrait from 1658 in the Frick Collection, New York (cat. no. 71), to which the drawing has been compared, in fact bears less of a resemblance (see Giltaij 1988, p. 102, note 4).

220 Others have seen a maulstick diagonally over the hand. Giltaij believes, however, that this mark is a fold of the cloak (1988, p. 102, note 2).

221 White/Boon 1969, no. B. 273.

222 M. Bisanz-Prakken in New York 1997, no. 60, was the first to give an extensive account of the technical details of this drawing.

223 Haverkamp Begemann 1961, p. 87.

224 Benesch 1973, vol. V, no. 1177.

225 See W. Liedtke in New York 1995–6, vol. II, p. 76, and *Corpus*, vol. IV, under no. 20.

226 Van Thiel 1969. According to Chapman (1990, p. 168, note 104) the letters cannot be read in this way. On the basis of the allusions to the Epistle to the Ephesians incorporated into this painting, however, Van Thiel's hypothesis deserves serious reconsideration; see *Corpus*, vol. IV, under no. 21.

227 See also *Corpus*, vol. I, pp. 148–9.

228 *Corpus*, vol. I, no. A 11.

229 Goeree 1682, p. 107. A face with raised eyebrows and a frowning brow is also found, albeit less pronounced than here, in the self portrait from 1660 in New York (cat. no. 80).

230 *Corpus*, vol. I, no. A 26. For a characteristic depiction of Paul, made in Rembrandt's workshop around 1635, see Bredius/Gerson 1969, no. 603, and Van de Wetering 1997, p. 111, fig. 134.

231 For the painting from 1661, see Bredius/Gerson 1969, no. 309. For a list of other paintings with the same model as in the painting in Washington (our fig. 81b), see Wheelock 1995, p. 244.

232 This is suggested in De Vries 1989.

233 Quoted from Gaehtgens 1987, p. 438; see also J. van der Veen in Melbourne/Canberra 1997–8, p. 73.

234 Quoted from Chapman 1990, p. 126; see also pp. 120 and 126–7 for an even more elaborate psychological explanation. See also Tümpel 1986, pp. 367–8.

235 See e.g. Bredius/Gerson 1969, nos. 297 (our fig. 81c), 615 and 618.

236 See Chapman 1990, p. 121, and *Corpus*, vol. IV, under no. 21.

237 See note 271.

238 Van Mander 1604a, fol. 301 recto. Van Mander based his account on the Roman writer Marcus Verrius Flaccus; see Blankert 1973, p. 35.

239 Van Hoogstraten 1678, pp. 78 and 110.

240 Dordrecht/Cologne 1998–9, no. 22B.

241 The first to relate the painting discussed here to the story of Zeuxis laughing himself to death was Blankert (1973, passim). For a summary of his persuasive interpretation and a few additional remarks, see A. Blankert in Melbourne/Canberra 1997–8, pp. 38–40. For other, less plausible interpretations, see Von Einem 1970; Pérussaux 1989; Vonessen 1992 and the literature cited in our note 246. For a survey of the complex historiography of this self portrait, see Vey/Kesting 1967, pp. 89–92; E. Mai in Dordrecht/Cologne 1998–9, pp. 99–108 and *Corpus*, vol. IV, no. 22.

242 A similar expression occurs in an etched self portrait made in 1630 (cat. no. 22) and *The Laughing Soldier* from the same period (p. 122, fig. 18a).

243 It is unclear whether the ribbon with the medal around Rembrandt's neck is intended to represent one of the gold insignia of honour that were presented to painters by sovereigns, or whether it is a more general allusion to the past, as in the case of earlier self portraits with gold chains (see cat. no. 10).

244 Aside from the hand with the brush raised to the level of the face, the X-radiograph also shows a second, lightly delineated shape resembling a hand with a brush, which is placed lower down in the pictorial plane. Chapman (1990, p. 102) takes this shape to indicate an earlier version of the maulstick.

245 As the painting is now covered with a thick layer of varnish, the figure on the left is hard to make out. Moreover, part of the head is no longer original, as the upper left corner (like the upper right) was lost in later years and pieces were added to replace them.

246 In Stechow 1944 the figure on the left is taken to represent the philosopher Heraclitus and Rembrandt himself the laughing Democritus; this interpretation is endorsed in Tümpel 1971, pp. 33–8 and Tümpel 1986, pp. 368 and 410. Białostocki (1966) identified the figure on the left as a bust of Terminus, the ancient god of death, and interpreted the scene as Rembrandt laughing in the face of death.

247 Between 1758 and 1808 Rembrandt's painting was described in this way at least six times; see A. Blankert in Melbourne/Canberra 1997–8, pp. 38 and 186–7.

248 Blankert 1973, p. 34.

249 *Corpus*, vol. IV, under no. 21. On cusping, see cat. no. 85.

250 See Dordrecht/Cologne 1998–9, no. 41.

251 First suggested by Blankert (1973, pp. 35–8); see also A. Blankert in Melbourne/Canberra 1997–8, pp. 38–40.

252 See *Corpus*, vol. IV, under no. 21. Pächt (1991, p. 78) previously related this self portrait to studies of facial expressions from Rembrandt's early years (see cat. nos. 20–3).

253 Rosenberg (1964, p. 55) even saw in this self portrait 'a faint hint of senility' (see also Chapman 1990, p. 104).

254 For an overview and discussion of the different interpretations, see Berlin/Amsterdam/London 1991–2, vol. I, pp. 284–7; De Jongh 1991b; *Corpus*, vol. IV, no. 23. For a purely mathematical approach to the composition, see Hussey 1990.

255 This link was first made by Broos (1971), who also saw an intentional contrast between the perfect form of the circle and Rembrandt's style of painting, which, on contemporaries, made the impression of

being unfinished. For reactions and additions to his theory, see Moffit 1984 and Chenault Porter 1988.

256 Van Mander 1604a, p. 96 verso. Van Mander took the anecdote from the Italian biographer Vasari; see also the literature listed in note 255.

257 See Schneider 1995.

258 On the execution of this painting, see also Van de Wetering 1997, p. 205.

259 Martin 1967. Only part of the last letter of Rembrandt's signature can still be seen at the left edge of the canvas. It may be concluded from this that the canvas was shortened along this side. The painting was probably also cut along the other sides, albeit to a lesser extent (see *Corpus*, vol. IV, under no. 24).

260 For the technical aspects of this painting, see London 1988–9, pp. 140–3.

261 It is not entirely certain whether the intended cap in the London painting was of exactly the same shape as in the three other paintings mentioned. Above and to the right of the head, several brushstrokes are visible, suggesting that the cap was initially intended to be larger and shaped more like a turban (see *Corpus*, vol. IV, under no. 24).

262 Chapman 1990, pp. 130–1, suggests that Rembrandt's self portrait from 1669 should be interpreted as a deliberate reference to the self portrait from 1640 (for a reaction to this suggestion, see *Corpus*, vol. IV, under no. 24). According to Broos (1987, p. 315) Rembrandt based the pose in this self portrait from 1669 on a print by Reinier van Persijn after Raphael's portrait of Baldassare Castiglione (for the painting, see p. 170, fig. 53b; for the print, see Broos 1987, p. 314, fig. 4 and Chapman 1990, fig. 105).

263 The diaries and documents relating to Cosimo's two journeys through the Netherlands have been published in Hoogewerff 1919; see also pp. 49–50.

264 As this catalogue went to press, a proposed cleaning of this self portrait had not yet been carried out, and the painting was still covered by later overpainting and a thick, blanched layer of varnish.

265 Chapman (1990, p. 130) and Langedijk (1992, p. 150) believe that he is wearing a chain, but according to the *Corpus*, vol. IV, under no. 25, it is probably a ribbon.

266 With thanks to Marieke de Winkel for pointing out these details.

267 Langedijk 1992, p. 149.

268 The painting was probably reduced in size by about 15 cm on all sides (*Corpus*, vol. IV, under no. 25). On cusping, see also Van de Wetering 1997, pp. 111–23.

269 Van Gelder 1948, p. 58. For other quotations, see De Vries/Tóth-Ubbens/Froentjes 1978, p. 187, note 8; Broos 1987, pp. 311–15, and *Corpus*, vol. IV, under no. 26.

270 Berlin/Amsterdam/London 1991–2, vol. I, p. 290.

271 The information given here has been derived from a preliminary report of this research, which was conducted in 1998 by Caroline van der Elst and Carol Pottasch in the Mauritshuis. For the findings of previous technical research, see De Vries/Tóth-Ubbens/Froentjes 1978, pp. 179–87. A black border has been applied along three sides of the canvas. The absence of this border along the lower edge indicates that the picture was trimmed there and that the present, almost square format, is not the original

one. The function of this border, which was applied directly onto the ground before painting commenced, has not yet been clarified. In the *Self Portrait as the Apostle Paul*, Rembrandt also added a border, but only after the work's completion (see cat. no. 81).

272 See cat. no. 73.

273 During the restoration of the painting in 1996–7, it became clear that only a few traces remained of the original paint of the signature and year; the latter is now illegible. With thanks to Jos Deuss for this information.

274 Bol was already documented in Dordrecht as a painter in December 1635 (see Blankert 1982, p. 71). In or around 1636 he appears to have been active in Rembrandt's workshop, according to a note on the back of one of the latter's drawings (Benesch 1973, vol. II, no. 448).

275 In his monograph on Bol, Blankert (1982) still had doubts as to whether this piece could be identified as a self portrait, but in Canberra/Melbourne 1997–8, no. 45, he seems to have been convinced.

276 Blankert 1982, nos. 151–2.

277 Sumowski 1979–92, vol. I, no. 107.

278 The author is extremely grateful to Marieke de Winkel for her valuable comments on the costumes worn by Rembrandt's pupils in the works described here.

279 Blankert 1982, nos. 61–2; see also Blankert 1982, nos. 63–4 and Hollstein, vol. III, p. 26, no. 12. Compare also *Corpus*, vol. III, pp. 380–1.

280 Sumowski 1979–92, vol. I, no. 142.

281 See note 176.

282 Hollstein, vol. III, p. 35, no. 2. For the provenance of the drawing described here, see Sumowski 1979–92, vol. I, no. 106.

283 Orlers 1641, p. 380.

284 Hunnewell 1987, pp. 279–81, appendix A, nos. 1–10, p. 283, appendix B, no. 5, pp. 286–7, appendix C, nos. 5 and 8.

285 The composition with a basket and a gourd in the right foreground displays similarities to a painting depicted in the *Painter in his Studio*, which is attributed to Dou's pupil Adriaen van Gaesbeeck (Leiden 1988, no. 17) and may have been produced in Dou's workshop.

286 Sumowski 1983–95, vol. I, no. 301.

287 Sumowski 1983–95, vol. I, no. 274.

288 According to Marieke de Winkel, this costume dates, at the earliest, from the second half of the 1640s (oral communication).

289 Martin 1913, p. 18, left; Hunnewell 1987, pp. 286–7, appendix C, no. 8, as a copy. At least three copies of this self portrait are dated 1652.

290 For pieces believed to be self portraits by Drost, see Sumowski 1983–95, vol. I, nos. 326, 334 and 341.

291 See also the drawing attributed to Nicolaes Maes (Sumowski 1979–92, vol. VIII, no. 1758) and a drawn self portrait by Heyman Dullaert (Sumowski 1979–92, vol. III, no. 570).

292 See P. Schatborn in Berlin/Amsterdam/London 1991–2, vol. II, p. 142.

293 Dudok van Heel (1992) discovered Drost's year of birth and compiled his family tree (see also Houbraken 1718–21, vol. III, p. 61).

294 Langedijk 1992, pp. 32–7, no. 6; Sumowski 1983–95, vol. I, no. 341.

295 The authenticity of the signature has recently been called in question (see M. van Berge-Gerbaud in Paris/Haarlem 1997–8, p. 118). The inscription nonetheless displays the artist's characteristic handwriting, although the 'D' is rare (for another example, compare Sumowski 1979–92, vol. II, no. 401).

296 Compare Sumowski 1979–92, vol. II, no. 520.

297 Houbraken 1718–21, vol. I, p. 174; vol. II, pp. 100–1.

298 It has been suggested that Van den Eeckhout's self portrait could in fact portray Ferdinand Bol (see Broos 1984, p. 180; M. van Berge-Gerbaud in Paris/Haarlem 1997–8, no. 51).

299 For possible portraits, or self portraits, of Van den Eeckhout, see Sumowski 1979–92, vol. II, no. 524; Hollstein, vol. VI, p. 134, no. 5 (both dubious as self portraits); Houbraken 1718–21, vol. II, facing p. 102, no. 3.

300 Sumowski 1983–95, vol. II, no. 609.

301 The X-radiograph of the painting reveals white contours below the chin, possibly interpretable as the outline of a white collar that was later painted over (see Giltaij/Jansen 1988, fig. 7a).

302 Van Hoogstraten 1678, p. 11.

303 Brown 1981, p. 147, document no. 6.

304 Corpus, vol. III, nos. C 97, C 106–7 and C 114. The attribution of the painting at Pasadena (no. C 97) to Carel Fabritius has not been accepted by other art historians (cat. no. 56).

305 Brown 1981, pp. 121–2, no. 1.

306 Dendrochronological examination of the panel is indicative of a date of origin no earlier than 1629 (report by Dr P. Klein, 27 January 1993).

307 If the painting is indeed identical to a panel auctioned as a Flinck in 1878, this false signature must have been added after that year (on the provenance, see MacLaren/Brown 1991, vol. I, p. 141).

308 Houbraken 1718–21, vol. II, p. 21.

309 Houbraken 1718–21, vol. II, pp. 20–1.

310 This painting is dated 163(.), although the Rembrandt Research Project dates it c.1641 on the basis of a (doubtful) attribution to Carel Fabritius. Flinck's Portrait of a man from 1643 (Sumowski 1983–95, vol. II, no. 680; London 1988–9, p. 82, fig. 65), which displayed a very close resemblance to Rembrandt's Self Portrait from 1640, was apparently 'destroyed' during cleaning work (Sumowski 1983–95, vol. VI, p. 3608).

311 De Bruyn Kops 1965, figs. 7–8.

312 De Bruyn Kops 1965, p. 27.

313 Sumowski 1979–92, vol. IV, no. 868.

314 Dordrecht/Cologne 1998–9, no. 58 (compare The Entrance of a Temple, The Hague, Mauritshuis, inv. no. 737; Dordrecht/Cologne 1998–9, no. 6).

315 P. Schatborn in Dordrecht/Cologne 1998–9, pp. 110–21.

316 Sumowski 1983–95, vol. II, no. 749; Dordrecht/Cologne 1998–9, no. 22 B.

317 Weyerman 1729–69, vol. III, p. 44.

318 For self portraits of Maes, see Sumowski 1983–95, vol. III, no. 1437; Sumowski 1979–92, vol. VIII, no. 1758 (attribution uncertain).

319 P. Schatborn in Dordrecht/Cologne 1998–9, p. 114.

320 Sumowski 1979–92, vol. V, no. 1110. Various authors have expressed doubt as to whether this painting can be identified as a self portrait.

321 Sumowski 1983–95, vol. II, nos. 847 and 851; his no. 852 is probably not by Van Hoogstraten (Brusati 1995, pp. 43–4 and fig. 31 as Willem Drost [?]).

322 Van Hoogstraten 1678, p. 257. Roscam Abbing (1993, p. 34, no. 9) assumed that Van Hoogstraten arrived at Rembrandt's workshop no earlier than 1642.

323 For contracts of painters pupils who were sometimes allowed to do their own work for a profit, see De Jager 1990, p. 100 (contracts Amsterdam 1698, Delft 1621), p. 101 (contract Dordrecht 1675) and p. 103 (contract Utrecht 1611).

324 Sumowski 1979–92, vol. V, p. 2780, no. 1256^x and White/Boon 1969, no. B 193.

325 Compare Melbourne/Canberra 1997–8, no. 61. See Broos 1981, pp. 135–8 for several drawings by Van Hoogstraten from 1646–8.

326 Roscam Abbing 1993, p. 36, nos. 13–15.

327 De Jongh 1967, pp. 87, 90, fig. 76.

328 Miedema 1975, pp. 13–16; for an interpretation of this painting along these lines, see Brusati 1995, pp. 44–5; Popper-Voskuil 1973, pp. 63–5.

Bibliography

ALPERS 1988
S. Alpers, *Rembrandt's Enterprise: The Studio and the Market*, Chicago/London 1988

AMSTERDAM 1976
E. de Jongh *et al.*, *Tot leering en vermaak: Betekenissen van Hollandse genrevoorstellingen uit de zeventiende eeuw*, Amsterdam, Rijksmuseum 1976

AMSTERDAM 1984–5
P. Schatborn, E. Ornstein-van Slooten, *Bij Rembrandt in de leer / Rembrandt as Teacher*, Amsterdam, Museum Het Rembrandthuis 1984–5

AMSTERDAM 1985–6
B.P.J. Broos, *Rembrandt en zijn voorbeelden / Rembrandt and his sources*, Amsterdam, Museum Het Rembrandthuis 1985–6

AMSTERDAM 1986
W. Kloek, J.P. Filedt Kok, W. Halsema, *Kunst voor de beeldenstorm: Noordnederlandse kunst 1525–1580*, Amsterdam, Rijksmuseum 1986

AMSTERDAM 1989–90
P. Hecht, *De Hollandse fijnschilders: Van Gerard Dou tot Adriaen van der Werff*, Amsterdam, Rijksmuseum 1989–90

AMSTERDAM 1991
A. Tümpel, P. Schatborn *et al.*, *Pieter Lastman: Leermeester van Rembrandt*, Amsterdam, Museum Het Rembrandthuis 1991

AMSTERDAM 1996
C. Schuckman, M. Royalton-Kisch, E. Hinterding, *Rembrandt & Van Vliet: A Collaboration on Copper*, Amsterdam, Museum Het Rembrandthuis 1996

AMSTERDAM/GRONINGEN 1983
A. Blankert *et al.*, *The Impact of a Genius: Rembrandt, his Pupils and Followers in the Seventeenth Century. Paintings from Museums and Private Collections*, Amsterdam, Waterman Gallery; Groningen, Groninger Museum 1983

ANGEL 1642
P. Angel, *Lof der schilder-konst*, Leiden 1642

ASH/FLETCHER 1998
N. Ash, S. Fletcher, *Watermarks in Rembrandt's Prints*, Washington 1998

B.
A. von Bartsch, *Catalogue raisonné de toutes les estampes qui forment l'oeuvre de Rembrandt, et ceux de ses principaux imitateurs*, 2 vols., Vienna 1797

J. VAN B. 1662
J. van B., *Een onderscheyt boeckje ofte tractaetje vande fouten en dwalingen der politie in ons vaderlant*, Amsterdam 1662

BADT 1957–8
K. Badt, 'Drei plastische Arbeiten von Leone Battista Alberti', *Mitteilungen des Kunsthistorischen Institutes in Florenz 8*, 1957–8, pp. 78–87

BAER 1990
R. Baer, *The Paintings of Gerrit Dou (1613–1675)*, diss., New York 1990

BAILEY 1992
M. Bailey, 'Rembrandt's Alexander the Great: A salutary warning', *Apollo 136*, 1992, no. 365, pp. 35–6

BAL 1991
M. Bal, *Reading "Rembrandt": Beyond the World-Image Opposition*, Cambridge, Mass. 1991

BALDINUCCI 1686
F. Baldinucci, *Cominciamento e progresso dell'arte dell'intagliare in rame, colle vite di molti de' più eccelenti Maestri della stessa Professione*, Florence 1686

BALDWIN 1985
R.W. Baldwin, ' "On earth we are beggars, as Christ himself was": The protestant background of Rembrandt's Imagery of Poverty, Disability, and Begging', *Konsthistorisk Tidskrift 54*, 1985, pp. 122–35

BAUCH 1960
K. Bauch, *Der frühe Rembrandt und seine Zeit*, Berlin 1960

BAUCH 1962
K. Bauch, 'Ein Selbstbildnis des frühen Rembrandt', *Wallraf-Richartz-Jahrbuch 24*, 1962, pp. 321–32

BAUCH 1966
K. Bauch, *Rembrandt: Gemälde*, Berlin 1966

BAUER 1977
H. Bauer, 'Rembrandt vor der Staffelei', *Festschrift Wolfgang Braunfels*, Tübingen 1977, pp. 1–11

BECK 1624
D. Beck, S.E. Veldhuyzen (ed.), *Spiegel van mijn leven: Een Haags dagboek uit 1624*, Hilversum 1993

BENESCH 1947
O. Benesch, *Rembrandt: Teekeningen verzameld door Otto Benesch*, Oxford/London 1947

BENESCH 1973
O. Benesch, enlarged and edited by E. Benesch, *The Drawings of Rembrandt*, 6 vols., London/New York 1973

BERGSTRÖM 1966
I. Bergström, 'Rembrandt's double-portrait of himself and Saskia at the Dresden Gallery', *Nederlands Kunsthistorisch Jaarboek 17*, 1966, pp. 143–69

BERLIN/AMSTERDAM/LONDON 1991–2
C. Brown, J. Kelch, P.J.J. van Thiel (eds.), *Rembrandt: The Master & His Workshop*, vol. I: *Paintings*; H. Bevers, P. Schatborn, B. Welzel (eds.), vol. II: *Drawings & Etchings*, Berlin, Altes Museum; Amsterdam, Rijksmuseum; London, National Gallery 1991–2

BIAŁOSTOCKI 1966
J. Białostocki, 'Rembrandt's "Terminus"', *Wallraf-Richartz-Jahrbuch 28*, 1966, pp. 49–60

BIDLOO 1720
L. Bidloo, *Panpoëticon Batavum, Kabinet, waar in de Afbeeldingen van Voornaame Nederlandsche Dichteren, verzameld, en Konstig Geschilderdt door Arnoud van Halen, en onder Uytbreyding, en Aanmerkingen, over de Hollandsche Rym-Konst, geopendt, door Lamb. Bidloo*, Amsterdam 1720

DE BIE 1661
C. de Bie, *Het gulden cabinet van de edel vrij schilder-const*, Antwerp 1661

BIENTJES 1967
J. Bientjes, *Holland und der Holländer im Urteil deutscher Reisender*, Groningen 1967

BLANKERT 1973
A. Blankert, 'Rembrandt, Zeuxis and Ideal Beauty', J. Bruyn, J.A. Emmens, E. de Jongh, D.P. Snoep (eds.), *Album Amicorum J.G. van Gelder*, The Hague 1973, pp. 32–9

BLANKERT 1982
A. Blankert, *Ferdinand Bol 1616–1680: Rembrandt's Pupil*, Doornspijk 1982

BLUNT 1964
A. Blunt (ed.), *Nicolas Poussin: Lettres et propos sur l'art*, Paris 1964

VON BODE 1876
W. [von] Bode, 'Notizen: Die ersten Selbstporträts des Rembrandt van Rijn', *Zeitschrift für bildende Kunst 11*, 1876, pp. 125–6

BOEHM 1985
G. Boehm, *Bildnis und Individuum: Über den Ursprung der Porträtmalerei in der italienischen Renaissance*, Munich 1985

BOON 1963
K.G. Boon, *Rembrandt de etser*, Amsterdam 1963

BOON 1969
K.G. Boon, 'Rembrandt's laatste geëtste zelfportret', *Kroniek van het Rembrandthuis 23*, 1969, no. 1, pp. 4–9

BORGHINI 1584
R. Borghini, *Il riposo*, Florence 1584

BREDIUS 1915–22
A. Bredius, *Künstler-Inventare: Urkunden zur Geschichte der holländischen Kunst des XVI[ten], XVII[ten] und XVIII[ten] Jahrhunderts*, 8 vols., The Hague 1915–22

BREDIUS/GERSON 1969
A. Bredius, revised by H. Gerson, *Rembrandt: The Complete Edition of the Paintings*, London 1969

BROOS 1971
B.P.J. Broos, 'The "O" of Rembrandt', *Simiolus 4*, 1971, pp. 150–84

BROOS 1975–6
B.P.J. Broos, 'Rembrandt and Lastman's Coriolanus: The history piece in 17th-century theory and practice', *Simiolus 8*, 1975–6, pp. 199–228

BROOS 1981
B.P.J. Broos, *Rembrandt en tekenaars uit zijn omgeving (Oude tekeningen in het bezit van de Gemeentemusea van Amsterdam waaronder de collectie Fodor, vol. III)*, Amsterdam 1981

BROOS 1981–2
B.P.J. Broos, review of *Strauss/Van der Meulen 1979*, *Simiolus 12*, 1981–2, pp. 245–62

BROOS 1983
B.P.J. Broos, 'De bronnen over Rembrandt anno 1983', *Kroniek van het Rembrandthuis 35*, 1983, pp. 1–31

BROOS 1984a
B.P.J. Broos, 'De bronnen over Rembrandt anno 1984', *Tableau 6*, 1984, no. 5, pp. 34–45

BROOS 1984b
B.P.J. Broos, review of *Sumowski 1983–95*, vol. I, *Oud Holland 98*, 1984, pp. 146–86

BROOS 1987
B.P.J. Broos, *Meesterwerken in het Mauritshuis*, The Hague 1987

BROOS 1995
B.P.J. Broos, 'Jan van Beuningen: een heer van stand in de kunst / a gentleman of standing in the art world', *Mauritshuis in focus* 8, 1995, pp. 20–6

BROWN 1981
C. Brown, *Carel Fabritius: Complete Edition with a catalogue raisonné*, Oxford 1981

BROWN 1995
J. Brown, *Kings and Connoisseurs: Collecting Art in Seventeenth-Century Europe*, New Haven/London 1995

BRUNSWICK 1979
J. Białostocki, S. Jacob, R.E.O. Ekkart, *Jan Lievens: Ein Maler im Schatten Rembrandts*, Brunswick, Herzog Anton Ulrich-Museum 1979

BRUNSWICK 1980
H.-J. Raupp, *Selbstbildnisse und Künstlerporträts von Lucas van Leyden bis Anton Raphael Mengs*, Brunswick, Herzog Anton Ulrich-Museum 1980

BRUNSWICK 1995
T. Döring, *Rembrandt als Radierer: Die Selbstbildnisse*, Brunswick, Herzog Anton Ulrich-Museum 1995

BRUNSWICK 1997
T. Döring et al., *Ansichten vom Ich. 100 ausgewählte Blätter der Sammlung. Künstler sehen sich selbst: Graphische Selbstbildnisse des 20. Jahrhunderts*, Brunswick, Herzog Anton Ulrich-Museum 1997

BRUSATI 1995
C. Brusati, *Artifice and Illusion: The Art and Writing of Samuel van Hoogstraten*, Chicago/London 1995

BRUSSELS MANUSCRIPT 1635
M.P. Merrifield (ed.), *Original Treatises on the Arts of Painting*, New York 1967, vol. II, pp. 759–841

BRUYN 1987
J. Bruyn, 'Nog een suggestie voor het onderwerp van Rembrandts historiestuk te Leiden: De grootmoedigheid van Alexander', *Oud Holland* 101, 1987, pp. 89–94

DE BRUYN KOPS 1965
C.J. de Bruyn Kops, 'Vergeten zelfportretten van Govert Flinck en Bartholomeus van der Helst', *Bulletin van het Rijksmuseum* 13, 1965, pp. 20–9

BUBERL 1916
P. Buberl, *Die Denkmale des Gerichtsbezirkes Salzburg* (*Österreichische Kunsttopographie*, vol. XI), Vienna 1916

BUIJSEN 1993
E. Buijsen, 'Schildersportretten in een Antwerpse kunstkamer', *Tableau* 16, 1993, pp. 100–3

CAMPBELL 1971
C.G. Campbell, *Studies in the Formal Sources of Rembrandt's Figure Compositions*, diss., London 1971

CAMPBELL 1990
L. Campbell, *Renaissance Portraits: European Portrait-Painting in the 14th, 15th and 16th Centuries*, New Haven/London 1990

CAMPBELL 1998
L. Campbell, *The Fifteenth-Century Netherlandish Schools*, London 1998

CASTIGLIONE 1528
A. Haakman (ed.), *Il libro del Cortegiano 1528*, Amsterdam 1991

CHAMBERLAIN 1994
E. Chamberlain (ed.), *Catalogue of the Pepys Library at Magdalene College, Cambridge*, vol. III (*Prints and Drawings*), Cambridge 1994

CHAPMAN 1989
H.P. Chapman, 'Rembrandt's "Burgerlijk" Self-portraits', *Leids Kunsthistorisch Jaarboek* 8, 1989, pp. 203–15

CHAPMAN 1990
H.P. Chapman, *Rembrandt's Self-Portraits: A Study in Seventeenth-Century Identity*, Princeton 1990

CHENAULT PORTER 1988
J. Chenault Porter, 'Rembrandt and His Circles: More About the Late *Self-Portrait* in Kenwood House', R.E. Fleischer, S.S. Munshower (eds.), *The Age of Rembrandt: Studies in Seventeenth-Century Dutch Painting, Papers in Art History from The Pennsylvania State University* 3, 1988, pp. 188–212

CHILD 1990
G. Child, *World mirrors 1650–1900*, London 1990

CLARK 1978
K. Clark, *An Introduction to Rembrandt*, London 1978

CORPUS
J. Bruyn, B. Haak, S.H. Levie, P.J.J. van Thiel, E. van de Wetering, *A Corpus of Rembrandt Paintings*, I– , Foundation Rembrandt Research Project 1982–

CORSON 1965
R. Corson, *Fashions in hair: The first five thousand years*, London 1965

COTGRAVE 1611
R. Cotgrave, *A Dictionarie of the French and English Tongues*, London 1611

COUPRIE 1994
L.D. Couprie, 'De jonge Rembrandt in zijn atelier', *Leids Jaarboekje* 86, 1994, pp. 69–96

DAVIES 1968
M. Davies, *National Gallery Catalogues: The Early Netherlandish School*, London 1968

VAN DEURSEN 1991
A.T. van Deursen, *Mensen van klein vermogen*, Amsterdam 1991

DEZALLIER D'ARGENVILLE 1745–52
A.-J. Dezallier d'Argenville, *Abrégé de la vie des plus fameux peintres*, 3 vols., Paris 1745–52

DICKEY 1994
S.S. Dickey, *Prints, Portraits and Patronage in Rembrandt's Work around 1640*, diss., New York 1994

DONATO 1987
M.M. Donato, 'Famosi Cives: Testi, frammenti, e cicli perduti a Firenze fra Tre e Quattrocento', *Ricerche della storia dell'Arte* 30, 1987, pp. 27–42

DORDRECHT/COLOGNE 1998–9
Arent de Gelder (1645–1727): Rembrandts laatste leerling, Dordrecht, Dordrechts Museum; Cologne, Wallraf-Richartz-Museum 1998–9

DUDOK VAN HEEL 1978
S.A.C. Dudok van Heel, 'Mr Joannes Wtenbogaert (1608–1680): Een man uit remonstrants milieu en Rembrandt van Rijn', *Jaarboek Amstelodamum* 70, 1978, pp. 146–69

DUDOK VAN HEEL 1992
S.A.C. Dudok van Heel, 'Willem Drost, een ongrijpbaar Rembrandt-leerling', *Maandblad Amstelodamum* 79, 1992, pp. 15–21

VAN DUUREN 1996
D. van Duuren, *De kris*, Amsterdam 1996

VON EINEM 1970
H. von Einem, 'Das Kölner Selbstbildnis des lachenden Rembrandt', *Festschrift für Gert von der Osten*, Cologne 1970, pp. 177–88

EKKART 1989
R.E.O. Ekkart, 'Jan Cornelisz. van 't Woudt als portretschilder', *Oud Holland* 103, 1989, pp. 223–38

EMMENS 1964
J.A. Emmens, *Rembrandt en de regels van de kunst*, diss., Utrecht 1964

EMMENS 1968
J.A. Emmens, *Rembrandt en de regels van de kunst*, Utrecht 1968

ERPEL 1967
F. Erpel, *Die Selbstbildnisse Rembrandts*, Vienna/Munich 1967

EWALD 1976
G. Ewald, 'Appunti sulla Galleria Gerini e sugli affreschi di Anton Domenico Gabbiani', *Kunst des Barock in der Toskana: Studien zur Kunst unter den letzten Medici (Italienische Forschungen*, vol. IX), Munich 1976, pp. 344–58

FOUCART 1982
J. Foucart, *Les peintures de Rembrandt au Louvre*, Paris 1982

FRERICHS 1970
L.C.J. Frerichs, 'Nieuw licht op een oud opschrift', *Kroniek van het Rembrandthuis* 24, 1970, pp. 35–44

FROENTJES 1969
W. Froentjes, 'Schilderde Rembrandt op goud', *Oud Holland* 84, 1969, pp. 233–7

FURETIÈRE 1690
A. Furetière, *Dictionnaire Universel*, The Hague/Rotterdam 1690

G. / GERSAINT
E.-F. Gersaint, *Catalogue raisonné de toutes les pièces qui forment l'oeuvre de Rembrandt*, Paris 1751

GAEHTGENS 1987
B. Gaehtgens, *Adriaen van der Werff*, Munich 1987

GARAS 1981
K. Garas, 'Christian Seybold und das Malerbildnis in Österreich im 18. Jahrhundert', *Bulletin du Musée Hongrois des Beaux-Arts* 56–7, 1981, pp. 113–37

GASKELL 1990
I. Gaskell, *The Thyssen-Bornemisza Collection. Seventeenth-century Dutch and Flemish painting*, London 1990

GASSER 1961
M. Gasser, *Das Selbstbildnis*, Zurich 1961

VAN GELDER 1943
H.E. van Gelder, 'Marginalia bij Rembrandt. Rembrandts geëtst zelfportret "teekenend aan een lessenaar"', *Oud Holland* 50, 1943, pp. 34–5

VAN GELDER 1948
H.E. van Gelder, *Rembrandt en zijn portret*, Amsterdam [1948]

Van Gelder 1953
J.G. van Gelder, 'Rembrandt's vroegste ontwikkeling', *Mededelingen der Koninklijke Nederlandse Akademie van Wetenschappen, afd. Letterkunde* new series, 16, 1953, no. 5, pp. 273–300

Genootschap 1773
Arnoud van Halen's Pan Poëticon Batavum verheerlijkt door Lofdichten en Bijschriften; grootendeels getrokken uit het Stamboek van Michiel de Roode; en nu eerst in 't licht gebragt door het Genootschap, onder de Spreuk: Kunst wordt door arbeid verkreegen, Leiden 1773

Gerson 1968
H. Gerson, *Rembrandt*, Amsterdam 1968

Giltaij 1988
J. Giltaij, *The Drawings by Rembrandt and His School in the Museum Boymans-van Beuningen*, Rotterdam 1988

Giltaij/Jansen 1988
J. Giltaij, G. Jansen, *Een gloeiend palet: Schilderijen van Rembrandt en zijn school / A glowing palette: Paintings of Rembrandt and his School*, Rotterdam 1988

Glaser/Lehmann/Lubos 1973
H. Glaser, J. Lehmann, A. Lubos, *Wege der deutschen Dichtung*, Frankfurt am Main/Berlin/Vienna 1973

Goeree 1670
W. Goeree, *Inleydingh tot de practyck der Al-gemeene Schilder-konst*, Middelburg 1670

Goeree 1682
W. Goeree, *Natuurlyk en schilderkonstig ontwerp der menschkunde*, Amsterdam 1682

Goldscheider 1936
L. Goldscheider, *Fünfhundert Selbstporträts von der Antike bis zur Gegenwart*, Vienna 1936

Van Gool 1750–1
J. van Gool, *De nieuwe schouburg der Nederlantsche Kunstschilders en schilderessen*, 2 vols., The Hague 1750–1

Gregory 1998
S. Gregory, *Vasari, Prints and Printmaking*, diss., Courtauld Institute of Art, London 1998

Grimm 1991
C. Grimm, *Rembrandt selbst: Eine Neubewertung seiner Porträtkunst*, Stuttgart/Zurich 1991

Groen 1988
K. Groen, 'The examination of the *Portrait of Rembrandt in a Flat Cap*', *The Hamilton Kerr Institute Bulletin* 1, 1988, pp. 66–8

De Grouchy 1894
Vicomte de Grouchy, 'Everhard Jabach collectionneur parisien (1695)', *Mémoires de la Société de l'Histoire de Paris et de l'Ile de France* 21, 1894, pp. 217–92

Haarlem 1986
E. de Jongh, *Portretten van echt en trouw: Huwelijk en gezin in de Nederlandse kunst van de zeventiende eeuw*, Haarlem, Frans Halsmuseum 1986

The Hague 1992
P. Huys Janssen, W. Sumowski, *Rembrandt's Academy*, The Hague, Hoogsteder & Hoogsteder Gallery 1992

The Hague 1997–8
P. van der Ploeg, C. Vermeeren *et al.*, *Vorstelijk verzameld: De kunstcollectie van Frederik Hendrik en Amalia*, The Hague, Mauritshuis 1997–8

The Hague/Münster 1974
G. Langemeyer *et al.*, *Gerard ter Borch. Zwolle 1617. Deventer 1681*, The Hague, Mauritshuis; Münster, Landesmuseum für Kunst und Kulturgeschichte 1974

Van Hall 1963
H. van Hall, *Portretten van Nederlandse beeldende kunstenaars*, Amsterdam 1963

Harrison 1992
C. Harrison, 'Rembrandt: "De kunstenaar in zijn atelier"', *Kunst & Museumjournaal* 4, 1992, no. 1, pp. 28–33

Harte 1976
N.B. Harte, 'State control of Dress and Social change in Pre-Industrial England', D.C. Coleman, A.H. John (eds.), *Trade, Government and Economy in Pre-Industrial England: Essays Presented to F.J. Fisher*, London 1976, pp. 132–65

Haskell 1989
F. Haskell, 'Charles I's Collection of Pictures', *MacGregor 1989*, pp. 203–31

Haverkamp Begemann 1961
E. Haverkamp Begemann, review of O. Benesch, *The Drawings of Rembrandt*, 6 vols., Oxford/London 1954–7, *Kunstchronik* 14, 1961, pp. 10–28, 50–7, 85–91

Haverkamp Begemann 1982
E. Haverkamp Begemann, *Rembrandt: "The Nightwatch"*, Princeton 1982

Heeren 1919
J.J.M. Heeren, 'Het "Panpoëticon Batavum"', *Oud Holland* 37, 1919, pp. 230–40

Heesakkers 1987
C.L. Heesakkers (ed.), *Constantijn Huygens: Mijn jeugd*, Amsterdam 1987

Heesakkers 1994
C.L. Heesakkers (ed.), *Constantijn Huygens: Mijn jeugd*, Amsterdam 1994

Held 1984
J.S. Held, 'A Rembrandt "Theme"', *Artibus et historiae* 10, 1984, pp. 21–34

Hervey 1921
M.F.S. Hervey, *The life correspondence & collections of Thomas Howard, Earl of Arundel*, Cambridge 1921

Heyns 1601
Z. Heyns, *Dracht-Thoneel*, Amsterdam 1601

Hind
A.M. Hind, *A Catalogue of Rembrandt's Etchings*, second edition, 2 vols., London 1923

Hinterding 1995
E. Hinterding, *The history of Rembrandt's copperplates*, Zwolle 1995

Hoff 1935
U. Hoff, *Rembrandt und England*, diss., Hamburg 1935

Hofstede de Groot 1895
C. Hofstede de Groot, 'Bijlage: Aan den Directeur van het Koninklijk Kabinet van Schilderijen te 's-Gravenhage', *Verslagen omtrent 's Rijks Verzamelingen van Geschiedenis en Kunst XVI. 1893*, The Hague 1895, pp. 48–57

Hofstede de Groot 1906
C. Hofstede de Groot, *Die Urkunden über Rembrandt (1575–1721)*, The Hague 1906

Hollstein
F.W.H. Hollstein, *Dutch and Flemish Etchings, Engravings and Woodcuts, ca. 1450–1700*, I– , Amsterdam 1949– (for the vols. on Rembrandt, see: *White/Boon 1969*)

Hondius 1610
H. Hondius, *Pictorum aliquot celebrium praecipuae Germaniae inferioris effigies*, The Hague 1610

Hoogewerff 1919
G.J. Hoogewerff, *De twee reizen van Cosimo de' Medici Prins van Toscane door de Nederlanden (1667–1669): Journalen en documenten*, Amsterdam 1919

Van Hoogstraten 1678
S. van Hoogstraten, *Inleyding tot de hooge schoole der schilderkonst*, Rotterdam 1678

Hope 1985
C. Hope, 'Historical Portraits in the Lives and in the Frescoes of Giorgio Vasari', *Giorgio Vasari: Tra decorazione ambientale e storiografia artistica. Convegno di studi, Arezzo 1981*, Florence 1985, pp. 321–38

Houbraken 1718–21
A. Houbraken, *De groote schouburgh der Nederlantsche konstschilders en schilderessen*, 3 vols., Amsterdam 1718–21 (second edition The Hague 1753)

Hoyle/Miedema 1996
M. Hoyle (translation), H. Miedema (introduction and commentary), 'Philips Angel, *Praise of painting*', *Simiolus* 24, 1996, nos. 2–3, pp. 227–58

Huidobro/Santiago 1998
C. Huidobro, H. Santiago, *De lo divino a lo humano: Rembrandt en la biblioteca nacional*, Madrid 1998

Hunnewell 1987
R. Whittier Hunnewell, *Gerrit Dou's Self Portraits and Depictions of the Artist*, diss., Boston 1983, 2 vols., Ann Arbor 1987

Hussey 1990
H. Hussey, *The Rembrandt Self Portrait: Kenwood*, Henley-on-Thames 1990

Jacobowitz/Stepanek 1983
E.S. Jacobowitz, S.L. Stepanek, *The Prints of Lucas van Leyden & his Contemporaries*, Washington 1983

De Jager 1990
R. de Jager, 'Meester, leerjongen, leertijd: Een analyse van zeventiende-eeuwse Noord-Nederlandse leerlingcontracten van kunstschilders, goud- en zilversmeden', *Oud Holland* 104, 1990, pp. 69–111

Janson 1980
A.F. Janson, *Indianapolis Museum of Art: 100 Masterpieces of Painting*, Indianapolis 1980

Janson 1981
A.F. Janson, 'Rembrandt in the Indianapolis Museum of Art', *Perceptions* 1, 1981, pp. 7–21

De Jonge 1918
C.H. de Jonge, 'De Kleederdracht in de Nederlanden in de XVIe eeuw: Het mannencostuum, Hoofdbedekking', *Oud Holland* 36, 1918, pp. 137–48

De Jonge 1919
C.H. de Jonge, 'De Kleederdracht in de Nederlanden in de XVIe eeuw: Het mannencostuum', *Oud Holland* 37, 1919, pp. 1–207

DE JONGH 1967
E. de Jongh, *Zinne- en minnebeelden in de schilderkunst van de zeventiende eeuw*, sine loco 1967

DE JONGH 1969
E. de Jongh, 'The Spur of Wit: Rembrandt's response to an Italian Challenge', *Delta: A Review of Arts, Life and Thought in the Netherlands* 12, 1969, no. 2, pp. 49–67

DE JONGH 1991a
E. de Jongh, 'De Mate van Ikheid in Rembrandts Zelfportretten', *Kunstschrift* 35, 1991, no. 6, pp. 13–23

DE JONGH 1991b
E. de Jongh, 'Van Kabbala tot Picturale Structuur', *Kunstschrift* 35, 1991, no. 6, pp. 40–1

DE JONGH 1995
E. de Jongh, *Kwesties van betekenis: Thema en motief in de Nederlandse schilderkunst van de zeventiende eeuw*, Leiden 1995

JOOST-GAUGIER 1982
C.L. Joost-Gaugier, 'The Early Beginnings of the Notion of "Uomini Famosi" and the "De viribus Illustribus" in Greco-Roman Literary Tradition', *Artibus et historiae* 6, 1982, pp. 97–115

JUNIUS 1638/1694
K. Aldrich, P. Fehl, R. Fehl (eds.), *Franciscus Junius. The Literature of Classical Art. I: The Painting of the Ancients. II: A Lexicon of Artist and Their Works* (originally published in 1638 and 1694 respectively), Oxford 1991

KEMP 1976
M. Kemp, '"Ogni dipintore dipinge sé": A Neoplatonic Echo in Leonardo's Art Theory?', C.H. Clough (ed.), *Cultural Aspects of the Italian Renaissance: Essays in Honour of Paul Oskar Kristeller*, New York 1976, pp. 311–23

KEMP 1989
M. Kemp, *Leonardo on Painting*, New Haven/London 1989

VAN KEULEN 1996
C. van Keulen, 'Liefhebbers van de schilderkunst in het Lucasgilde', *Simulacrum* 5, 1996, no. 2, pp. 21–3

KINGSTON 1982
W. McAllister Johnson, *French Royal Academy of Painting and Sculpture: Engraved Reception Pieces 1672–1789*, Kingston, Agnes Etherington Art Centre 1982

KLINGER 1991
L. Klinger, *The Portrait Collection of Paolo Giovio*, diss., Princeton University, Princeton 1991

KLINGSÖHR 1986
C. Klingsöhr, 'Die Kunstsammlung der "Académie Royale de Peinture et de Sculpture" in Paris', *Zeitschrift für Kunstgeschichte* 49, 1986, pp. 556–83

KNUTTEL 1892
W.P.C. Knuttel, *Catalogus van de pamfletten-verzameling berustende in de Koninklijke Bibliotheek*, 9 vols., The Hague 1892

KOERNER 1986
J.L. Koerner, 'Rembrandt and the epiphany of the face', *Res* 12, 1986, pp. 5–32

KOSLOW 1975
S. Koslow, 'Frans Hals's Fisherboys: Exemplars of Idleness', *The Art Bulletin* 57, 1975, pp. 418–32

KULTZEN 1996
R. Kultzen, *Michael Sweerts, Brussels 1618 – Goa 1664*, Doornspijk 1996

L. / LUGT
F. Lugt, *Les marques de collections de dessins & d'estampes*, Amsterdam 1921

DE LAIRESSE 1707
G. de Lairesse, *Het Groot Schilderboeck*, 2 vols., Amsterdam 1707 (second edition 1740)

LAMPSONIUS/COCK 1572
D. Lampsonius with engravings by Hieronymus Cock et al., *Pictorum aliquot celebrium Germaniae inferioris effigies*, Antwerp 1572

LANGEDIJK 1992
K. Langedijk, *Die Selbstbildnisse der Holländischen und Flämischen Künstler in der Galleria degli Autoritratti der Uffizien in Florenz*, Florence 1992

LEIDEN 1968
Rondom Rembrandt: De verzameling Daan Cevat, Leiden, Stedelijk Museum De Lakenhal 1968

LEIDEN 1976–7
M.L. Wurfbain *et al.*, *Geschildert tot Leyden Anno 1626*, Leiden, Stedelijk Museum De Lakenhal 1976–7

LEIDEN 1988
E.J. Sluijter, M. Enklaar, P. Nieuwenhuizen *et al.*, *Leidse fijnschilders: Van Gerrit Dou tot Frans van Mieris de Jonge, 1630–1760*, Leiden, Stedelijk Museum De Lakenhal 1988

LEIDEN 1991–2
C. Vogelaar *et al.*, *Rembrandt & Lievens in Leiden*, Leiden, Stedelijk Museum De Lakenhal 1991–2

LIEBENWEIN 1977
W. Liebenwein, *Studiolo: Die Entstehung eines Raumtyps und seine Entwicklung bis um 1600* (*Frankfurter Forschungen zur Kunst*, vol. 6), Berlin 1977

LIEDTKE 1996
W. Liedtke, 'Reconstructing Rembrandt and His Circle: More on the Workshop Hypothesis', *Rembrandt, Rubens and the Art of their Time: Recent Perspectives, Papers in Art History from The Pennsylvania State University* 11, 1996, pp. 37–59

LIEURE 1924–7
J. Lieure, *Jacques Callot*, 4 vols., Paris 1924–7

LIVERPOOL 1994–5
X. Brooke, *Face to Face: Three Centuries of Artists' Self-Portraiture*, Liverpool, Walker Art Gallery 1994–5

LOMAZZO 1590
G.P. Lomazzo, *Idel Tempio della Pittura*, Milan 1590

LONDON 1988–9
D. Bomford, C. Brown, A. Roy, *Art in the Making: Rembrandt*, London, National Gallery 1988–9

LOWENTHAL 1986
A.W. Lowenthal, *Joachim Wtewael and Dutch Mannerism*, Doornspijk 1986

MACGREGOR 1989
A. MacGregor (ed.), *The Late King's Goods: Collections, Possessions and Patronage of Charles I in the Light of the Commonwealth Sale Inventories*, London/Oxford 1989

MACLAREN/BROWN 1991
N. MacLaren, revised and expanded by C. Brown, *National Gallery Catalogues: The Dutch School, 1600–1900*, 2 vols., London 1991

MAHON 1967
D. Mahon, *I disegni del Guercino della collezione Mahon*, Bologna 1967

VAN MANDER 1604a
K. van Mander, *Het Schilder-Boeck*, Haarlem 1604

VAN MANDER 1604b
K. van Mander, *Den grondt der edel vry schilder-const*, Haarlem 1604

VAN DER MARCK 1773
Catalogus Van een Uitmuntend en Overheerlyk Kabinet Konstige Schilderyen, Door de voornaamste Nederlandsche Meesters ... Alles in veele Jaaren byeen verzamelt en nagelaaten door wylen den Wel Ed. Gestrenge Heer Mr. Johan van der Marck Aegidz., Amsterdam, De Winter, Yver, 25 August 1773 et seq.

MARTIN 1913
W. Martin, *Gerard Dou: Des Meisters Gemälde in 247 Abbildungen* (*Klassiker der Kunst*, vol. 14), Stuttgart/Berlin 1913

MARTIN 1923–4
W. Martin, 'Rembrandt zelf op de Nachtwacht', *Oud Holland* 41, 1923–4, pp. 1–4

MARTIN 1967
G. Martin, 'A Rembrandt Self Portrait from his last year', *The Burlington Magazine* 109, 1967, p. 355

MAUQUOY-HENDRICKX 1956
M. Mauquoy-Hendrickx, *L'iconographie d'Antoine van Dyck: Catalogue raisonné*, 2 vols., Brussels 1956

MELBOURNE/CANBERRA 1997–8
A. Blankert (ed.), *Rembrandt: A Genius and His Impact*, Melbourne, National Gallery of Victoria; Canberra, National Gallery of Australia 1997–8

MELONI TRKULJA 1978
S. Meloni Trkulja, 'La collezione Pazzi (autoritratti per gli Uffizi): Un'operazione sospetta, un documento malevolo', *Paragone* 29, 1978, no. 343, pp. 79–123

MIDDLETON 1878
C.H. Middleton, *A descriptive Catalogue of the etched Work of Rembrandt van Rijn*, London 1878

MIEDEMA 1969
H. Miedema, review of *Emmens 1964*, *Oud Holland* 84, 1969, pp. 249–56

MIEDEMA 1973
H. Miedema, *Karel van Mander: Den grondt der edel vry schilder-const*, 2 vols., Utrecht 1973

MIEDEMA 1975
H. Miedema, 'Over het realisme in de Nederlandse schilderkunst in de zeventiende eeuw naar aanleiding van een tekening van Jacques de Gheyn II (1565–1632)', *Oud Holland* 89, 1975, pp. 2–18

MIEDEMA 1989
H. Miedema, *Kunst historisch*, Maarssen 1989

MIEDEMA 1994–
H. Miedema (ed.), *Karel van Mander: The lives of the illustrious Netherlandish and German painters*, I– , Doornspijk 1994–

MILAN 1977
Omaggio a Tiziano: La cultura milanese nell'eta di Carlo V, Milan, Palazzo Reale 1977

MILLAR 1958–60
O. Millar (ed.), 'Abraham van der Doort's Catalogue of the Collections of Charles I', *The Walpole Society* 37, 1958–60, pp. 1–243

MOFFIT 1984
J.F. Moffit, '"Più tondo che l'O di Giotto": Giotto, Vasari, and Rembrandt's Kenwood House "Self-Portrait"', *Paragone* 35, 1984, no. 407, pp. 63–70

VON MOLTKE 1965
J.W. von Moltke, *Govaert Flinck, 1615–1660*, Amsterdam 1965

MONTIAS 1982
J.M. Montias, *Artist and artisans in Delft: A Socio-Economic Study of the Seventeenth Century*, Princeton 1982

MÜNSTER 1997
K. Ahrens *et al.*, *Künstler im Spiegel einer Sammlung: Graphische Bildnisse von Malern, Bildhauern und Kupferstechern aus dem Porträtarchiv Diepenbroick*, Münster, Westfälisches Landesmuseum für Kunst und Kulturgeschichte 1997

MÜNZ
L. Münz, *A Critical Catalogue of Rembrandt's Etchings*, 2 vols., London 1952

MÜLLER HOFSTEDE 1989
J. Müller Hofstede, 'Rubens und das Constantia-Ideal: Das Selbstbildnis von 1623', M. Winner (ed.), *Der Künstler über sich in seinem Werk: Internationales Symposium der Bibliotheca Hertziana Rom 1989*, Weinheim 1992, pp. 365–405

MÜLLER HOFSTEDE 1992–3
J. Müller Hofstede, 'Peter Paul Rubens 1577–1640: Selbstbildnis und Selbstverständnis', E. Mai and H. Vlieghe (eds.), *Von Bruegel bis Rubens: Das goldene Jahrhundert der flämischen Malerei*, Cologne, Wallraf-Richartz-Museum; Antwerp, Koninklijk Museum voor Schone Kunsten; Vienna, Kunsthistorisches Museum 1992–3, pp. 103–20

NAUMANN 1981
O. Naumann, *Frans van Mieris the Elder (1635–1681)*, 2 vols., Doornspijk 1981

NEW HOLLSTEIN
The New Hollstein: Dutch & Flemish etchings, engravings and woodcuts, 1450–1700, Rotterdam 1996–

NEW YORK 1982
M.W. Ainsworth, J. Brealey, E. Haverkamp-Begemann, P. Meyers, *Art and Autoradiography: Insights into the Genesis of Paintings by Rembrandt, Van Dyck and Vermeer*, New York, The Metropolitan Museum of Art 1982

NEW YORK 1995–6
H. von Sonnenburg, W. Liedtke, C. Logan, N.M. Orenstein, S.S. Dickey, *Rembrandt / Not Rembrandt in The Metropolitan Museum of Art: Aspects of Connoisseurship*, 2 vols., New York, The Metropolitan Museum of Art 1995–6

NEW YORK 1997
M. Bisanz-Prakken *et al.*, *A Quintessence of Drawing: Masterworks from the Albertina*, New York, The Solomon R. Guggenheim Museum 1997

NEW YORK 1998–9
M.W. Ainsworth *et al.*, *From Van Eyck to Bruegel: Early Netherlandish Painting in The Metropolitan Museum of Art*, New York, The Metropolitan Museum of Art 1998–9

ORENSTEIN 1996
N.M. Orenstein, *Hendrick Hondius and the Business of Prints in Seventeenth-Century Holland*, Rotterdam 1996

ORLERS 1641
J.J. Orlers, *Beschrijvinge der Stadt Leyden*, Leiden 1641

ORNSTEIN-VAN SLOOTEN/HOLTROP/SCHATBORN 1991
E. Ornstein-van Slooten, M. Holtrop, P. Schatborn, *The Rembrandt House: The Prints, Drawings and Paintings*, Zwolle/Amsterdam 1991

OZAKI 1989
A. Ozaki, 'A New Look at the *Bust of a young man* in the MOA Museum', *Art History: Tohoku University* 11, 1989, pp. 1–14

PÄCHT 1991
O. Pächt, *Rembrandt*, Munich 1991

PARIS 1986
S. de Bussiere, *Rembrandt: Eaux-fortes*, Paris, Musée du Petit Palais 1986

PARIS/HAARLEM 1997–8
M. van Berge-Gerbaud, *Rembrandt en zijn school: Tekeningen uit de Collectie Frits Lugt*, Paris, Institut Néerlandais; Haarlem, Teylers Museum 1997–8

PARIS/LYON 1991
H. Buijs, M. van Berge-Gerbaud, *Tableaux Flamands et Hollandais du Musée des Beaux-Arts de Lyon*, Paris, Institut Néerlandais; Lyon, Musée des Beaux-Arts 1991

PELS 1681
A. Pels, *Gebruik en misbruik des tooneels*, Amsterdam 1681

PÉRUSSAUX 1989
C. Pérussaux, 'L'énigme du "Portrait de Rembrandt vieillard"', *Gazette des Beaux-Arts* 131, 1989, no. 114, pp. 123–6

PHILADELPHIA/BERLIN/LONDON 1984
P. Sutton *et al.*, *Masters of Seventeenth-Century Dutch Genre Painting*, Philadelphia, Philadelphia Museum of Art; Berlin, Staatliche Museen Preußischer Kulturbesitz; London, Royal Academy of Arts 1984

PHOENIX/KANSAS CITY/THE HAGUE 1998–9
Copper as Canvas: Two Centuries of Masterpiece Paintings on Copper, 1525–1775, Phoenix, Phoenix Art Museum; Kansas City, The Nelson-Atkins Museum of Art; The Hague, Mauritshuis 1998–9

PINDER 1943
W. Pinder, *Rembrandts Selbstbildnisse*, Leipzig 1943

PINDER 1950
W. Pinder, *Rembrandt's Selbstbildnisse*, Leipzig 1950

PLINY 1968
G. Plinius Secundus, H. Rackham (ed.), *Naturalis Historia*, London/Cambridge, Mass. 1968

PLOMP 1997
M.C. Plomp, *The Dutch Drawings in the Teyler Museum: Artists Born Between 1575 and 1630*, Haarlem/Ghent/Doornspijk 1997

POPPER-VOSKUIL 1973
N. Popper-Voskuil, 'Selfportraiture and vanitas still-life painting in 17th-century Holland in reference to David Bailly's vanitas oeuvre', *Pantheon* 31, 1973, pp. 58–74

PRINZ 1966
W. Prinz, *Vasaris Sammlung von Künstlerbildnissen (Beiheft zu den Mitteilungen des Kunsthistorischen Institutes in Florenz 12)*, Florence 1966

PRINZ 1971
W. Prinz, *Die Sammlung der Selbstbildnisse in den Uffizien*, vol. I: *Geschichte der Sammlung (Italienische Forschungen, third series, vol. V)*, Berlin 1971

RAGGHIANTI-COLLOBI 1971
L. Ragghianti-Collobi, 'Il Libro de' disegni ed i ritratti per le Vite del Vasari', *Critica d'Arte* 18, 1971, pp. 37–64

RAGGHIANTI-COLLOBI 1972
L. Ragghianti-Collobi, 'Aggiunta ai ritratti nel Libro de' disegni del Vasari', *Critica d'Arte* 19, 1972, pp. 57–8

RAUPP 1984
H.-J. Raupp, *Untersuchungen zu Künstlerbildnis und Künstlerdarstellung in den Niederlanden im 17. Jahrhundert*, Hildesheim/Zurich/New York 1984

VAN RIJCKEVORSEL 1932
J.L.A. van Rijckevorsel, *Rembrandt en de traditie*, Rotterdam 1932

RIPA 1644
C. Ripa, *Iconologia of uijtbeeldinghe des verstands, uit het Italiaans vertaelt door D. Pietersz Pers*, Amsterdam 1644

ROSCAM ABBING 1993
M. Roscam Abbing, *De schilder & schrijver Samuel van Hoogstraten 1627–1678: Eigentijdse bronnen & oeuvre van gesigneerde schilderijen*, Leiden 1993

ROSENBERG 1964
J. Rosenberg, *Rembrandt: Life & Work*, second revised edition, London 1964 (first edition 1948)

ROYALTON-KISCH 1991
M. Royalton-Kisch, 'Rembrandt's Self-Portraits' (review of *Chapman 1990*), *Print Quarterly* 8, 1991, pp. 304–8

ROYALTON-KISCH 1992
M. Royalton-Kisch, *Drawings by Rembrandt and his circle in the British Museum*, London 1992

S.
W. von Seidlitz, *Kritisches Verzeichniss der Radierungen Rembrandts*, Leipzig 1895

VON SANDRART 1675
J. von Sandrart, *L'Academia Todesca della Architectura, Scultura et Pictura: oder Teutsche Academie der Edlen Bau-, Bild- und Mahlerey-Künste*, 2 vols., Nuremberg 1675

VON SANDRART 1925
A.R. Peltzer (ed.), *Joachim von Sandrarts Academie der Bau-, Bild- und Mahlerey-Künste von 1675: Leben der Berühmten Maler, Bildhauer und Baumeister*, Munich 1925

SCHATBORN 1981
P. Schatborn, 'Van Rembrandt tot Crozat: Vroege verzamelingen met tekeningen van Rembrandt', *Nederlands Kunsthistorisch Jaarboek* 32, 1981, pp. 1–54

SCHATBORN 1985
P. Schatborn, *Tekeningen van Rembrandt, zijn onbekende leerlingen en navolgers / Drawings by Rembrandt, his anonymous pupils and followers (Catalogus van de Nederlandse Tekeningen in het Rijksprentenkabinet, Rijksmuseum, Amsterdam, vol. IV)*, The Hague 1985

SCHATBORN 1986
P. Schatborn, review of *Corpus*, vol. I, *Oud Holland* 100, 1986, pp. 55–63

SCHELLER 1969
R.W. Scheller, 'Rembrandt en de encyclopedische kunstkamer', *Oud Holland* 84, 1969, pp. 132–42

SCHILLEMANS 1987
R. Schillemans, 'Gabriel Bucelinus and "The Names of the Most Distinguished European Painters"', *Hoogsteder-Naumann Mercury* 6, 1987, pp. 25–37

SCHILLEMANS 1991
R. Schillemans, '"Rimprant, nostrae aetatis miraculum" (Rembrandt, het wonder van onze tijd)', *Kroniek van het Rembrandthuis* 43, 1991, pp. 17–20

VON SCHLOSSER 1924
J. von Schlosser, *Die Kunstliteratur: Ein Handbuch zur Quellenkunde der neueren Kunstgeschichte*, Vienna 1924

VON SCHLOSSER 1978
J. von Schlosser, *Die Kunst- und Wunderkammern der Spätrenaissance: Ein Beitrag zur Geschichte des Sammelwesens*, Brunswick 1978 (first edition 1908)

SCHNEIDER 1995
C.P. Schneider, 'Rembrandt Reversed: Reflections on the early Self-Portrait Etchings', *Shop Talk: Studies in Honor of Seymour Slive, Presented on his Seventy-Fifth Birthday*, Cambridge, Mass. 1995, pp. 224–6, 402–3

SCHNEIDER/EKKART 1973
H. Schneider, with a supplement by R.E.O. Ekkart, *Jan Lievens: Sein Leben und seine Werke*, Amsterdam 1973

SCHWARTZ 1977
Gary Schwartz, *Rembrandt: Alle etsen op ware grootte afgebeeld*, Maarssen/The Hague 1977

SCHWARTZ 1984
G. Schwartz, *Rembrandt: Zijn leven, zijn schilderijen*, Maarssen 1984

SCHWARTZ 1993
G. Schwartz, 'Lady Pictura painting flowers', *Tableau* 15, 1993, pp. 66–80

SCHWEIKHART 1993
G. Schweikhart, 'Das Selbstbildnis im 15. Jahrhundert', J. Poeschke (ed.), *Italienische Frührenaissance und nordeuropäisches Spätmittelalter*, Munich 1993, pp. 7–39

SIX 1706
Catalogus Istructissimae Bibliothecae Nobilissimi et Amplissimi Domini Do. Joannis Six, Amsterdam 1706

SLIVE 1953
S. Slive, *Rembrandt and his Critics*, The Hague 1953

SLIVE 1964
S. Slive, 'Rembrandt's "Self-Portrait" in a studio', *The Burlington Magazine* 106, 1964, pp. 483–6

SLUIJTER 1998
E.J. Sluijter, 'The painter's pride: the art of capturing transience in self-portraits from Isaac van Swanenburgh to David Bailly', K. Enenkel *et al.* (eds.), *Modelling the Individual: Biography and Portrait in the Renaissance, With a Critical Edition of Petrarch's Letter to Posterity*, Amsterdam/Atlanta 1998, pp. 173–96

SMALL 1996
A. Small, *Essays in Self-Portraiture: A comparison of Technique in the Self-Portraits of Montaigne and Rembrandt*, New York 1996

SMITH 1982
D.R. Smith, *Masks of Wedlock: Seventeenth-Century Dutch Marriage Portraiture*, Ann Arbor 1982

SPRINGELL 1963
F. Springell, *Connoisseur and Diplomat: The Earl of Arundel's Embassy to Germany in 1636*, London 1963

STECHOW 1944
W. Stechow, 'Rembrandt-Democritus', *Art Quarterly* 7, 1944, pp. 233–8

STERNBERG 1977
P.R. Sternberg, 'Rembrandt: Two new States', *The Print Collector's Newsletter* 8, 1977, p. 143

STOLKER 1786
Catalogus van eene uitmuntende verzameling ... schilderijen en een kabinetje met de Pourtraiten der Oude Hoog en Nederduitsche kunstschilders en schilderessen ... nagelaten door wylen den Heere Jan Stolker in leven kunst schilder te Rotterdam, Rotterdam, Holsteyn, 27 March 1786 et seq.

VAN STRATEN 1991
R. van Straten, 'Rembrandts "Leidse Historiestuk": Een iconografisch standpunt', *Leids Jaarboekje* 83, 1991, pp. 89–107

STRATTON 1986
S. Stratton, 'Rembrandt's Beggars: Satire & Sympathy', *The Print Collector's Newsletter* 17, 1986, pp. 77–82

STRAUSS/VAN DER MEULEN 1979
W.L. Strauss, M. van der Meulen (eds.), *The Rembrandt Documents*, New York 1979

VAN STRIEN 1989
C.D. van Strien, *British travellers in Holland during the Stuart period*, Amsterdam 1989

STUMPEL 1988
J. Stumpel, 'Wie is de grootste meester in de kunst?: Eeuwenlang vergelijken door kunstenaars en connaisseurs', *Kunstschrift* 32, 1988, pp. 148–9

SULLIVAN 1980
S.A. Sullivan, 'Rembrandt's Self-portrait with a Dead Bittern', *Art Bulletin* 62, 1980, pp. 236–43

SUMOWSKI 1979–92
W. Sumowski, *Drawings of the Rembrandt School*, 10 vols., New York 1979–92

SUMOWSKI 1983–95
W. Sumowski, *Gemälde der Rembrandt-Schüler*, 6 vols., Landau/Pfalz 1983[–95]

SUSINO 1974
S. Susinno, 'La Galleria: I ritratti degli accademici', *L'Accademia Nazionale di San Luca*, Rome 1974, pp. 201–70

TACKE 1995
A. Tacke, *Die Gemälde des 17. Jahrhunderts im Germanischen Nationalmuseum*, Mainz 1995

TEELLINCK 1620
W. Teellinck, *Den Spieghel der Zedigheyt*, Middelburg 1620

VAN THIEL 1969
P.J.J. van Thiel, 'Zelfportret als de apostel Paulus. Rembrandt van Rijn (1606–1669)', *Openbaar Kunstbezit* 13, 1969, pp. 1 a–b

VAN THIEL 1976
P.J.J. van Thiel *et al.* (eds.), *All the paintings of the Rijksmuseum in Amsterdam: A completely illustrated catalogue*, Amsterdam/Maarssen 1976

TÜMPEL 1968
C. Tümpel, 'Ikonographische Beiträge zu Rembrandt I', *Jahrbuch der Hamburger Kunstsammlungen* 13, 1968, pp. 95–126

TÜMPEL 1971
C. Tümpel, 'Ikonographische Beiträge zu Rembrandt: Zur Deutung und Interpretation einzelner Werke (II)', *Jahrbuch der Hamburger Kunstsammlungen* 16, 1971, pp. 20–38

TÜMPEL 1986
C. Tümpel, *Rembrandt*, Amsterdam 1986

DE VECCHI 1977
P.L. de Vecchi, 'Il Museo Gioviano e le "Vera Imagines" degli uomini illustri', *Milan* 1977, pp. 87–96

VEY/KESTING 1967
H. Vey, A. Kesting, *Katalog der niederländischen Gemälde von 1550 bis 1800 im Wallraf-Richartz-Museum*, Cologne 1967

VIENNA 1969–70
Die Rembrandt-Zeichnungen der Albertina, Vienna, Graphische Sammlung Albertina 1969–70

VIS 1965
D. Vis, *Rembrandt en Geertje Dircx: De identiteit van Frans Hals' portret van een schilder en de vrouw van de kunstenaar*, Haarlem 1965

VLIEGHE 1987
H. Vlieghe, *Rubens Portraits of Identified Sitters Painted in Antwerp (Corpus Rubenianum Ludwig Burchard, vol. XIX, 2)*, London/New York 1987

VONESSEN 1992
F. Vonessen, 'Selbstporträt und Selbsterkenntnis: Zu Rembrandts Selbstdarstellung als "Lachender Alter"', *Zeitschrift für Ästhetik und Allgemeine Kunstwissenschaft* 37, 1992, pp. 123–52

DE VRIES 1883
A.D. de Vries, 'Aantekeningen naar aanleiding van Rembrandts etsen', *Oud Holland* 1, 1883, pp. 292–310

DE VRIES 1989
L. de Vries, 'Tronies and other Single Figured Netherlandish Paintings', *Leids Kunsthistorisch Jaarboek* 8, 1989, pp. 185–202

DE VRIES/TÓTH-UBBENS/FROENTJES 1978
A.B. de Vries, M. Tóth-Ubbens, W. Froentjes, *Rembrandt in the Mauritshuis*, Alphen aan de Rijn 1978

VAN DER WAALS 1984
J. van der Waals, 'The Print Collection of Samuel Pepys', *Print Quarterly* 1, 1984, pp. 236–57

WAETZOLDT 1908
W. Waetzoldt, *Die Kunst des Porträts*, Leipzig 1908

VAN DE WETERING 1976–7
E. van de Wetering, 'Leidse schilders achter de ezels', *Leiden* 1976–7, pp. 21–31

VAN DE WETERING 1982
E. van de Wetering, 'Painting materials and working methods', *Corpus*, vol. I, pp. 11–33

VAN DE WETERING 1986
E. van de Wetering, 'Problems of apprenticeship and studio collaboration', *Corpus*, vol. II, pp. 45–90

VAN DE WETERING 1991–2
E. van de Wetering, 'De symbiose van Lievens en Rembrandt', *Leiden 1991–2*, pp. 39–47

VAN DE WETERING 1995
E. van de Wetering, 'Rembrandt's "Satire on Art Critisism" reconsidered', *Shop Talk: Studies in Honor of Seymour Slive, Presented on his Seventy-Fifth Birthday*, Cambridge, Mass. 1995, pp. 264–70

VAN DE WETERING 1997
E. van de Wetering, *Rembrandt: The Painter at Work*, Amsterdam 1997

VAN DE WETERING/BROEKHOFF 1996
E. van de Wetering, P. Broekhoff, 'New directions in the Rembrandt Research Project, Part I: the 1642 self-portrait in the Royal Collection', *The Burlington Magazine* 138, 1996, pp. 174–80

WEYERMAN 1726
J.C. Weyerman, *Maandelyksche 't zamenspraaken tusschen de dooden en de leevenden*, Amsterdam 1726

WEYERMAN 1729–69
J.C. Weyerman, *De levens-beschryvingen der Nederlandsche konst-schilders en konst-schilderessen, met een uytbreyding over de schilder-konst der ouden*, 4 vols., The Hague/Dordrecht 1729–69

WHEELOCK 1995
A.K. Wheelock, Jr., *Dutch Paintings of the Seventeenth Century (The Collections of the National Gallery of Art Systematic Catalogue)*, Washington/New York/Oxford 1995

WHITE 1962
C. White, 'Did Rembrandt ever visit England?', *Apollo* 76, 1962, pp. 177–84

WHITE 1969
C. White, *Rembrandt as an Etcher: A Study of the Artist at Work*, 2 vols., London 1969

WHITE 1982
C. White, *The Dutch Pictures in the Collection of Her Majesty the Queen*, Cambridge 1982

WHITE 1984
C. White, *Rembrandt*, London 1984

WHITE/BOON 1969
C. White, K.G. Boon, *Rembrandt's Etchings: An illustrated critical catalogue in two volumes (Hollstein's Dutch and Flemish Etchings, Engravings and Woodcuts*, vols. XVIII–XIX), Amsterdam/London/New York 1969

WILDE 1988
O. Wilde, Donald L. Lawler (ed.), *The Picture of Dorian Gray*, New York/London 1988

DE WINKEL 1995
M. de Winkel, '"Eene der deftigsten dragten": The Iconography of the "Tabbaard" and the Sense of Tradition in Dutch Seventeenth-century Portraiture', *Nederlands Kunsthistorisch Jaarboek* 46, 1995 (*Beeld en Zelfbeeld in de Nederlandse kunst, 1550–1750*), pp. 145–67

WINKLER 1957
F. Winkler, 'Echt, falsch, verfälscht', *Kunstchronik* 10, 1957, pp. 141–7

WOORDENBOEK DER NEDERLANDSCHE TAAL
M. de Vries, L.A. te Winkel (eds.), *Woordenboek der Nederlandsche Taal*, I– , The Hague/Leiden 1882–

WOODS-MARSDEN 1998
J. Woods-Marsden, *Renaissance Self-Portraiture: The Visual Construction of Identity and the Social Status of the Artist*, New Haven/London 1998

WRIGHT 1982
C. Wright, *Rembrandt: Self-Portraits*, London/Bedford 1982

ZOET 1648
J. Zoet, *Sabynaja of vermomdeeloosheid*, Amsterdam 1648

ZÖLLNER 1989
F. Zöllner, '"Ogni pittori dipinge sé": Leonardo da Vinci and "Automimesis"', M. Winner (ed.), *Der Künstler über sich in seinem Werk: Internationales Symposium der Bibliotheca Hertziana Rom 1989*, Weinheim 1992, pp. 137–60

Concordance

to previous publications on the self portraits: Bredius/Gerson 1969, Corpus (paintings), Bartsch / Hollstein (etchings) and Benesch 1973 (drawings).

PAINTINGS

Bredius/Gerson 1969	Corpus	cat. no.
-	A 14	5
1	A 14 (copy 1)	[fig. 5b]
2	A 19	7
-	A 22	[fig. 8a]
3	A 22 (copy 1)	8
4	C 35	-
5	C 34	[fig. 22a]
6	A 21	14b
-	A 21 (copy 1)	14a
7	C 36	16
8	A 20	10
9	C 37	-
10	C 38	-
11	B 5	18
12	A 33	26
13	C 39	-
[14]	C 40	-
[15]	C 33	-
16	A 40	29a
-	A 40 (copy 1)	29b
17	A 58	33
18	A 71	35
19	A 72	36
20	B 11	52
21	A 96	39
22	A 97	40
23	C 56	37
24	C 98	[Manuth fig. 16]
25	C 92	-
26	C 99	

27	C 96	48
[28]	-	-
29	B 10	51
30	A 111	43
31	A 133	50
32	C 97	56
33	C 93	55a
-	C 94	55b
34	A 139	54
35	IV 3	-
36	IV 2	59
37	IV 1	57
38	IV 5	60
39	IV 6	-
40	IV 4	-
41	IV 7	-
42	IV 8	65
43	IV 9	66
44	IV 11	67
45	IV 12	68
46	IV 10	70c
47	IV 10	70a
47A	IV 10	70b
48	IV 15	74
49	IV 13	69
50	IV 14	71
51	IV 18	73
52	IV 23	83
53	IV 19	79
54	IV 20	80
55	IV 24	84
56	-	-
57	-	-
58	IV 16	75
[Bauch 337]	IV 17	76
59	IV 21	81
60	IV 25	85
61	IV 22	82

62	IV 26	86
[157]	IV, add. no. 2	34
410	A 146	[Van de Wetering figs. 47-8 and cat. no. 1, fig. 1h]
419	A 18	17
433	A 120	-
460	A 6	1 [and fig. 1d]
488	A 9	[fig. 1c]
499	A 109	[fig. 1g]
501	A 116	[fig. 1g]
531A	A 1	[Van de Wetering fig. 28 and cat. no. 1, fig. 1b]
547	A 68	[fig. 1g]
548	A 69	[Van de Wetering fig. 27 and cat. no. 1, fig. 1f]
550	A 65	[fig. 1g]
555	A 106	[fig. 1g]
632	A 7	[fig. 1g]

The editors do not subcribe to the opinion of Chapman (1990, fig. 42) that the print by Lambertus Claessens illustrates a lost self portrait by Rembrandt.

Picture Credits

Index

Numbers in *italics* refer to illustrations; catalogue entries (all illustrated) are in **bold**

Lenders

Her Majesty Queen Elizabeth II 57

His Grace The Duke of Sutherland 74

Musée Granet, Aix-en-Provence 75

Museum Het Rembrandthuis, Amsterdam 29b, 63

Rijksmuseum, Amsterdam 5, 81

Rijksmuseum, Rijksprentenkabinet, Amsterdam 2-4, 9, 11-12, 15, 19-25, 27-8, 30-2, 38, 41-2, 44, 46, 49, 53, 58, 61-2, 64, 90, 95

Staatliche Museen, Kupferstichkabinett, Berlin 47

Isabella Stewart Gardner Museum, Boston 10

Museum of Fine Arts, Boston 17

Wallraf-Richartz-Museum, Cologne 82

Dordrechts Museum, Dordrecht 87

Galleria degli Uffizi, Florence 52, 85

Glasgow Museums, The Burrell Collection, Glasgow 33

Teylers Museum, Haarlem 6

Royal Cabinet of Paintings Mauritshuis, The Hague 14b, 86, 89

Indianapolis Museum of Art, Indianapolis 8

Staatliche Kunstsammlungen, Schloss Wilhelmshöhe, Kassel 40

Stedelijk Museum De Lakenhal, Leiden 1

Walker Art Gallery, Liverpool 26

British Museum, London 2, 4, 6, 9, 11, 13, 15, 19, 20, 21, 22, 23, 24, 25, 27, 28, 30, 31, 32, 38, 41, 42, 44, 46, 49, 53, 58, 61, 62, 64

Courtauld Institute of Art, London (Prince's Gate Collection) (not in catalogue)

English Heritage, The Iveagh Bequest, Kenwood House, London 83

The National Gallery, London 54, 84, 93

Museo Thyssen-Bornemisza, Madrid 59

Bayerische Staatsgemäldesammlungen, Alte Pinakothek, Munich 7

Germanisches Nationalmuseum, Nuremberg 14a

Institut Néerlandais, Frits Lugt Collection, Paris 91

Musée du Petit Palais, Paris 29a, 72

Museum Boijmans Van Beuningen, Rotterdam 77, 92, 96

Nationalmuseum, Stockholm 18

Staatsgalerie, Stuttgart 76

Graphische Sammlung Albertina, Vienna 78, 88

Kunsthistorisches Museum, Vienna 65

National Gallery of Art, Washington 45, 73

Schlossmuseum, Weimar 94

as well as private owners who wish to remain anonymous 34, 89.

This catalogue has been generously supported
by the Basil Samuel Charitable Trust

This book was published to accompany
an exhibition at the National Gallery, London
entitled *Rembrandt by Himself*
9 June 1999 – 5 September 1999 and at
Royal Cabinet of Paintings Mauritshuis,
The Hague, 25 September 1999 – 9 January 2000

First published in Great Britain by
National Gallery Publications Limited
St Vincent House
30 Orange Street
London WC2H 7HH
and in the Netherlands by
Royal Cabinet of Paintings Mauritshuis

ISBN   1 85709 252 x hardback
            525309

ISBN   1 85709 270 8 paperback
            525453

British Library Cataloguing-in-Publication Data.
A catalogue record is available from the British
Library.
Library of Congress Catalogue Card Number:
99–70647

MANAGING EDITORS: *Suzie Burt and Quentin Buvelot*
DESIGNER: *Isambard Thomas*
ASSISTANT EDITORS: *John Jervis, Mandi Gomez,
Emma Shackleton, Tessa Daintith*
PICTURE RESEARCHER: *James Mulraine*

Printed in the Netherlands by Waanders, Zwolle
Bound in the Netherlands by De Ruiter, Zwolle

Front cover: *Self Portrait with Beret and Turned-Up
Collar*, 1659 (cat. no. 73)
Frontispiece: *Self Portrait with Beret and Turned-Up
Collar*, 1659? (cat. no. 74)